ANIMATION
FROM CONCEPT TO PRODUCTION
HANNES RALL

T0138768

CRC Press
Taylor & Francis Group
Boca Raton London New York

CRC Press is an imprint of the
Taylor & Francis Group, an **informa** business

A FOCAL PRESS BOOK

CRC Press
Taylor & Francis Group
6000 Broken Sound Parkway NW, Suite 300
Boca Raton, FL 33487-2742

© 2018 by UVK Verlagsgesellschaft mbH (Proprietor)
CRC Press is an imprint of Taylor & Francis Group, an Informa business

No claim to original U.S. Government works

Printed on acid-free paper

International Standard Book Number-13: 978-1-138-04222-3 (Hardback) 978-1-138-04119-6 (Paperback)

Visit the Taylor & Francis Web site at
http://www.taylorandfrancis.com

and the CRC Press Web site at
http://www.crcpress.com

Printed and bound in the United States of America by Sheridan

Acknowledgments

Prof. Alan Chan, Dean, College of Humanities, Arts and Social Sciences (HASS), Nanyang Technological University Singapore.

Prof. Vibeke Sorensen, Chair, School of Art, Design and Media (ADM), Nanyang Technological University Singapore,

For their continuous support and encouragement.

Hans Bacher and Ishu Patel, for many years of inspiration, collaboration and friendship.

Thomas Silbereis, for designing the wonderful original layout for this book.

All the BFA Digital Animation students at the School of Art, Design and Media at Nanyang Technological University Singapore, who keep amazing me since I started teaching there in 2005.

Introduction

Animation is a fascinating art form. Unlike any other medium, it allows filmmakers to have complete artistic control over each image. This book is designed to help beginners in getting started, and to provide those with advanced skills and "old hands" with new and surprising insights.

In order to best achieve this, the focus of this volume has been clearly defined: It is about the animator in the role of filmmaker - that is, the methodology of using artistic concepts to implement content-specific objectives. With regard to its content, the book follows roughly the general production process of an animation film and later explores the individual major production techniques and animation styles.

Some may rightly argue that job descriptions for those who just completed training in the field of animation, particularly coming from major studios, are characterized by extreme specialization requirements to individual areas. However, I am convinced that knowledge of the larger context is helpful, if not indispensable, for seasoned filmmakers seeking specialization as well. A character animator, for example, must understand the principles of film editing in order to provide continuity between scenes.

In addition, most animation study programs worldwide include the production of an animated short film as a major part of the final exam. For the artistic quality, it is essential to understand how to utilize one's creative resources for the optimal communication of content, whether they be linear/narrative or abstract/experimental in nature.

A comprehensive book about animation on

Hannes Rall

only 300 pages also requires that it be limited to the major points. Nevertheless, I hope that we have succeeded in bringing transparency to complex correlations, while still providing detailed and practical information.

This book is not a software manual, and for good reason. For one thing, it would go beyond the realm of possibility, and secondly, software in the field of animation is changing too quickly and cannot be reflected adequately in just one book. I believe that understanding the basic design concepts is much more important than the knowledge of purely technological details. Other media are much better suited for teaching this kind of information, and our work gives relevant pointers by naming and describing the currently most important programs for every technique.

The main focus, however, is clearly on artistic themes, which will continue to be relevant for years to come. I am pleased and proud to be able to feature excellent contributors for special topics: Guest author Kathrin Albers is a renowned and award-winning animation filmmaker and stop-motion expert as well as Assistant Professor at the School of Art, Design and Media at Nanyang Technological University in Singapore. I also wish to thank Melanie Beisswenger for her chapter. She is a professor for 3D computer animation at the University of Applied Sciences, Mainz. My book designer Thomas Silbereis and I have placed great emphasis on the optimal combination of text and image, an essential approach for this topic. Numerous illustra-

tions, which I designed specifically for the book, are complemented with relevant examples from the work of other animators. Therefore, thanks also to the numerous animation film makers, studios and animation students, who have made pictures of their work available to us.

The high-profile interviewees, who include Annie Award Winner Hans Bacher, star animator Andreas Deja and Oscar Award Winner VFX Volker Engel virtually represent a triumvirate of the German animation film. Then there is the internationally renowned computer animation expert Isaac Kerlow, who provides some thoughts about the future of the medium.

I sincerely hope that this book will enthuse and inspire many aspiring and established animators to implement, expand, and even challenge the methods shown. Because animation, like almost no other medium, depends on the continuous progression and reinvention: We are just at the beginning of an exciting development. To use the words of a famous spacefaring colleague: *"To infinity and beyond."* Or something like that.

Stuttgart, December 2014

Hannes Rall

Guest authors

Melanie Beisswenger

Prof. Melanie Beisswenger teaches computer animation at the University of Applied Sciences Mainz and works also as a freelance 3D character animator, supervisor and director. She has been involved in a variety of international animation and VFX films, including the Academy Award winner "Happy Feet" and its sequel "Happy Feet 2", the TV clip for the BioShock game as well as "Iron Man 3" (Oscar nomination for the category "Best Visual Effects"), "Riddick", "The 7th Dwarf" and "Sapphire Blue", where she was the lead animator for the digital character. Her animated short film "There's Bliss in the Kiss" has won many international awards.

Kathrin Albers

Kathrin Albers has worked as a stop-motion filmmaker for over 13 years and has produced many short films, trailers, spots and music videos under the label Stoptrick. Since 2012, she has been working as Assistant Professor for Digital Animation at the Nanyang Technological University in Singapore.

Technical terms that are not explained in the text and are highlighted as follows– example term – (in the respective chapter color), are explained in the glossary.

Overview

Script and Storyboarding

The script, the idea and the story for an animated film are almost always developed with a storyboard. The storyboard forms the framework, the basis for a successfully animated film. It is all about visual storytelling: communicating a story through the sequence of images.

The topic of developing and writing a story for animation film is so broad and complex that it would require a book of its own and cannot be covered in its entirety here. Therefore, we have provided a list of recommended readings in the appendix.

Nevertheless, I want to share some important thoughts and principles: Assuming that this is an in-house development, it usually starts with an idea, the beginning or end of a story - maybe just an image, a visual or narrative situation. Now, before proceeding with the actual writing, it is important to have a clear idea on a few things:

- Which format? (short film, feature film, TV series)
- Which narrative format? (Linear narrative or experimental)
- Which target group? (For whom do I write/develop the story - who is the audience?)
- What do I want to communicate? (Do I want to thrill my audience with entertainment or unsettle them with experiments?)

Of course, the idea or content also determines or leads to the format. Deciding on a final format is very important, since the style and form of writing largely depend on it. Likewise, let us never forget that movies are not primarily made for oneself, but for an audience. (Exceptions prove the rule.)

Therefore, my story has to communicate something, that is, it has to be comprehensible (more on this later).

The majority of this book's readers will develop short formats, i.e. animated short films, whether in a degree program, as an independent animation filmmaker or for a commissioned work. An animated short film should meet certain criteria:

- The story must be visually attractive: many outstanding animation short films are based on a basic concept that is relatively simple, but visually concise.
- Why as animation film? Or: What makes my story more special when it is told as an animation film? In other words: Tell a story in such a way, that it can only be told effectively as an animation film.
- Clear and simple: A short film of 2 to 10 minutes in length does not allow for a complex introduction of characters or an overload with too many narrative threads and/or characters.

There is this widespread misconception - particularly among beginners - that complexity equals quality, when the opposite is actually the case!

Telling a simple story in a comprehensible manner is often most difficult. You can certainly compare this to a well-prepared dish. More ingredients don't improve the recipe; it is all about the correct balance of a few, but properly selected ingredients!

As with anything, there are exceptions here as well, but as a rule, such films are made by professionals with years of experience in visual storytelling.

I think it is important that you first learn to master the smaller and simpler structure by applying the proper rules, before being able to modify or break those rules.

Some examples of well-designed animation shorts with a relatively clear and simple structure are:

■ Michael Dudok de Wit: "Le Moine et le Poisson" (1994)
A monk chasing a fish (with the chase becoming increasingly surreal).

■ Mark Baker: "The Hill Farm" (1989)
A day on a farm: When visitors from the city disrupt the everyday life on an English farm, it is marked with bizarre events. Cyclical narrative structure, which returns to the starting point of the narrative.

■ Cordell Baker: "The Cat Came Back" (1988)
You cannot kill a cat, and an attempt to do so will only make things worse. The story is resolved in a very striking visual gag - very specific to animation film!

■ Christoph und Wolfgang Lauenstein: "Balance" (1989)
A downright exemplary idea for animation film: Five characters must keep a free-floating platform in constant balance to keep from falling. A visually very striking idea, and very well suited as an allegory!

Analyzing well animated commercials can be very helpful as well: It is amazing how well you can tell a story in 30 or 60 seconds, if you stick to the right narrative economy.

A story for animation film, particularly for the short form, is rarely developed as a classic script, but often comes about exclusively as a storyboard:

Storyboard - the Blueprint for Animated Films

What is a storyboard?
A storyboard is often described as the "comic strip version" of the script - this works for a quick descriptive explanation, but it is actually not quite accurate:

A storyboard translates the description of the script into images and defines "visual storytelling".
In doing so, each shot is represented by at least one image. Long or complex shots can be illustrated with multiple images.

COMIC STRIP

*Comparison of Story-
boards and Comic Strips
by Hannes Rall*

This storyboard illustrates a tracking shot, combined with zooms for a continuous shot. It is important to understand that although the storyboard format can change in size, it never changes the relative aspect ratio.

When projected as a movie or video, everything is shown in the same size! (illustrations right)

TV

4:3
(1.33:1)

"CLASSIC-TV"-FORMAT:
COMMON UNTIL THE 1980s.
OUTDATED TODAY.

16:9
(1.77:1)

"STANDARD-TV"-FORMAT:
THIS IS THE STANDARD
FORMAT FOR MODERN
TV PRODUCTIONS.

MOVIE

1.33:1
"ACADEMY
STANDARD"

FILM FORMAT ESTABLISHED
BY THE ACADEMY OF MOTION
PICTURES AND SCIENCES IN
THE 30s. TODAY IT IS RARELY
USED.

1.85:1
"ACADEMY FLAT"

Screen format, which is still often
used today. Introduced in the 40/50s
to curb the competition of TV.
Examples: "The Birds", "The English
Patient."

2.35:1
CINEMASCOPE/PANAVISION

INTRODUCED 1953 (FOR THE BIBLICAL
EPIC "THE ROBE") IT IS STILL WIDELY
USED TODAY. EXAMPLES: "THETHIN RED
LINE", "STAR WARS", "BLADE RUNNER".
ANAMORPH = THE FILM IMAGE IS
"COMPRESSED" AND IS ONLY CORRECTED
BY PROJECTION WITH ANAMORPHIC LENS.

WHEN TO USE EACH FORMAT?
TV- TODAY'S TV PRODUCTIONS
DON'T ALLOW TOO MUCH CHOICE:
16:9 IS THE ESTABLISHED STANDARD.
CINEMA: WIDE-SCREEN (1:1,85) OR
SUPER WIDESCREEN (1:2,35) = CINEMASCOPE

Formats for storyboard
While a comic strip can stand alone and already represents the final "product", a story-board is a planning tool for the film to be produced. It must therefore take into account the requirements of the film format. This includes, for example, the constant movie or TV screen format, in which a film is produced, the so-called aspect ratio. Here is an overview of the most common formats.

When which format?
■ TV productions:
  Today, there is hardly a choice: 16:9 is the estab-lished standard today
■ Movie theater:
  Wide-screen (1.85:1) or super wide-screen (2.35:1) (Cinemascope)

Aspect Ratio
„Aspect Ratio" is the term for the projection or screen format of a movie or video. It is extremely important to un-derstand that a composition for film - and thus animation - must always be "thought of" in those terms.

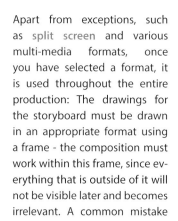

Split Screen

A "split screen" is an additional segmentation of the actual image format into additional windows: several formats within a format. This variation, which is not unlike a comic strip, is often used to show concurrence of actions. Examples can be found in the TV series "24" or the motion picture film "Hulk" by Ang Lee: Here, the stylistic element was deliberately used to create a "comic-strip-like" appearance.

Apart from exceptions, such as split screen and various multi-media formats, once you have selected a format, it is used throughout the entire production: The drawings for the storyboard must be drawn in an appropriate format using a frame - the composition must work within this frame, since everything that is outside of it will not be visible later and becomes irrelevant. A common mistake for beginners is to neglect this simple rule and draw the individual storyboards randomly in various formats, something that does not work for filmmaking.

Choosing a format

Choosing the "correct" type of movie or TV screen format depends on several factors. The decision can either be motivated artistically or financially, or include technical production considerations. The key is to decide on the format at the beginning of the production and to stick with it throughout the entire process. ■

CHAMBERPLAY ⟵⟶ EPIC/BLOCKBUSTER

— SIGNIFICANTLY EXPANDED COMPARED TO THE "OLD" 1:1,33 FORMAT.
— COST-SAVING, BECAUSE THERE IS LESS CANVAS THAT HAS TO BE "FILLED".

— ALLOWS IMPRESSIVE LANDSCAPE AND CROWD SCENES (→ INTRODUCED FOR BIBLICAL EPICS).
— HAS THE EFFECT TO STRONGLY IMMERSE THE VIEWER IN THE FILMIC ENVIRONMENT.

— ALLOWS DYNAMICS OF MOVEMENT IN THE FORMAT.
— EASY COMPOSITION OF CLOSE-UPS.

— WIDE BANDWIDTH/RANGE OF CAMERA MOVEMENTS/DYNAMIC MOVEMENT WITHIN THE FORMAT.
— CLOSE-UPS NEED TO BE LAYED OUT AND PLANNED VERY CAREFULLY.

Cut-Off Area – the "Safety Clearance" in Movie and Television Formats

Due to the so-called projection cut-off area for film projectors as well as different screen dimensions and standards for TV formats, it is important to take into account a certain "safety clearance" when configuring film images: important image elements or components of titles should not be positioned outside this "title safe area". This does not necessarily have to be observed precisely in the storyboard, if the positions of the image elements are exactly defined in a layout stage later. However, the storyboard illustrator can take into account the important image elements such as heads, etc., making sure that they are not placed at the extreme edge of the format. If the sole purpose of the storyboard is to develop the story, then such technical factors can be completely ignored. If, however, the storyboard is adopted almost unchanged as a layout, or if individual storyboard drawings are adopted as key frames, then it is safer to consider the respective cut-off areas from the beginning.

PARTICULARLY IMPORTANT FOR TITLES TO MAKE SURE THAT THEY ARE NOT "CUT OFF"!

These two drawings show, where important image information for 2.35 : 1 (CinemaScope) and wide-screen TV (16 : 9) should be and where they should not be.

"TITLE -SAFE -AREA" IN CINEMASCORE

IMPORTANT ELEMENTS OF THE IMAGE SHOULD NOT BE PLACED OUTSIDE THIS RANGE.

TITLE MUST BE PLACED WITHIN.

IMPORTANT PARTS OF THE IMAGE MUST BE PLACED INSIDE!

16 : 9 FORMAT. INSIDE : "TITLE-SAFE-AREA".

A storyboard translates or develops the story for an animated film into the drawn version of the individual shots: It is about visual narration, visual storytelling. Here is an example of how choosing different camera angles for the individual shots can create an entirely different impression of the same story.

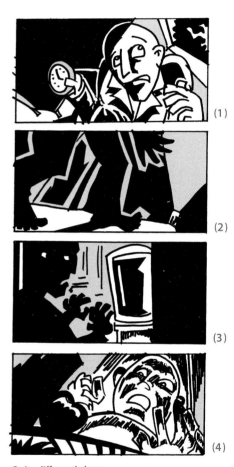

(1)

(2)

(3)

(4)

There is hardly a change in the camera's angle:
Although the camera changes between long, medium and close-up shots, it always remains roughly at eye level to the viewer and never "tilts" in perspective. The lighting of the scene is also very uniform and lacks dramatic accents. Since the stylistic means create an emotionally neutral effect, it leaves the viewer with a documentary-style impression.

Quite differently here:
Dramatic/extreme lighting (e.g. the classic "horror under-lighting") and highly varied camera angles (from above/below) are used: this creates the impression of threat (down-shot [1]), suspense (silhouette, lighting [3]) and shock/horror (under-lighting, up-shot [4]).

Assignment:

- Create two versions of an identical or similar story, for example a comedy and a horror version. Use the above-mentioned stylistic means such as camera angles, shot sizes and lighting/light and shadow.
  An example for such a story might be:
  A man/woman walking with a dog. The man/woman throwing a ball and the dog returning it (or something else?).

- You can also experiment by changing place and time: City or nature? Night or day?

- But start with those versions, which are set in a similar environment and time, and only later try out bolder variations: In this way it becomes clear, how much you can greatly change the effect of visual storytelling with only limited resources!

Why a Storyboard?

For live-action film, shots are usually repeated and sometimes covered with multiple cameras or camera angles. During the editing process, the director can then select the desired versions and continuity from a surplus of footage. For animation film, the process is very different: The elaborate frame-by-frame production process generally does not allow for the repeated production of scenes for cost reasons alone. Therefore, the film has to be planned visually exact in advance, in order not to lose time and money during the actual production process. It is equally important that an animation film be edited at least approximately when still in the storyboard format. Continuity and transitions between individual scenes can already be defined in the storyboard.

Last but not least, the storyboard is often the crucial communication tool between film producers/authors and potential investors, on the basis of which the approval of financing is decided: A script alone is not sufficient to apply for granting subsidies for animation films, the same applies to private and commercial investors. The storyboard is a relatively inexpensive way to present the visual implementation of the story the most precise way.

Because of this precise planning method, the storyboard has also been used in live-action filmmaking since the 40s and 50s, mainly for visually elaborate productions and those associated with special effects. The use of storyboards is now standard in complex feature film productions, but it is also being widely replaced by so-called previsualization (short: previz) when it comes to the planning of elaborate effects sequences or hybrid forms of CG animation and live-action film.

An animated TV series such as "Star Wars: The Clone Wars" (Filoni, 2008-2014) is now exclusively developed using previz - storyboards are no longer used. Newer CG animations, on the other hand, like Pixar's "Brave" (Andrews, Chapman, 2012) still use storyboards: This is probably due to the fact that drawings have an original expressive power that can present the charm of a story in a much more attractive manner.

Historically, the storyboard has been a medium that was first invented and used for animated film and later was used increasingly for live-action film as well. The name comes from the original form, where many small drawings in the format of the film are pinned to a board with needles.

The drawings represented the various shots of the film and enabled the production staff

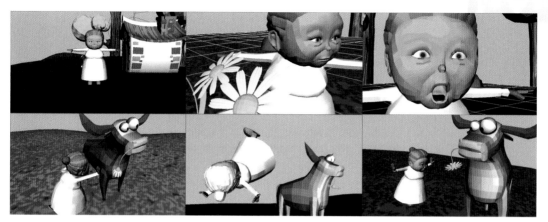

Example:
Excerpts from the previz version of the student film "Daisy" by Renald Taurusdi and Michael King Sutanto, School of Art, Design and Media, Nanyang Technological University Singapore, 2010.

to examine and exchange them, or to replace them quickly with new versions. This allowed for a constant evolution of the story process, in which the story was continuously evolving until, ultimately, a final version of the story in drawn form had emerged.

The Oscar-winning CG animation feature film "Rango" (Industrial Light and Magic, 2011) was first developed fully as a storyboard together with director Gore Verbinski. Even composition and camera angles were roughly defined in the storyboard. However, both were greatly modified and improved in the subsequent stage of the 3D layout. ▪

Animatic: Filmed version of a storyboard, which frequently already includes key frames, generally highlighted with provisional sound as well. The key is the ability to develop the timing of the film.

Leica Reel: Animatic in feature film length. Initially consisting of only the storyboards, these are replaced in the course of production by layout images, animation tests, and lastly, the final animation. A Leica reel allows everyone involved in production to keep in mind the structure of the overall film. An absolutely indispensable planning tool.

Previz/3D layout: An animatic, which does not use drawings, but very rough computer models in a 3D environment. This is where in the work process of computer animation, the positions of the characters and shot angles are often finalized.

Fundamentals of Cinematic Design

If you want to tell a linear story through film that the audience can understand, it is necessary to speak the same language the audience understands: Since the introduction of the film medium, certain conventions of visual language have been established that the audience can understand. By adhering to these conventions with regard to shots and editing, the audience can follow the action. If these conventions are violated, the understanding of the events on the screen is made difficult or impossible.

A classic example is the editing of shot and reverse shot.

It is an established cinematic convention that the close-up of a face is followed by a shot that shows what that person sees.

If you want to tell a traditionally structured story, you will stick to these established rules and expand/modify them in a playful manner. There are, of course, numerous examples, especially from the recent past and postmodernism, in which these rules were deliberately broken in order to achieve a certain effect. Masters of cinematics are able to integrate this in such a way that the story is still - or maybe even better - understood. This works, because the breaks with convention are used deliberately to support a certain narrative statement. For beginners, however, it is imperative to first familiarize themselves with the established rules of the film language before they can begin to purposefully override them. Starting out, it is difficult enough to combine all the skills needed to draw an attractively designed and narrated storyboard that is clear and comprehensible. You can compare this to a jazz musician, who must first master all the scales before he can begin to improvise at all. If your work is about a purely improvisational, i.e. experimental animation film, which is not designed to tell a conventionally structured and intelligible story, then these rules can be ignored. However, many experimental abstract animation films by masters such as Oskar Fischinger ("Motion Painting No.1", 1947) or Michel Gagné ("Sensology", 2010) have a sequential graphic structure - which can certainly be planned in and with storyboards. Graphic contrasts and tension and relief through rhythmic

variations are used to structure a film in a storyboard rather than classic rules of narrative film language. Other experimental animated artists are completely abandoning storyboards for some of their films and are improvising: One image follows another, everything in straight-ahead animation. ■

Composition

Storyboards are about the appealing and functional arrangement of image elements in a given format: That is why a good storyboarder must master the **basic rules of composition**. Students starting out often forget that drawing for storyboards is always about the composition in a defined frame:

It is important to show exactly, what the viewer will later see on a movie or TV screen!

Important image elements are placed on "thirds". Contrast between the diagonal lines and the vertical line of the right figure.

PERFECT SYMMETRY

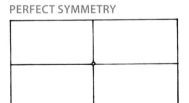

Symmetry can work very well!

COMPOSITION BASED ON "THIRDS"

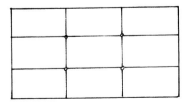

Contrast between symmetry and irregular distribution of objects = irritation, draws attention.

*If a **strong** base composition forms the basis, ...*

... then the added visual themes will work.

***Even** when detailed texture(s) and color are added (= higher demand for realism). Color can also **support** the composition.*

It is important to understand that composition can not be regarded in isolation: The idea is to choose the composition of a scene so that it supports and highlights the appropriate content of the story. The design should ultimately benefit **visual storytelling**. Form follows function. If that is achieved, then this alone will often result in a good composition, since it is based on a well thought-out concept. Successful compositions are usually based on an organized system for optimal communication of the image content: Artistic styling means and tools such as lighting, line thickness, density of detail and scaling are used to achieve this effect.

This can be seen in the following example: **In Figure1 ,** objects are placed in the foreground as silhouettes, there is more detail at the mid-ground, which decreases with increasing distance. Likewise, the line thickness is varied to emphasize the essentials (thick lines) and to mark the less important "accessories" (thin lines, gray/blue outlines in the background).

Figure 1

In Figure2, none of these stylistic means are used; each element is treated the same way: There is no system, the composition appears confusing and not well organized - and was therefore not successful.

Additional note:
Of course, there may be artistic reasons to have a shot appear "flat" and "one-dimensional", perhaps even confusing - there are exceptions to the rule.

Always important:
The compositional implementation must meet the artistic/content-related intention! ■

Figure 2

Composition for the Purpose of Visual Storytelling

FRAMING

Image elements draw attention to the central motif.

POSITIVE AGAINST NEGATIVE:
small positive figure against large nega-
tive surface; also works in reverse:

VARIED SPATIAL LAYOUT:
irregular distribution of parallel
curves + size contrast.

- BALANCE OF NEGATIVE SURFACES
- TRIANGLE AS COMPOSITIONAL
* ELEMENT*

VARIATION + CONTRAST OF BASIC SHAPES + SIZE DIFFERENCE:
central figure slightly offset against symmetry:
* Contrast to diagonals.*

Drawing attention with framing and the use of vanishing point perspective.

VERTICAL LINE/CURVES Repetition of shapes as decorative elements.

Convex/Concave

Round/Rectangular

Dynamic Composition

Animation film is not about static compositions: A composition can change within a scene, be it through tracking shots or, in the case of animation film, by metamorphoses. Unlike, for example, in a comic, a character moves through a scene, or the camera moves horizontally, vertically, or zooms: Ideally, there should always be a well-designed image composition at any point within a scene.

Over time, the character moves through the scene, while the camera moves at the same time: For each resulting shot, there should be a perfect composition. Animated film in particular, offers the possibility of absolute control, since each frame is individually generated. However, it should be mentioned that this control is significantly easier with (digitally or traditionally) drawn animated film than with 3D computer animated film. This is because, as a rule, virtual backgrounds are modeled in computer animations in which the characters move - similar to a live-action shoot. Changing these backgrounds within a scene or adapting them is quite difficult, if not impossible.

This "composition" shows how positions of characters change within a single, unedited shot, and how camera angle and image frame adjust. It becomes apparent that the balance between the dynamic image elements and the background must be taken into account. On the following page, the shot is shown in three separate sequential storyboard drawings. As you can see, such a complex and dynamic shot requires multiple drawings in order to illustrate it intelligibly.

THIS PART OF THE BACKGROUND (TAKELAGE) IS DELIBERATELY ONLY HINTED AT TO AVOID OVERLOADING THE IMAGE WITH UNNECESSARY DETAIL THAT MIGHT CONFLICT WITH A FOREGROUND CHARACTER.

IN A FILM FIGURES OR OTHER ELEMENTS CAN POP UP MOMENTARILY TO ACHIEVE A MORE BALANCED COMPOSITION.

IF THE PIRATE GOES TO THE BOW OF THE SHIP, THE WHALE CAN DIVE TO AVOID UNFAVORABLE OVERLAPS. ELEMENTS CAN APPEAR IN THE PICTURE AND THEN DISAPPEAR AGAIN. (= DYNAMIC COMPOSITION).

THE DYNAMIC COMPOSITION TAKES THE CHANGED POSITIONS OF THE FIGURES WITHIN THE SETTING INTO ACCOUNT.

THE CAMERA VIEW SHIFTS TO CREATE SPACE FOR THE UFOS THAT ENTER THE IMAGE. THE REQUIREMENTS OF THE **VISUAL NARRATIVE** DETERMINE THE **COMPOSITION**!

THE OVERLAP OF THE UFOS WITH THE TAKELAGE IS NOT IDEAL FOR THE COMPOSITION, BUT THIS IS ACCEPTABLE, AS IT ONLY AFFECTS THE IMAGE FOR A SHORT MOMENT.

AFTER THE PIRATE HAS CRASHED INTO THE MAST, ONE WOULD PRESUMABLY QUICKLY CUT TO THE NEXT SHOTS — OTHERWISE THE RIGHT HALF OF THE IMAGE WOULD APPEAR "EMPTY".

THIS ELEMENT OF **COUNTER-MOVEMENT** OF PIRATE AND PARROT INCREASES THE DYNAMIC AND ENSURES AN APPEALING CINEMATIC COMPOSITION.

Film Takes - How Do I Find the Right Shot?

A film usually consists of single **shots, which are connected through** film **editing**. It is the purpose of the storyboard to break down the described action of the script (if available) into shots. Choosing the right shots is extremely important in order to achieve the desired emotional and narrative effect on the audience.

Cut and Editing

The most important **basic rule** for film editing is: **Cuts must be motivated!** Since a cut means changing the shot, then there must be a reason why a new shot is selected. As a rule, it is about **communicating information relevant** to the **action**:

- A new place of action is being introduced.
- A detail is shown.

- The relationship between two people in a particular environment is shown.
- Time has passed.

These are just a few examples, but an edit should always be motivated by the need for visual storytelling. It is of vital importance to preserve the narrative continuity in this process. For example, in the storyboard, the characters in the drawings must always be recognizable - otherwise the story becomes unintelligible.

Break in continuity:
Different clothing of the same character for implied simultaneity and for the same environment leads to irritation (= perceived as an error by the audience).

Or:
Used deliberately by the filmmaker in order to suggest a "leap in time" in contrast to visual conventions.

The traditionally "correct" version: Edit of close-up to medium shot with change of camera angle. Continuity through left-right distribution and unchanged lighting/colors completely appropriate.

In this edit of a continuous movement (= direct continuity) and an unchanged environment, the viewer perceives the change in dress color as a continuity error.

When keeping the same characters, but changing the environment, then a different version emerges: By using a match cut, the situation shown is communicated as a temporally continued or a repeated dispute.

Simply changing the lighting implies the passing of time: A mistake turns into an interesting version. Although the continuous motion suggests immediate continuity, the changed time of day creates a **new context**.

An edit can, of course, be graphically/aesthetically motivated as well; ideally, the aesthetic component connects perfectly with the narrative intention.

When there is a complete change in the environment, without continuity of movement and a completely different situation, then the change in the dress color does not constitute an error in continuity: Narratively speaking, continuity is not intended here.

Below is a description of the **most important types of shots** based on a continuous scene, and connected through editing. Shot selec- tions are closely linked to the kind of editing from one shot to the next.

The *long shot (wide shot or extreme wide shot)* informs the audience about the place of action. It is also called the **establishing shot**. This kind of shot is ideal to establish the **atmosphere** and **mood** about the story's **location**.

The *medium shot* is well suited to highlight the relationship between two characters, while the surrounding context remains distinguishable. The storyboard also highlights the important relationship of the actors in shades of gray. Insignificant characters "fade". (In the final film, this can be replaced by other means, such as varying focus.)

The **close-up** is the best way to show the emotions of a character. The viewing direction of the character here "meets" the gaze of the character in the next shot. This is achieved with the established cinematic convention of **reverse shot:** The following shot shows the gaze of the character in a close-up that the other character sees.

An **extreme close-up** shows details that would otherwise not be recognizable or where the information would be lost (here, how the eyes become slits).

Over-the-shoulder shot: This shot, often used for dialogues, joins two characters in a foreground-background combination. Traditionally, these shots are edited and combined to alternate for the left and right character in dialogue.

A **down shot** from the "bird's eye perspective"
- a special type of **long shot**.
The shooter in the foreground is accentuated by
position, scale, and harsh contrast.

Over-the-shoulder shot, again combined with a "more
distanced"medium shot. This grants the audience the
view, how the cowboy on the left gets hit. At the same
time, the audience can see the reaction of the character
in the foreground. Again, the use of light and shadow
supports the narrative intention. The position of the
gaze on the 2D picture plane of the image format ...

... is identical to the
position of the fleeing
shooter in the next shot.
This again communi-
cates that this shot shows what the character from
the previous shot sees.

An **up shot** or low-angle shot focuses on the face of the
wounded, the touching hand and the reaction of the
other character in the center. From a purely graphic point
of view, this change of perspective offers an appealing
option.

This long shot combined with tracking shot is
action motivated: We are suddenly in a completely
different scenario, the identity of the isolated
horseman is deliberately unclear. The shot communicates the isolation of the horseman by using
the contrast of the monumental landscape. The
cinematic stylistic means of the tracking shot is
used to show additional information: During the
course of the scene it is revealed that Indians are
lurking in the foreground. This creates a completely new contextual layer of suspense.

The composition takes into account the tracking shot and
change of position of the character during the course of the
scene: There are no background details in the direction, in which
the horseman is moving. In film, this can be achieved by different
focal planes (few details = out of focus).

For live-action film, the editing process is one of the last steps in production. The director and cutter create the final product from the existing material of the shoot - the film. Each scene is shot several times during a live action movie, there are several takes, often with various camera adjustments, from which the selection for the final cut is made.

In animation film, however, it is generally not possible to animate shots multiple times: That would be far too costly and inefficient. This is why edits for animation film are determined at a much earlier stage: during storyboard and/or animatic (Leica reel) or previz for 3D productions. The more detailed and comprehensive the planning in the early stage, the more smoothly and cost-effective the implementation of the actual production will be. With elaborate full-length productions, there is usually a final cut later, and it is certainly possible to change a scene for CG productions by using different shot angles. (As an additional note, it is more sensible to determine the shots during the previz or layout stage, in order to create the most efficient and suitable background/environment). Film editing follows certain rules which have been established as viewing conventions with the audience:

It is indispensable for the (animation) filmmaker to know, understand, and apply these rules so that the audience understands the action shown according to the filmmaker's intentions:

Classic examples are the **shot/reverse shot** editing or the avoidance of **crossing the line**.

These rules are often deliberately violated or ignored in postmodern film, in order to achieve certain effects. In order to do this sensibly and balanced, the filmmaker has to know the traditional rules and know how to tell his story in a visually intelligible manner. However, this seems to be very difficult for beginners or students. Therefore, I think it is very important to learn first how conventional editing rules should be applied before they are broken.

Tip: **Always** show the **storyboard** or **animatic** of an animation film to someone who is completely unfamiliar with the story. If this person does not understand the story based on the storyboard or animatic, then it must be corrected:

- Are the drawings clear enough?
- Did I show all the elements/scenes relevant to the actions?
- Did I choose the correct shots?
- Did I make the right cuts/transitions?
- Do I need more drawings to make a certain shot more intelligible?

Important Editing Rules

Contrast between shots
As a rule, joining together two very similar shots should be avoided.

(1) - (2)

Here, it is better to combine them by **zooming** in.

With regard to composition, a cut should include a contrast between shots.
(1) - (3)
A cut should always be justified in terms of content: The new shot communicates important image information for the narrative:

In this close-up the character looks at the 2D position of the observer from (3). This makes it clear that he has noticed the observer.

A close-up reveals an important detail of the story that is otherwise lost (and vice versa: a close-up or extreme close-up of a detail automatically imparts contextual significance).

The cut of 1 to 2 works, because of the contrast between the opposing diagonals on which the image elements are based.

CONVEX

The basic rules of composition work when applied to film editing: **Composition on the timeline!**

CONCAVE – CONTRAST

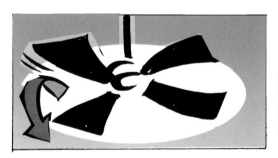

Abstract/graphic image transitions: Two shots can also be joined by two graphically similar themes. This effect is reinforced by precise continuity editing in the movement.

In animation, you are free to choose, since you do not have to rely on material from the shoot, and are therefore able to plan each edit in great detail!

CONTINUATION OF MOVEMENT

Because of the orientation on the 2D plane of the movie screen, it is important to adhere to the direction of movement between cuts (①→②A), if you want to give the impression of a continuous movement.

A cut becomes even less noticeable, if the exact movement is continued after the edit.

Changing the character's direction immediately following continuity has a disorienting effect, and should therefore be avoided as a rule.

①——→②B)

If a character leaves the image to the right, it will return to the image from the left in the next shot as the movement direction continues.

One of the "classic" violations in editing is the so-called crossing the line. As a result, the two characters exchange their position between shot (1) and shot (2).
This has an irritating and disorienting effect on the viewer.

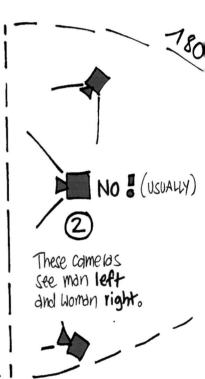

These cameras see man **right** and woman **left**.

These cameras see man **left** and woman **right**.

NO ! (USUALLY)

Crossing the line has a disorienting effect, because the viewer registers the position of a figure on a 2D picture plane.

Crossing the line occurs, when the camera skips an imaginary line at an angle of 180° - that is, when the next shot comes from an angle at which the actors "jump" from left to right (or vice versa).

Crossing the line can be avoided by using a tracking shot around the characters, or by ...

... inserting a neutral shot without a clear right-left positioning.

CREATIVE TRANSITIONS OF SCENES

*By precisely matching the position and the exact continuation of the movement after the cut, a **connection** between similar image themes can be established: a **match cut.***

The most famous example: The transition from a flying bone to a spaceship from Kubrick's "2001 - A Space Odyssey" (1968). In addition, a graphically elegant contrast is created by switching to the black of the universe.

*Not a **match cut** in the strict sense, but another famous edit is the cut to blowing out a match to a sunset in the desert from David Leans "Lawrence of Arabia" (1962).*

The warm yellow-orange color of the match "jumps" to the right towards the sunrise, while all the other image elements are replaced by an empty space.

This accentuates the dominance and importance of the new image motif. The composition of the new shot follows the 1/3- to 2/3 rule.

Fast, hard cuts between very different shots suggest simultaneous events: **parallel editing** or **cross-cutting**.

Example: In close-up, the character tells of his dream of emigrating to America.

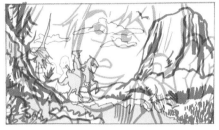

In addition to hard cuts, shots can be connected by using soft transitions: **Dissolves** and **fade out/fade in**. These transitions are often used to suggest the lapse of time:

Typically, a scene might fade out in the black of night, and in the next shot, fade in to the morning of the next day. ▪

A cross dissolve indicates that time has passed.

The following shot shows a horseman in long shot in an American landscape: The narrative thus suggesting that the narrator has made his dream come true.

"CLASSIC" FADE IN AND FADE OUT

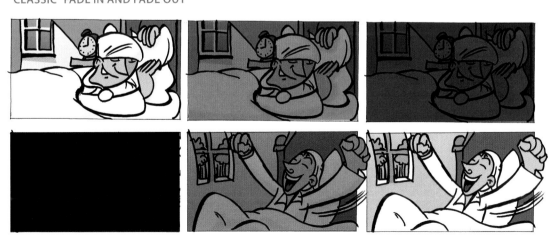

Camera in Motion

As pointed out in the examples, camera movement is another essential means of film design with regard to editing: This applies as a component within a shot, as well as for transitions between scenes. Tracking shots can be done freely in all directions, particularly in animation film. No real movement, but a similar effect is achieved by zooming. In addition, there are effects such as rack focus/partial blurring.

It is interesting to note that in 2D and 3D animation film real cameras or lenses are no longer used, but a software that virtually " replicates" these effects. This has eliminated all the "physical" limitations of a real camera, thus opening up a world of new possibilities for animation film:

In animation film, unconventional and innovative transitions between shots, which differ from conventional cutting techniques, are also possible. In fact, the animation filmmaker has all the freedom to explore his creativity! The digital revolution and the convergence between animated and live-action film have opened many doors for smooth scene transitions in live-action film as well.

Creative transitions for animated film

As opposed to live-action film, animation film provides unlimited possibilities in creating transitions between two shots:

- Unlimited use of tracking shots, which are not limited by physical objects or locations
- Metamorphoses
- Abstract graphic/shape-based opposites or matches

My former Professor Albrecht Ade has repeatedly said: *"The place where they cut in live-action film, is where it gets interesting in animation film."* I fully agree with this observation, would like to add, however, that these stylistic means for innovative transitions should be implemented in such a way that the story remains intelligible. This only applies, if you want to tell a traditional and narratively linear story; for a strictly experimental animation film, the purely visual/aesthetic elements may dominate.

This technique has almost become a "trademark" for my own films (here examples from the "The Cold Heart", 2013): not only does it link extreme perspectives by means of animated (and hand-drawn) tracking shots, but it also implements the changes in perspective in a way that it supports the story's effect. Instead of using a vanishing point perspective, a perspective of importance is used to illustrate the status of the various characters as the story unfolds. ∎

Animated transitions can be used so that certain aspects of the story become more clear and obvious: If, for example, you don't "split" two shots by editing, but join them directly with an animated tracking shot, then the issue of crossing the line can be avoided and you have created a visually appealing sequence.

What is the Difference Between a Storyboard and a Layout?

A layout or 3D layout goes one step further than the storyboard, and precisely specifies field of view, tracking shots and angles during a shot. Layouts provide the basis for the subsequent animation of the shots. This is not a "one-way street", since the animator might want to break up the scene differently later (e.g. placement of characters/camera angles), which would require changes. A layout can therefore be modified later. A 2D layout is created in a traditionally or digitally drawn form. A 3D layout is created as previsualization: generally rendered as low-resolution versions of the character models, or even with rough geometric shapes as "doubles" of the characters. This allows for each shot to be planned

STORYBOARD

SKETCHY HINT ON THE
STORYBOARD IS OK. IT
IS ABOUT UNDERSTANDING
OF THE STORY, ABOUT SPEED
AND FLEXIBILITY FOR
CONSTANT CHANGE.

IN THIS CASE THE STORYBOARD
DOES NOT SUGGEST THE FINAL
LAYOUT OR THE EXACT STAGING
- THE NARRATIVE IS MOST IM-
PORTANT.

USUALLY IT IS ENTIRELY SUFFICIENT
FOR THE STORYBOARD TO SKETCH
A ROUGH IDEA OF THE ENVIRONMENT-
AS LONG AS THE DRAMATURGIC
IMPORTANCE AND THE RELEVANT
ACTION IS COMMUNICATED CLEARLY.

ONLY THE LAYOUT PROVIDES FINAL
CLARITY ABOUT THE WAY ACTIONS
ARE LINKED THROUGH CAMERA
MOVEMENTS OR ZOOMS WITHIN
THE SAME SHOT.

so precisely that, during the actual production of a computer animation, backgrounds, for example, have to be modeled only as far as they are visible later in the film due to the pre-specified camera positions.

LAYOUT For the storyboard, it is generally sufficient to convey a rough idea of the environment, as long as the dramaturgical significance and the actual action(s) are clearly communicated. A typical 2D layout often sets up backgrounds with such details, that the background artist can use them as an exact template!

BY USING **DIFFERENT COLORS**, THE DIFFERENT CAMERA POSITIONS WITHIN A SHOT CAN BE CLEARLY MARKED.

OF COURSE, (ESPECIALLY IN SMALL TEAMS OR ON YOUR OWN FILMS) YOU CAN ALSO WORK WITH A HYBRID FORM OF LAYOUT AND STORYBOARD.

NO BACKGROUND MUST BE CREATED BEYOND THE ZONE THAT IS RELEVANT FOR THE CAMERA - VIEW(S).

In comparison to the overall picture, here is an insertion of the "wrong" vanishing point perspective, which works in the tracking shot, since it only shows the respective field of view and not the whole background as shown here. The exaggerated vanishing point perspective supports the sense of "dropping off".

THE LAYOUT ALSO HELPS TO DETERMINE WHERE DETAILS ARE RELEVANT AND WHERE THEY CAN BE LEFT OUT.

Once the **camera movements** have been precisely defined in the layout, you only need to create the background, which can also be "seen" by the camera throughout the scene. Accurate layout planning can help avoid unnecessary work and save money: It just has to be drawn/painted (2D) as background or modeled as surroundings (3D), which will show up later in the film!

The layout serves as a template and working basis for background painters and animators using the 2D process. For more complex productions, the layout procedure remains "negotiable", especially in terms of animation. The animator may have a different or better idea of how the camera is supposed to "see" the character in his scene.

NATURALLY, IF YOU WANT **COMPLETE FLEXIBILITY** FOR CAMERA MOVEMENTS, YOU HAVE TO CREATE A COMPLETE ENVIRONMENT.

LAYOUT AND STAGING

A good layout should also help to avoid any unfavorable overlapping of the acting characters with too many details in the background: Backgrounds should function as a stage for the actors of the scene and should not compete with them visually. This must be planned for the entire shot and for all character placements in the layout!

TOO MANY SIMILAR SHAPES AND TEXTURES ARE OVERLAPPIN ALL CLARITY IS LOST. NO STAGE FOR THE CHARACTER = BAD **STAGING**.

"DEAD ZONE" WITHOUT FUNCTIONALITY FOR THE STORYTELLING.

NO DETAILS = EMPTY. THE **STAGE** (→ **STAGING**) FOR THE MAIN CHARACTER.

ATTENTION IS DIRECTE TO THE MAIN FIGURE

CONTRAST NEGATIVE FORM ←→ POSITIVE BACKGROUND

LATER THE CORRECT USE OF **COLOR** CAN FURTHER ENHANCE THIS EFFECT, HERE: **COLOR CONTRAST** ←→ COLD.

Transitions between the storyboard and layout are fluid, depending on technology and size of production: For smaller 2D productions, the storyboard is often planned with the precision needed to fulfill the task of the layout. The more task-specific the process and the larger the studio, the more the 2D story production separates visual storytelling of the storyboard and refinement later in the layout. Large studios like Disney had established a specialized work step for this:

They created a workbook that meticulously converts/converted the storyboards into detailed layouts of each shot. Overall, the importance of a layout stage in 2D production has somewhat diminished. While predefining camera positions is still an indispensable step

in order to determine, for example, the size of a background to be created, new digital means of production have made this process much more adaptable and flexible:

- Shots can be repeated or varied relatively easy.
- Thanks to fast computers and large hard drives, high-resolution background files can be used for extreme zooming in and out without compromising quality. In 3D production, a drawn storyboard is often created first, followed by a 3D layout in pre-visualization. This is an essential step, since a hand-drawn storyboard can never reflect the actual technical circumstances and virtual "reality" of 3D models and backdrops.

A VERY IMPORTANT FUNCTION OF THE **LAYOUT** IS, OF COURSE, TO PLAN SCENES IN SUCH A WAY THAT CONFLICTS BETWEEN THE POSITION OF THE ACTORS AND THE BACKGROUND **ARE AVOIDED** IN THE COURSE OF A SHOT.

OUTSIDE THE FRAME / ASPECT RATIO = INVISIBLE IN THE FILM!

Animatic and Leica Reel

Simply put, an animatic is a filmed version of the storyboard with the approximate timing of the subsequent movie. Added to this are sounds and layout music (temp tracks). Where final dialogue has been pre-recorded, or the final music exists, they should, of course, be included!

An animatic is indispensable in order to try out the story as closely as possible to its cinematic form with sound: A test audience should be able to follow the story in this version already, and the appeal of the story should come across. The animatic should certainly be revised and improved throughout, until timing combined with storytelling functions well, above all. There are no fixed rules on how detailed or precise an animatic must be worked out: However, the more it resembles the subsequent key frames (extremes) of the animation, the more convincing it is. In addition to the storyboard, the animatic is also the medium of choice in "selling" an animation film without having to go into the costly production stage.

This applies internally to studios, as well as externally with potential financial backers. The advantage over the storyboard is, that by incorporating time and sound, an animatic conveys a better idea of the cinematic version to come: With a perfect animatic, the viewer can simply sit back and understand the presented story without any complicated explanations (and might even laugh in the right places). A Leica reel is an animatic, in which the shots throughout the production are replaced step-by-step with the latest version of the production: in 2D, the storyboard drawing is replaced with rough animation; rough animation is replaced by clean-up, clean-up is replaced by the final rendered/colored version. In 3D accordingly, storyboard is replaced with previz, previz with playblast, playblast by the final rendered version.

■

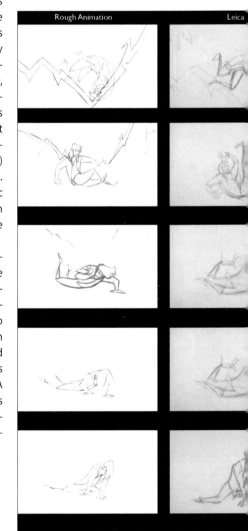

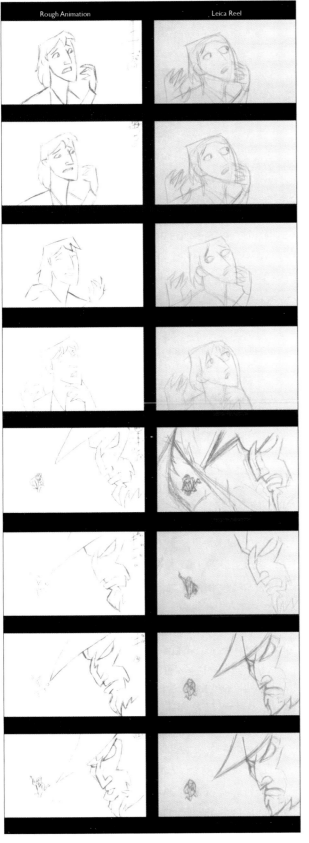

Rough Animation | Leica Reel

*This example from my film **"The Cold Heart"** illustrates the principle of an animatic or Leica reel:*

*On the **left side**, you see the **fully animated** version of the drawings (Davide Benvenuti, Tan Wei Keong), as they appear later (cleaned up and colored) in the film. The **right side** shows the **Leica reel version** of the film, which is based on my **storyboards** and **layouts**: A drawing here serves as a placeholder, so to speak, for several animation drawings represented in the actual length to be inserted later.*

You can also see, how the layout drawings provide a working basis for the animation, and how camera perspectives have been precisely defined. It is easy to see how the animation of extremes (key frames) changes as it leads to improved or smoother movements. The Leica reel produces a "pre-version" of the film to come, an ever-changing "work in progress", which can be used throughout the process to test the length of certain shots, showing them within a larger context. Another essential tool: It is the only way to maintain an overview of the emerging film as a whole (!).

This is so important, because the effect of a single shot can only be assessed adequately within the given context. I often ask my students to insert a new animated scene into the Leica reel, as it is the only way to assess an animation correctly and to make suitable suggestions for improvement. This helps significantly in determining priorities for the production process and for improvement of individual shots:

An animation that raises questions when considered in isolation, can work or sometimes only be correctly understood when viewed within its given context.

Figure Drawing
for Storyboard and Animation

Drawing for storyboard and animation requires a different focus in education than the classic academic training: The quick grasp and understanding of form and movement becomes essential.

Drawing remains an indispensable means of expression for almost everyone who is involved in animation. A quick, simple but expressive sketch is still the most effective way to present visual thinking and use it as a basis for discussion: "A picture is worth a thousand words." In this instance, it's not about refined "finalized" drawings, but about clarity, which communicates an idea in a visually comprehensible manner. Practicing your own drawing talents still remains an important aspect in the 21st century - whether with a digital drawing tablet or the good old pencil does not matter much. ■

Gestural Approach:
Quick Sketching = The Essence of Movement

Animators and storyboarders must practice the skill of fast perception and communication through drawing. In figure drawing, it is crucial to pay attention to the appropriate accents: What is important for the animator is usually very different from the main focus of a painter or other "classically" trained visual artist: the animator is interested in the overall impression of the body in the pose, expressed by line(s) of action. The key is not to get lost in details in terms of nuances and detailed structures, but to understand the big picture. Quick sketching and capturing impressions in just a few minutes should become a daily routine and always be part of the figure drawing process. Keeping a sketch book, either digital or analog, also helps in training this skill. This type of drawing is called gestural drawing.

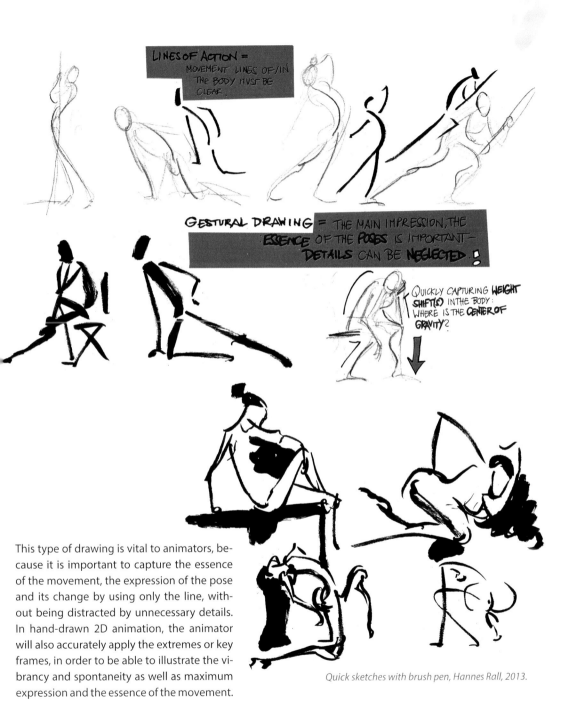

LINES OF ACTION = MOVEMENT LINES OF/IN THE BODY MUST BE CLEAR.

GESTURAL DRAWING = THE MAIN IMPRESSION, THE ESSENCE OF THE POSES IS IMPORTANT — DETAILS CAN BE NEGLECTED.

QUICKLY CAPTURING WEIGHT SHIFT(S) IN THE BODY: WHERE IS THE CENTER OF GRAVITY?

This type of drawing is vital to animators, because it is important to capture the essence of the movement, the expression of the pose and its change by using only the line, without being distracted by unnecessary details. In hand-drawn 2D animation, the animator will also accurately apply the extremes or key frames, in order to be able to illustrate the vibrancy and spontaneity as well as maximum expression and the essence of the movement.

Quick sketches with brush pen, Hannes Rall, 2013.

This is also very useful for 3D animators, who learn in this way how to recognize the essentials for animation, to see the lines of movement, and to block in figures or anatomy in basic shapes. This is an important approach for the animator, since it allows him to carry out complex movement sequences in figures by connecting the changes of basic shapes in the figure.

How do I draw for animation?
Always from rough to refined: If the primary changes of the lines of action are correct, the changes of the form defined by the lines - in the sense of the "bigger picture" - then any details added later as part of this concept will work as well.

If, on the other hand, you get lost in minor details and your drawings lack expressive contrast, the animation will turn out disappointing. The following drawings illustrate the different key aspects between rendering figurative studies for animation and classical academic figure drawing. In this context: Many animators use thumbnails to roughly conceive and try out the sequence of a scene,

FOR THE ANIMATOR, QUICKLY CAPTURING THE ESSENCE OF THE POSE IS CRUCIAL:
- HOW IS THE WEIGHT DISTRIBUTED, WHERE LIES THE CENTER OF GRAVITY?
- WHICH LINES COMMUNICATE THE POSE MOST EFFICIENTLY?
- WHAT ARE THE LINES OF ACTION?
- THE TENSION IN THE BODY MUST BE EMPHASIZED IN THE DRAWING.
DETAILS ARE DELIBERATELY NEGLECTED.

since they often possess an incredible vitality and spontaneity. These thumbnails can also be created as fast sketches of complex sequences of movements with a model - a great way to achieve credible animation by using reality as the basis. However, stylization, simplification and exaggeration should be used even when nature sketching! For 2D animation, you can simply use the copier to "blow up" the sketches in size, then mount them to the peg bar and use them directly as extremes. Even 3D animators can use thumbnails as a reference to check if the 3D animation has retained the fresh look, strong silhouettes and the essence of the expression! ■

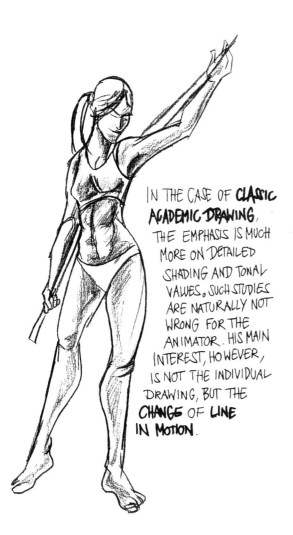

IN THE CASE OF **CLASSIC ACADEMIC DRAWING**, THE EMPHASIS IS MUCH MORE ON DETAILED SHADING AND TONAL VALUES. SUCH STUDIES ARE NATURALLY NOT WRONG FOR THE ANIMATOR. HIS MAIN INTEREST, HOWEVER, IS NOT THE INDIVIDUAL DRAWING, BUT THE **CHANGE** OF **LINE IN MOTION**.

Expression and silhouette
For the classical academic training in the traditional visual or fine arts, poses are often drawn for hours, if not days: It involves the meticulous study of shading and a perfect representation of "reality". In contrast, it is more important for the future or professional animator to quickly grasp the expression of a pose, reduce it to the essentials and, if necessary, to exaggerate it for maximum expression. While drawing, he will also look for the angle that provides the strongest silhouette, and prepare several versions from different perspectives.

Figure Drawing for Animation

Figure Drawing for Animation and Storyboard - Done Right!

In my opinion, figure drawing remains an important aspect of animation: For 2D animation, it is vital to be able to draw human (and animal) anatomy credibly. But it is helpful for 3D- and stop-motion animators as well.

An animator's lack of knowledge of how the center of gravity in the body can be displaced during movement, for example, will result in unnatural and incorrect animation. In 3D animation, it is noticeable that the figures of many hopeful beginners move - as if drawn by magic - from a static pose (such as sitting) into an upright position with mechanically inserted in-betweens. Again, this is because of the lack of knowledge about how weight in the body can and must be shifted in order to make standing up possible at all: Bearing weight on one body part is accompanied by the relief of another; an upward movement of the body is prepared with a counteraction. The anatomy defines which body parts are used for this and how it affects the interaction of bones, muscles and joints. Frequent figure drawing, that is, the sketching with a model, helps the animator to develop a repertoire of credible poses and stages of movement, which he can then "recall" and vary in his animation.

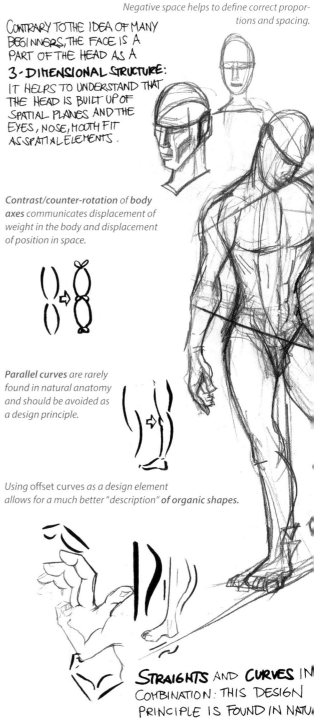

Negative space helps to define correct proportions and spacing.

CONTRARY TO THE IDEA OF MANY BEGINNERS, THE FACE IS A PART OF THE HEAD AS A **3-DIMENSIONAL STRUCTURE**: IT HELPS TO UNDERSTAND THAT THE HEAD IS BUILT UP OF SPATIAL PLANES AND THE EYES, NOSE, MOUTH FIT AS SPATIAL ELEMENTS.

Contrast/counter-rotation of body axes communicates displacement of weight in the body and displacement of position in space.

Parallel curves are rarely found in natural anatomy and should be avoided as a design principle.

Using offset curves as a design element allows for a much better "description" **of organic shapes.**

STRAIGHTS AND **CURVES** IN COMBINATION: THIS DESIGN PRINCIPLE IS FOUND IN NATU... DUE TO ANATOMICAL STRUCTU... AND GRAVITY. VISIBLE AND APPLICABLE IN ARMS, LEGS, FIN...

For the animator, it is of primary importance to create movement and a three-dimensional illusion by using the **line** as a means of expression.

In each drawing, the **essence** of the pose should be clearly identifiable, ideally the pose should be clearly distinguishable as a silhouette as well.

The animator has to know how **weight** is distributed in the body.

Details are **neglected** in favor of the overall impression: The animator selects what is essential for his drawing, and "overlooks" anything that distracts from it.

Depicting light and shadow through **tonal values in hatching** and textures is secondary, unlike classical/academic figure drawing.

A three-dimensional illusion is produced only by **overlapping, scaling and foreshortening** of lines connected to the body axes.

THE **LINES OF ACTION** ARE CLEARLY DEFINED THROUGH/BY ELEGANT LINES AND ARE STRONG IN CONTRAST. THEY DEMONSTRATE THE TENSION IN THE BODY.

OVERLAPS OF LINES (SMALL "Ts") SUGGEST THE POSITIONING (BEFORE/BEHIND) OF 3D VOLUME(S) IN SPACE.

FORESHORTENING CREATES THE ILLUSION OF SPATIALITY.

- What is the essence of the pose?
- Where is the center of gravity?
- If the model is in balance, how do I draw the figure correctly balanced?
- How does the center of gravity shift in movement?
- What are the various body axes I can see? (Counter-rotation)
- How can I see negative space correctly, to properly assess proportions and spacing?

E **ANGLE OF THE FEET** IN ²ACE IS EXTREMELY IMPORTANT CREATE THE CORRECT IMPRESSION F PERSPECTIVE AND WEIGHT F THE FIGURE.

Fingers and toes are often more realistic when using an **asymmetrical design.**

HANDS AND FINGERS, AS WELL AS FEET AND TOES, SHOULD FIRST BE "BLOCKED" AS "**PERSPECTIVE BOXES**". THIS MAKES IT EASIER TO UNDERSTAND THE OVERALL SHAPE. START WITH THE **ROUGH**, ADD **DETAIL** LATER!

THIS DRAWING ALSO WORKS FINE AS A **SILHOUETTE**.

Common Mistakes and How to Avoid Them

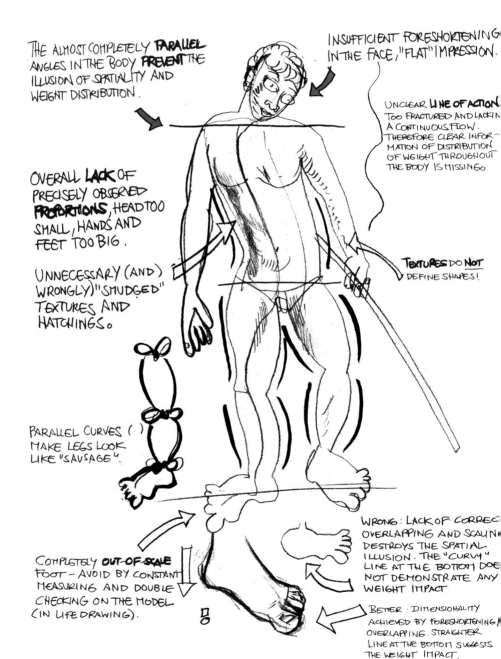

THE ALMOST COMPLETELY **PARALLEL** ANGLES IN THE BODY **PREVENT** THE ILLUSION OF SPATIALITY AND WEIGHT DISTRIBUTION.

INSUFFICIENT FORESHORTENING IN THE FACE, "FLAT" IMPRESSION.

UNCLEAR **LINE OF ACTION** TOO FRACTURED AND LACKING A CONTINUOUS FLOW. THEREFORE CLEAR INFORMATION OF DISTRIBUTION OF WEIGHT THROUGHOUT THE BODY IS MISSING

OVERALL **LACK** OF PRECISELY OBSERVED **PROPORTIONS**, HEAD TOO SMALL, HANDS AND FEET TOO BIG.

UNNECESSARY (AND) WRONGLY) "SMUDGED" TEXTURES AND HATCHINGS.

TEXTURES DO **NOT** DEFINE SHAPES!

PARALLEL CURVES ( ) MAKE LEGS LOOK LIKE "SAUSAGE".

WRONG: LACK OF CORRECT OVERLAPPING AND SCALING DESTROYS THE SPATIAL ILLUSION. THE "CURVY" LINE AT THE BOTTOM DOES NOT DEMONSTRATE ANY WEIGHT IMPACT

COMPLETELY **OUT-OF-SCALE** FOOT – AVOID BY CONSTANT MEASURING AND DOUBLE CHECKING ON THE MODEL (IN LIFE DRAWING).

BETTER: DIMENSIONALITY ACHIEVED BY FORESHORTENING/ OVERLAPPING. STRAIGHTER LINE AT THE BOTTOM SUGGESTS THE WEIGHT IMPACT.

EVEN AS A **SILHOUETTE** NOT VERY EXPRESSIVE!

For this purpose, it is important to draw firmly sweeping and continuous lines that are not interrupted in the middle of the momentum, thus destroying the definition of the shapes. In other words, no "splitting" the body into individual parts, but connecting through lines that overlap with one another. This takes into account the concept of line of action, that is, expressively curved lines, which connect various parts of the body. In order to be able to implement these connecting design concepts, it is important to avoid drawing exact parallel/symmetrical curves, but instead offsetting them: A trick that is copied from nature.

The recurring principle of contrast between lines and shapes can also be found when drawing anatomy: Straight lines against curves appear more graphically appealing and realistic, since this stylistic method is based on anatomical reality as well. For example, the top of a finger is closer to the bone (straight), which stabilizes it, while the underside is more fleshy and is "pulled down" by gravity (curve). This principle is found repeatedly in the body and can therefore be used as a design principle. Depending on the degree of stylization, this can be exaggerated or be left to remain relatively close to "reality".

The head is a good example for this:

Students often draw the head as an isolated "round squiggle" floating above the body. This usually results in a proportionally incorrect head that is not credibly integrated in the overall anatomy. But if you understand that the head, by being connected to the neck, is part and a continuation of the spine, then this will help you tremendously: The head should be included in the drawing from the outset as an element of the basic line(s) of action. This also means that you as the illustrator take notice of the frequently existing overlap with the shoulder line, integrating the head as a perspective projection in the spatial dimension of the body. Another common mistake is the reluctance to depict feet, often for fear of getting them wrong. This is awkward, because the axes of the feet on the floor and their spatial positioning to the body's center of gravity are decisive for the balance of the figure. Therefore, when drawing the main line of action of the body, always draw the axes of the feet as well: Even in a foreshortened position, it is possible to estimate the rough spatial orientation by measuring on the model, and: You can always correct it later. ■

Three-dimensionality

As a rule, figure drawing is about creating the illusion of three dimensional volume on a flat ("2D") sheet of paper. Understanding how this is done is immensely important and very helpful for any budding animator: Animators, working in 3D animations later on will also create their animations on a flat computer screen. Foreshortening and overlapping shapes are examples of methods with which this illusion can be achieved. The correct use of shading (more on this later) can strongly support the spatial impression as well.

TINTS AND **SHADES** ARE IMPORTANT STYLISTIC DEVICES TO CREATE THE **ILLUSION** OF **3-DIMENSIONALITY** IN THE DRAWING. THIS IS DUE TO THE FACT THAT IN THE REAL 3-DIMENSIONAL-OBJECT **PLANES** AND **SURFACES** ARE DIRECTED TOWARDS OR AWAY FROM THE **LIGHT SOURCES** - I.E. THEY ARE DIFFERENTLY OR BARELY ILLUMINATED. IN THE END, THIS MEANS THAT A SKILFULLY SHADED DRAWING CREATES THE ILLUSION THAT THE DRAWN OBJECT IS ACTUALLY BUILT UP IN SPATIALLY DISTRIBUTED **SURFACES** WHICH DEFINE A **VOLUME**.

HEAD IS **NOT FLAT**, IT CONSISTS OF **3-DIMENSIONAL-OBJECTS**.

The Mental Image and Reality

It is particularly important for long poses, (but also for sketching), not to stare constantly at the sheet, but to take time to really see the model: Very often what we are offered in "reality" in terms of directional changes, scale differences and foreshortening is much more extreme than what we are willing to accept. This often results in unintentionally trying to make the drawings more "normal" or "balanced" than the pose is in reality. This is because we have a mental image in our head of the human body in particular, which makes it harder for us to "see" reality, to accept the extremes of reality.

The only remedy is by abstracting what we see, i.e., to actually look at the model, to measure it, and to translate and draw what we see into lines, tilt angles, and spacing. The much-used "exaggeration" often is not really exaggerated, but a portrayal of reality. In addition to rapid sketching of expressive 2-to-3-minute poses, an animator should also practice "sequential figure drawing": the model follows a sequence of movements (i.e., getting up from a chair) into several short-held poses in succession. This allows the Animator to capture and study such sequential movements. This, of course, increases the understanding of how weight shifts during movements and how poses remain balanced. The drawings also demonstrate very well the already mentioned principle of bearing and relief of weight as well as the constant weight displacement during a movement.

We basically seem to be preconditioned to make "reality" "more normal" in our perception. Although we (could) see extreme foreshortening, differences in length and strong distortions, we tend to draw everything parallel, similar in size and "straight": Paradoxically, this mental disposition results in a false picture of "normality".

This kind of quick drawing focused on the overall pose uses the very appropriate expression of gestural drawing, a drawing intended to capture the gesture(s). A good starting point here is the already familiar concept of "lines of action": a rapid capturing of these "S-curves" and directional changes in the overall figure. This approach also prevents you from getting stuck in detailed sketching and drawing only parts of the figure during the short time.

If you look at bodies in poses, all parts of the body are connected, it's not about isolated parts, but about their synergy within the "overall concept". The goal for animation and storyboard is usually simplification in the interest of clarity and enhancement of effect. Just how deeply the animator wants to dive into the very detailed study of muscle structure depends entirely on his aspiration for realism. In my opinion, an overly detailed concept is a hindrance for expressive animation, since it often prevents a good grasp of the "big picture", and at worst, the drawings or animations

can appear stiff or unnatural. A 3D animator often uses a model predefined through rigging, a process that automates very complex anatomical details. However, this may not work for everyone, since other important factors should be considered, such as artistic appearance and production technique, as well as expectations for anatomical realism, some of which may need to be created by the animator alone. Of course, for someone who wants to specialize in 3D animation modeling, a detailed knowledge of all muscle groups in human anatomy is essential. ■

Gestural Drawing
This refers to the quick, sketchy capture of poses with only a few lines. For the animator, this form of figure drawing is very important because it allows him to capture the essence of a pose. A good animator must understand how to represent expressive poses. By constantly practicing gestural drawing, he acquires the necessary insight of such poses and develops a repertoire, which he then can draw from in animation.

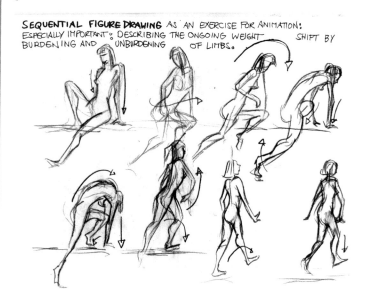

SEQUENTIAL FIGURE DRAWING AS AN EXERCISE FOR ANIMATION:
ESPECIALLY IMPORTANT: DESCRIBING THE ONGOING WEIGHT SHIFT BY BURDENING AND UNBURDENING OF LIMBS.

Longer Poses

Of course, an animator should also practice longer poses, more precisely defined drawings than those short 2-to-3-minute poses. Here in particular, the focus should be on the essential points for animation: Defining shape with the line, understanding anatomical structure, creating a 3D illusion on a 2D drawing plane, and the specific sketching of detailed anatomy. For this, **feet and hands are of great importance:** Hands lend expression of emotions, while both hands serve as supporting elements in the body. Proper positioning of the feet in space (angled) very often is key to presenting a pose in a credible manner. Drawing hands and feet is especially difficult for beginners, since they first must develop a functioning overall design for fingers and toes to prevent the disintegration into individual parts. ■

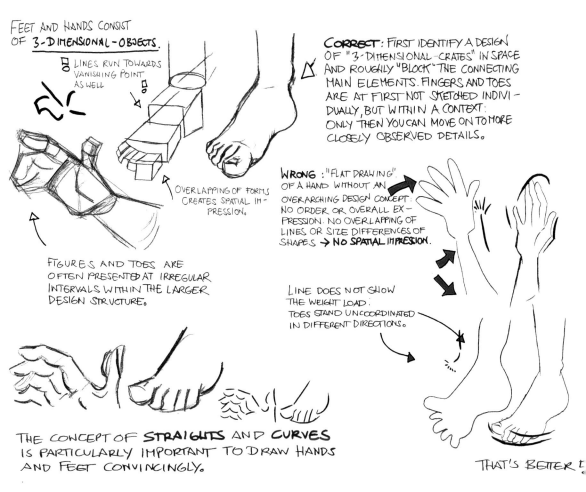

FEET AND HANDS CONSIST OF 3-DIMENSIONAL-OBJECTS.

LINES RUN TOWARDS VANISHING POINT AS WELL

OVERLAPPING OF FORMS CREATES SPATIAL IMPRESSION.

CORRECT: FIRST IDENTIFY A DESIGN OF "3-DIMENSIONAL-CRATES" IN SPACE AND ROUGHLY "BLOCK" THE CONNECTING MAIN ELEMENTS. FINGERS AND TOES ARE AT FIRST NOT SKETCHED INDIVIDUALLY, BUT WITHIN A CONTEXT. ONLY THEN YOU CAN MOVE ON TO MORE CLOSELY OBSERVED DETAILS.

WRONG : "FLAT DRAWING" OF A HAND WITHOUT AN OVERARCHING DESIGN CONCEPT: NO ORDER OR OVERALL EXPRESSION. NO OVERLAPPING OF LINES OR SIZE DIFFERENCES OF SHAPES → NO SPATIAL IMPRESSION.

FIGURES AND TOES ARE OFTEN PRESENTED AT IRREGULAR INTERVALS WITHIN THE LARGER DESIGN STRUCTURE.

LINE DOES NOT SHOW THE WEIGHT LOAD: TOES STAND UNCOORDINATED IN DIFFERENT DIRECTIONS.

THE CONCEPT OF **STRAIGHTS** AND **CURVES** IS PARTICULARLY IMPORTANT TO DRAW HANDS AND FEET CONVINCINGLY.

THAT'S BETTER !

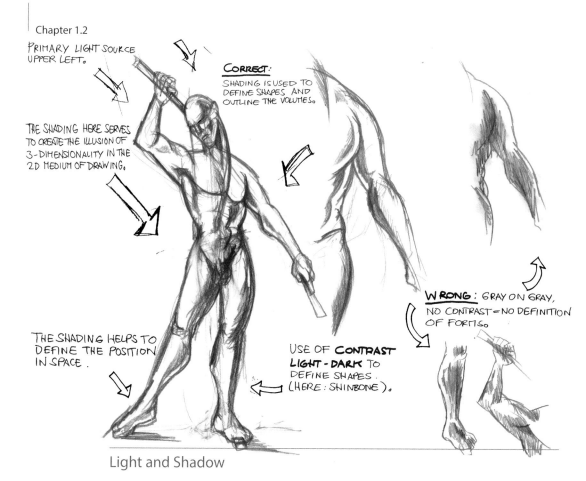

PRIMARY LIGHT SOURCE UPPER LEFT.

THE SHADING HERE SERVES TO CREATE THE ILLUSION OF 3-DIMENSIONALITY IN THE 2D MEDIUM OF DRAWING.

THE SHADING HELPS TO DEFINE THE POSITION IN SPACE.

CORRECT: SHADING IS USED TO DEFINE SHAPES AND OUTLINE THE VOLUMES.

USE OF CONTRAST LIGHT - DARK TO DEFINE SHAPES. (HERE: SHINBONE).

WRONG: GRAY ON GRAY, NO CONTRAST = NO DEFINITION OF FORMS.

Light and Shadow

For the animator in the classical sense, the line in particular is the focus in drawing: In essence, how do lines define volume, and how do lines change in motion? Shading is usually less important. However, it may well be both helpful and stylistically appealing to study through drawing, how the skillful use of tonal values and shading can define shape and reinforce three-dimensional illusion. The extended professional field of animation also includes such areas as lighting and rendering, where knowledge of light and shadow and surface structures is crucial, of course. Similarly, the proper use of light and shadow can greatly contribute to the effects of a storyboard. Anyone who works in the field of animation - or any artistic field - should understand and be able to apply the fundamental principles of tonal values, lighting and shading. Tonal values and shading in animation and storyboard should be used - just as the line - to define **volume and shapes** rather than obscuring them or complicating visual comprehension.

The key to this is working with adequate **contrasts** to help **distinguish** different shapes: A common beginner's mistake are drawings, which are covered extensively with a very similar shade of gray. It is important avoid drawings, where shapes do not clearly stand out against one another, and where the illusion of dimensionality is destroyed by incorrect or exaggerated shading.

In order to achieve sufficient contrast, the illustrator has to **select** from the overwhelming amount of information offered to the artist from the real world. For shapes to stand out clearly against one another, light must contrast dark - an arm will only stand out against an adjacent torso, if there is enough difference in their lightness. Therefore, more subtle shades often have to be neglected in favor of clarity - besides, a one-to-one rendition of the entire complexity of reality would be extremely difficult. A second key factor in a drawing is the **identification** and **consistent application** of **light sources**. An object or a figure is usually illuminated by one (sometimes even two) primary light sources, often in addition to diffuse ambient lighting. These light sources must be taken into account at all times and applied and implemented in the same way for all objects in the drawing. Therefore, you can not shade at your own discretion, but must follow a lighting concept. When sketching nature, you will identify these light sources naturally, but here too, the same rule applies: Select, simplify and provide sufficient contrast for the sake of effect!

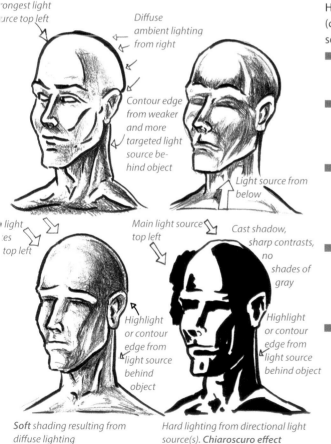

rongest light
urce top left

Diffuse
ambient lighting
from right

Contour edge
from weaker
and more
targeted light
source be-
hind object

Light source from
below

light
es
top left

Main light source
top left

Cast shadow,
sharp contrasts,
no
shades of
gray

Highlight
or contour
edge from
light source
behind
object

Highlight
or contour
edge from
light source
behind object

Soft shading resulting from
diffuse lighting

Hard lighting from directional light
source(s). **Chiaroscuro effect**

Here is a comparison between the correct (consistent) and incorrect application of light source(s) - please note:

- Used with a figure, light sources should be clearly structured - wildly changing shadows from left to right is incorrect.
- There is almost always a "ranking" of light sources: One main light source dominates, there is often a secondary light source and possible rim lighting and reflections.
- It is important to specify the main light source(s) and then apply it consistently(!) - different materials reflect light in different ways. Glass, for example, refracts light and reflects it with hard edges on the surface.
- Very important (!!): Always make sure, that there is sufficient contrast between each image element and simplify and over-emphasize, where necessary, in the interest of clarity!
- Shading a scene by using contrasts between each picture plane can also help to increase the spatial effect: for example very dark foreground, light main picture plane (middle ground) and gray/faded background (= aerial perspective).

CORRECT

Everything works well here:

1.) Careful attention to light source. Light enters clearly from the top right, all shading is consistently implemented in the appropriate manner: It is all applied in the same direction.

2.) Consistent spatial structure through directional lighting. High-contrast tonal values have been assigned to distinct spatial planes:

- Out-of-focus gray shapes very close to the "camera".
- Dark objects in foreground.
- Medium gray tones and lighter tones in "mid-ground", the most important picture plane.

- Increasingly gray and faded color values in the background - gray outlines or the omission of outlines and soft edges reinforce this effect.
- Gray values define shapes and objects and provide clarity.
- The silhouettes of trees and dog support the composition and frame the main actors, who are kept in lighter tonal values.

3.) Shading is used to define shapes and to accentuate them. All picture elements are easily "distinguishable", since sufficient contrast consistently makes them stand out from one another.

INCORRECT

This does not work:

1.) Shadows are placed in opposite directions, and there is no clearly identifiable concept for a light source. You can not tell from the drawing where the light is actually coming from - the directional lighting in itself is contradictory.

2.) The illusion of three-dimensionality is destroyed, since the different picture planes were not assigned any appropriately modified tonal values: The pictures flattens.

3.) Contrasts are missing, therefore characters and objects lose their distinguishability. This takes away considerably from the effect of the composition, which is strong in the line drawing.

Picture planes und Staging
A successful storyboard drawing puts the characters perfectly in the limelight and shows them clearly "distinguishable" against the background (if available). This "putting in the limelight" is called staging.
It is one of the most important basic principles of animation. If you want to create a spatial impression as well, then you must define distinct picture planes by using contrasting tonal values and density of detail. This can be done in different ways, but always in such a way that it appears convincing: Most importantly, the picture planes have to be very distinct, as can be seen in the examples on this double page.

Animal Drawings

All the above information also applies to the drawing of animals. For the animator, that is equally important, since the skillful animation of animal movements requires the knowledge of the relevant anatomy: We need only consider that the hind legs of dogs or horses "fold" in opposite directions than their own front legs or the legs of people. Many beginners also do not know that the leg of an animal is structured quite differently than that of humans: The place where one would expect the knee actually has the ankle or the equivalent of the wrist. When

it comes to drawing animals credibly and animating them later, even experienced animators usually need to first analyze the anatomy and movements of the relevant animal species through intensive studies of nature or reference material. The movements in horses, for example, are extremely complex. Nature studies can be very helpful in getting a feel for the animal's character beyond the purely technical analysis of movements, all of which can be incorporated into the artistic transformation. ▪

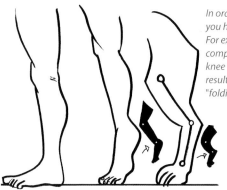

In order to animate or draw the movements of animals correctly, you have to know the differences with regard to human anatomy: For example, cats and dogs walk on the tips of their finger or toe (as compared to human anatomy). What we would first believe to be the knee of these animals, actually corresponds to the human ankle. As a result, the hind legs for the majority of animals "fold in" backwards in "folding-chair" fashion.

Horses even walk on what is the equivalent of human fingers or toe nails (= hooves).

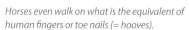

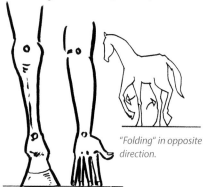

"Folding" in opposite direction.

*These sketches of mine are focused on capturing the **lines of action** of these animals without adding any shading. This is a good exercise for capturing the essence of poses and movements - as is necessary for animation. Drawing at the zoo enables you to discover typical and perhaps unusual movement patterns and poses, which differ from the cliché, yet are typical of the animal. Kangaroos or seals are ideal for studying lines of action; monkeys basically move constantly and are good objects for the quick capture of shapes.*

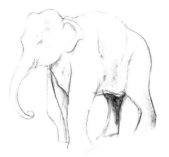

Here some quick sketches of movement, combined with loosely applied shading. Another very interesting aspect in addition to the elephant's very distinct skull structure is the shift in weight in the typical elephant's gait.

Assignment:

- Practice quick sketching of 2-to-3-minute poses during figure drawing: Focus on expressive poses and the line(s) of action!
- Draw only lines of action of the figure in 30 seconds!
- Draw quick poses as silhouettes with a brush pencil!
- Draw sequential poses, i.e. a movement (such as getting up, sitting down, hitting a golf ball) in several drawings, all as 2-to-3-minute poses
- For longer poses, concentrate on defining the dimensionality of shapes through lines!
- Practice sketching hands and feet and develop a design that works!
  ALWAYS PAY ATTENTION TO:
  lines of action; the body's center of gravity and balance; angles of the body axes; diagonals of the feet on the floor.

- Draw animals in the zoo in quick sketches!
  (The "actors" often don't give you a choice).
- Analyze displacement of the body's center of gravity in the motion of animals!

TOOLS: Brush pens are a good drawing tool for quick sketching and emphasizing action lines and silhouettes. Additionally, HB and 2B pencils, also for more detailed/longer poses, plus eraser.

TIP: These exercises should become part of a weekly routine throughout an artist's entire life - even though time and opportunities may vary for each person. If you don't have a way to practice figure drawing (even though many colleges and universities offer courses), going to the zoo or sketching from daily life are great alternatives.

Drawing for Storyboards

Storyboards require an easy-to-understand and quick-to-implement visual language: The drawings must communicate quickly and clearly content and camera perspective. For this, detail is less important, while communicating the context of the story, the sequence, is crucial! ■

Visual Storytelling
A storyboard is primarily a means of communication: Between story artist and director, between director and animator, between student and teacher, etc.. That is why the story must be intelligible through images: You have to be able to quickly and clearly understand what is shown. Figures must be recognizable, the continuity of the action must be maintained. If it is to be used for internal communication within a production team, then the primary goal is to be able to try out different versions of a story quickly: The images can even be sketchy and very informal, as long as they communicate the story!

As with comics , characters and figures in the storyboard have to be clearly and easily recognizable, ideally from all perspectives and vantage points. This is easier with highly stylized and caricatured figures than with very realistic characters in live-action movies, since they often even have to resemble real persons. This is an advantage of storyboards in animation: Animated characters can be drawn less realistic and more simplified.

In the storyboard, a character often does not have to be one-hundred-percent "on model", i.e., it does not have to look exactly like the final design - but each character must be clearly recognizable.

It may be better to stylize and reduce the styling in order to accommodate an existing complex design. This is especially true for computer-animated films, where a final design/model can be very detailed and would only complicate the storyboard. (In advertising, however, very detailed finish storyboards are sometimes required).

FINAL CHARACTER DESIGN/ MODEL.   SIMPLIFIED FOR STORYBOARD.

Spatial Representation: Perspective and Shortcuts for Perspective

It is essential to know the basic principles of perspective and spatial design: Characters and their surroundings must be presented in the storyboard across multiple viewing angles and the effects of different camera lenses have to be simulated. It is important to be able to master graphically the separation of foreground, midground and background. A more in-depth study of all aspects of perspective representation is highly recommended, for which additional literature is listed in the appendix. At this point, I would like to provide a brief overview of the most common methods of perspective representation (regarding the understanding of vanishing point perspectives):

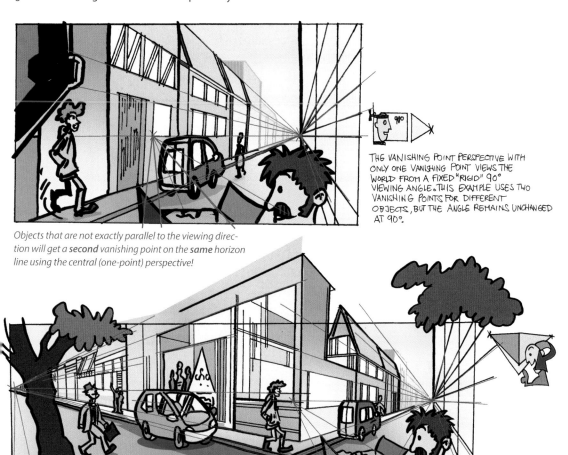

THE VANISHING POINT PERSPECTIVE WITH ONLY ONE VANISHING POINT VIEWS THE WORLD FROM A FIXED "RIGID" 90° VIEWING ANGLE. THIS EXAMPLE USES TWO VANISHING POINTS FOR DIFFERENT OBJECTS, BUT THE ANGLE REMAINS UNCHANGED AT 90°.

*Objects that are not exactly parallel to the viewing direction will get a **second** vanishing point on the **same** horizon line using the central (one-point) perspective!*

If you want to "look around the corner", it is better to work with two real different vanishing points: The viewer no longer looks at the screen at a rigid 90° angle: The angles of the horizontal line change accordingly.

IF YOU WANT TO SEE THE WORLD FROM "UP ABOVE" (OR "FROM BELOW"), A THIRD VANISHING POINT MUST BE USED!

THESE RULES CAN, OF COURSE, VARY. E.G. WITH BLURRED OBJECTS DIRECTLY IN FRONT OF THE CAMERA. HOWEVER, IT IS IMPORTANT TO CREATE **CONTRAST** BETWEEN THE VARIOUS IMAGE PLANES.

*The correct use of **light** and **color** can enhance the three-dimensional impression:*

*- Objects that are **close** to the camera are **dark** and **contrasted**.*

*- In the "mid-plane", between foreground and background, colors are **distinct** and **contrasted**.*

*- The further away the objects, the less distinctive the colors. Colors become **diffuse** and **bluish/gray** = the so-called **aerial perspective** (so called, because of the effect of the atmosphere with distant objects).*

*- Objects in the distance are **sketched**, only suggested and details omitted - even for color. This simulates the **decreasing** sharpness of more distanced objects or figures*

Shortcuts for Perspective

Storyboards often have to be developed quickly and with tight production deadlines. Therefore, a sketching method should be developed that allows for essential concepts to be quickly and easily identified: This presents the advantage of quickly creating, discarding and redrawing drawings for story development. That's why it is good to know some tricks, which you can use to suggest 3-dimensionality and perspective without having to construct a vanishing point perspective each time.

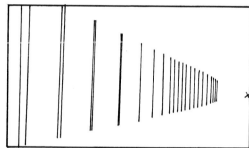

Lines already arranged at decreasing intervals, which are "trimmed" by imaginary diagonals, suggesting spatial depth as they approach an equally imaginary vanishing point. The latter is located on the equally imaginary horizon line, which corresponds to the **eye level** of the viewer.

Spatial effects are enhanced by adding other picture elements and structuring through various tonal values (see gray triangles, contrasted with white areas). Different line thicknesses are assigned to the various **picture planes** as well.

A very dark picture element combined with the appropriate scaling suggests an object very close to the camera and can be used to intensify depth perception. Other objects can go to additional vanishing points, but they must be on the **same** horizon line!

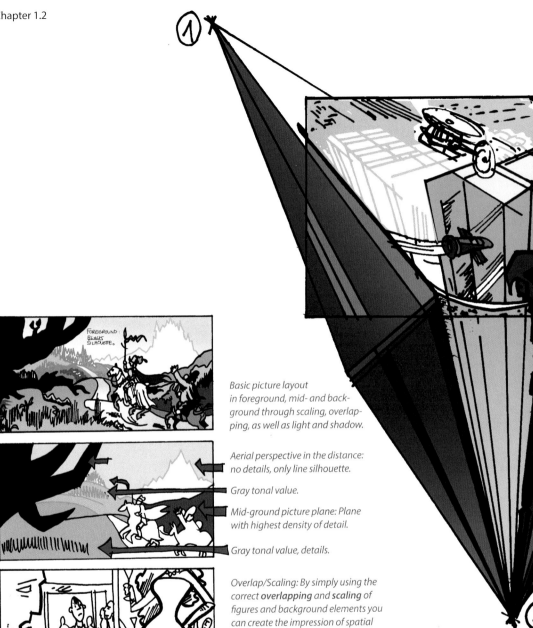

Basic picture layout
in foreground, mid- and background through scaling, overlapping, as well as light and shadow.

Aerial perspective in the distance:
no details, only line silhouette.

Gray tonal value.

Mid-ground picture plane: Plane
with highest density of detail.

Gray tonal value, details.

Overlap/Scaling: By simply using the
correct **overlapping** and **scaling** of
figures and background elements you
can create the impression of spatial
depth without having to construct a
perspective.

The deliberate use of tonal values
increases spatial impression
and separates the different picture
planes. The more distant the
elements should appear, the less
detailed they are drawn.

If you want to use vanishing points for construction, then it is better to first sketch out the general idea: This allows you to place vanishing points correctly and results in more powerful designs without appearing stilted.

DOWN SHOT = IT IS SUFFICIENT TO INDI-CATE A REDUCED BACKGROUND : YOU CAN SEE THE GROUND.

VANISHING POINT.

VANISHING POINT. UP SHOT : SAME SYSTEM, THE OTHER WAY ROUND. (YOU SEE THE CEILING).

VANISHING POINT.

IN THE UPSHOT, THE SPACING BECOMES SMALLER WITH IN-CREASING DISTANCE. THE SPACING CLOSER TO CAMERA BECOMES BIGGER . THE SAME PRINCIPLE BUT VICE VERSA.

THE REVERSE APPLIES TO THE DOWNSHOT.

IN ADDITION DIFFERENT LINE THICKNESS CAN SUGGEST PROXIMITY (THICKER) OR DISTANCE (THINNER) FROM THE CAMERA .

Light and Shadow for Storyboarding - Lighting for Atmosphere

The correct use of tonal values, i.e. the suggestion of certain lighting of a shot or a set is a very important means of expression for the storyboard: Appropriate lighting can effectively communicate the atmosphere as the story is told. The emotional and narrative effect of a shot in the storyboard can vary tremendously, depending on the lighting. Directional lighting can emphasize dramatically certain elements or figures of the image or make them almost disappear - thus lending more or less importance to the narrative statement as needed. To show a character, as is here, only as a silhouette, leaves the audience in the dark about the appearance of the character, implying almost instantly questions such as:

- Why is the character shown this way?
- Is something wrong with his/her look? Does he/she have shady intentions or a disfigured face?
- Or is it just about the gloomy atmosphere?

Lighting can be used deliberately to highlight individual characters, or to create a well lit "stage" for the characters to perform. Last but not least, you can also use alternating lighting effects to communicate the passing of time: A good example here is the contrast between day and night or the change of seasons. There are, of course, more subtle examples as well.
Here some examples on the opposite page: On the upper left you see the use of light tones to accentuate the main characters, otherwise the scenery is illuminated relatively evenly, which indicates diffused lighting from a cloudy sky. The picture below

could be a sunny autumn afternoon, the lighting is quite natural and follows classical principles, such as the dark elements in the foreground. The third drawing could be a foggy autumn or winter morning. An additional light source (street lamp) accentuates the dog. Background details disappear in the dark and fog. The very bottom shows the most extreme lighting: Night, in which the characters are visible only as silhouettes, hard contrasts are dominating. All these examples have in common that they can suggest a certain time, as well as evoke a mood. A visual narrator can use both in a logical correlation, but also contrary to expectations. ■

Assignment:

- ■ Imagine a storyboard when figure drawing:
- ■ To do this, first create a sufficient number of "blank" sheets with an aspect ratio, a TV screen or movie screen format, for example 16:9 or 1:2.35.
- ■ The model always adopts 10-minute poses.
- ■ In these frames, you now draw the poses of the model one by one, (that is, you create a composition) while imagining a story, e.g. a Western, a science fiction story or something similar.

This exercise practices a quick drawing out of the imagination in combination with the careful observation of a "real" model. If you are unable to find a figure drawing class, then finding friends, who are willing to pose dressed will work just as well.

Character Design – Virtual Casting Couch for Animated Film Stars

Character design is basically the same thing as the casting for a live-action movie: It is about finding the appropriate actors for a script or concept - for example, for an animated reinterpretation of a famous detective team.

The process of character design can have a significantly stronger influence on the content development of animation film than casting has in live-action film. It often goes hand in hand with story development during the storyboarding process: The visual development of the characters can affect the story to the same extent as the narrative requirements would inform the character development vice versa. The character design process usually begins with the traditional or digital sketch pad. Almost everyone working in the field of animation will encounter character design: Be it to develop characters for your own films, or to implement certain aspects of a character according to the specifications of the underlying character design in a studio context.

In a large studio production, one or more character designers will work closely with the director and production designer to come up with the right look for the characters. Or one specific artist may be commissioned for his/

her individual style in order to leave a mark on the production. Sometimes precise briefings are in place already, defining certain requirements for the characters: Since character design is one aspect of production design, the director and production designer, in the case of larger productions, will work closely with the character design-er(s), so that the character design fits into the overall concept of the project. The briefings are often very specific and may restrict suitable options, particularly in the area of advertising and similarly commissioned work. Such work is dominated by the taste and preferences of the customer, usually coupled with the ideas of an art director from the supervising advertising agency.

Illustration: Kathrin Albers, Michael Meier and Hannes Rall

Storyboarding
In storyboarding, the written script is "translated" into film shots (long shots, knee shots, close-up, etc.) and in the case of animation film, cuts are often pre-defined. Similar to a comic strip in appearance, it differs by the fact, that the image format is uniformly sized.

Briefing
A briefing (supplied either by the customer or internally) specifies the content of the assignment in detail: This can include concepts regarding graphic styles, animation techniques, length and costs, etc. The extent of the exact details depends largely on the interest and knowledge of the client.

For example, a briefing could be defined by embedding a historical element of a story ("animated comedy in Queen Victoria's England") and a desired graphic implementation ("references to contemporary copper engravings, strong contrast to painted backgrounds").

*A pencil **scribble** was deliberately not cleaned up, but scanned in its "raw" shape and slightly edited in Adobe Photoshop (contrast enhancement). The background is a classic painting, which was reworked as well: Modern digital programs allow for fast and straightforward experimenting of different stylistic combinations.*

The production team frequently "looks at every angle" to possibly define the tone and style of the planned film project first. In animated feature films, the character designer often gets involved very early in the process and plays an active role in determining the actual style of the film in collaboration with the production designer and director. Open and versatile experimentation during this stage is very important, so that all creative avenues can be explored.

Contrast is a basic design principle of animated film, which "runs through" character design, timing and sound - just think: small/large; thick/thin; fast/slow; loud/quiet. Lack of contrast usually leads to boredom or confusion for the audience!

It is also interesting to "cast" well-known characters "against the grain" - thus counteracting the expectations of the audience: Or arranging figures in an entirely different context. An approach that is frequently chosen in the "postmodern" 21st century.

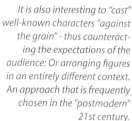

Public Domain
This term refers to artistic works where the copyright has expired (time span after the author's death varies for different territories) and thus can be used freely: Film versions of public domain books or characters, for example, can be produced without the cost of licensing fees.

This frequently results in a mutually supportive development process of story and character design: In contrast to straight live-action film, the actual story of animation film is often not developed until the storyboarding process - sometimes there is no "classic" script at all. In any case, a lot can change and a specific character design can provide inspiration for new (or different) gags and storylines.

In independent animation film production, you can often find the roles of author, director and character designer all wrapped up in one: In that case, the only limit is your own artistic intention. ■

Assignment:

Develop your own versions of a **public domain** character with the accompanying cast of "supporting actors":

- ■ Start by researching the history and interpretation of the characters during different time periods and in a contemporary context!
- ■ Research the era of the fictional characters, and draw up pertinent visual studies; decide what is important and useful for your own designs!
- ■ Return to your literary or historical sources and develop a concept for your own interpretation:
  - genuinely true to the original,
  - vaguely inspired, or
  - a drastic contradiction to the original?

Derive your own briefing from this, setting limitations for stylistic options.

Reference Material: Mood Boards and Reference Maps

Character design is rarely created in a vacuum. For the most part, it is necessary or required by the concept to first find historical or other reference material and study it in order to get inspired. Specific requirements for authenticity in terms of fashion, weapons, hairstyles, etc., are not uncommon. Even if you aspire a highly stylized version, it is often best to seek inspiration from the archetype first. This is especially true for less familiar characters, such as special animals.

The Internet is an excellent source for reference material. When looking for reference material, you need to distinguish between authentic historical image documents and artistic interpretations of an epoch or region from today's point of view and determine, which one it is you are looking for. Both can be skillfully combined into the design - but the composition of the elements must fit and ultimately result in a cohesive overall picture of the design.

Whether in the studio or independently: The character design process will usually begin with a collection of reference materials (for example, regarding fashion and culture of the Victorian era): It is helpful to compile so-called **mood boards** in order to narrow down the desired visual look by using examples or by bundling artistic reference material.

A compilation of Victorian menswear

Mood Board
The compilation of different image examples that visually communicate the desired mood of the film.

Reference Map
A collage of sometimes very different image references showing the graphic influences that are to be included in the film.
You should already have a concept in mind and not randomly select "anything you like". A thematic breakdown into different sections or elements of the film is also useful (backgrounds, characters, props).

A reference map compiles stylistic references that serve as inspiration for the final design. It is important to understand that this is by no means about copying styles but about an evolutionary development process: Combined with the individual style of the designer, a whole new design is to be created - one that is quoted at best, but never plagiarized!

Assignment:

■ Create reference maps that narrow down the stylistic direction of your cast of characters. This can and should be several maps for different stylistic directions.

Sketching Stage

A character designer will also draw as many loose sketches as possible in all kinds of stylistic variations in order to get closer to the optimal design.

Sketches for Character Development

It is not without reason that drawing is still firmly anchored in the curriculum of most animation programs: There is no faster and more direct form of visually implementing one's own artistic vision.

It is only of secondary importance whether the drawing is done traditionally, on paper, or in digital form (e.g., with a digital drawing tablet): The artistic handwriting always remains visible through the immediacy of the medium as the individuality of the designer transfers directly into the design. Quick sketching also has a spontaneity and expressive power, which is hardly attainable with any other medium. Good character designers will usually make a lot of fast sketches, presenting many variations of a character in different actions and moods.

Thanks to modern digital production methods, almost every "stroke" can be implemented in the production process unchanged. It is very attractive not having to "clean up" spontaneous scribbles first, but to be able to "blow them up" directly by copying them and using them as a template for the animation (works only for 2D animation, of course).

The results of the earlier research conducted, influence the artistically tried and tested style versions. Especially students and beginners tend not to make enough drawings for fear of producing the "wrong" versions or "bad" drawings: This is faulty reasoning, since even unsuitable designs help to find the right path and sort through the visual design process. In addition, designs often emerge as favorites, which are not perceived as such during the initial process of rapid sketching.

Assignment:

■ Using a pencil or brush pen (or digitally), draw as many scribbles and sketches as quickly and loosely as possible, in order to be able to select the best versions later. That should be in excess of 100 scribbles.

Particularly at the beginning of the pre-production or visual development stage, it may be quite possible, or even preferred, for one or more character designers to experiment with a wide-ranging variety of styles. The actual style of the film has yet to be found at this time and the open-mindedness of the process can lead to artistically extraordinary and outstanding results.

SILHOUETTE- LOTTE -
REINIGER-STYLE .

The classic detectives here in the style of Germany's famous pioneer of animated silhouette film, Lotte Reiniger.

Dynamic Ligne Claire and not a line too much! Maybe fancy that even for 3D?

Since the artists assigned to this first stage of development and experimentation often come from various stylistic backgrounds, many of these so-called exploratory designs end up in the drawer or will only be incorporated into certain aspects of the final design. The same applies to the individual designer, who will ultimately have to select one version from the multitude of designs he created.

Although hand-drawing is still the ideal first step towards an original character design, other means, mostly digital media and tools are added, depending on the animation technique:

Illustration: Michael Meier

For example, in Photoshop or similar programs, a character designed for 3D animation can be digitally painted or textured in a way that is close to the final "look" in the movie.

A stronger stylization and simplification of the character design does not necessarily mean a reduction in the aesthetic quality – it often can lead to the exact opposite: The figures acquire more of a "unique selling point" (more originality), since the "personal handwriting" of the designer is more clearly presented.

✳ Technically speaking the boundaries between 2D and 3D animation have become increasingly fluid. Modern 2D animation software also integrates 3D elements and has even become capable of including stereoscopy.

IN GENERAL: THE CHARACTER DESIGN SHOULD IDEALLY ANSWER TO THE REQUIREMENTS OF THE SCRIPT/NARRATIVE CONCEPT. IF A HIGHER LEVEL OF REALISM IS REQUIRED TO MAKE THE VISUAL STORYTELLING CREDIBLE, THE CHARACTER DESIGN MUST TAKE THIS INTO ACCOUNT.

The more details are used, the more distinguishable they have to be in order not to overwhelm the viewer visually. The "distinguishability" of the shapes in motion mustn't get lost in the detail. A principle that is often not sufficiently heeded, especially in contemporary computer animation.

Final Finishing Touches - Model Sheets and Character Turnarounds, Comparison Sheets and Character Maquettes

Final design by Michael Meier of the characters intended for a 3D computer animation film.

Additional refinements are usually required after the preliminary completion of the design process and the definition of basic character design:

- In 2D animation, an optimization of character design by the responsible lead animator (or character lead) is often used in larger productions. Here, very specific requirements of the design's "animability" come to fruition, and often particular aspects of the design are customized. Usually, the animator himself is an extremely talented designer, who can still make vital contributions for further improvements. A famous example is the legendary animator Milt Kahl who provided the finishing touches for character designs in many Disney films.

Once the actual design process has been completed, the look of the character has to be communicated in every detail and from very perspective to all parties involved in the production.

This is especially true for traditional 2D production, where the method used for drawing a character must be standardized. Otherwise the character would constantly change its appearance in the course of a film, depending on which animator had drawn it.

Model Sheet
A figure is presented in different poses and moods as well as analyzed visually in its basic graphic design.

Often, indications are also added for certain solutions in the animation, i.e. typical movement and behavioral patterns and their graphical solution. The intention is to ensure a stylistically coherent implementation of the character throughout the film.

For this purpose, the appearance of the character is stipulated in so-called **model sheets**, which is binding for all those involved in the production process: These are drawings of the character in different actions and emotional states, often with additional explanations of how certain details are to be handled. The drawings are produced mostly by the lead animator of a character, after experimental refinement of the character design through animation testing has taken place.

Above all, a good model sheet must reveal a character's construction of several basic geometric shapes in order to facilitate the animator's work:

It is easier, for example, to reshape a circle and to draw it in perspective, than having to deal with the entire complexity of a design all at once.

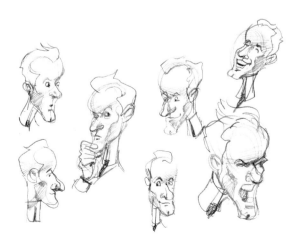

Model sheet of two characters, which primarily illustrate how the design changes to express certain moods of the character.
illustrations: Michael Meier

Character Comparison Sheet

Character Comparison Sheet
Shows the entire cast of a movie in size comparison, in order to avoid any fluctuations in proportion between the characters during production.

Character Turnaround
Shows the typical character from at least four different angles in a full 360° turn. In 3D computer animation, this is equivalent to the **character turntable**, a constant full 360° camera movement around the 3D model of the character.

In the **character comparison sheet**, the proportions of the individual characters to one another are fixed, which is particularly important in traditional 2D production in order to provide the animators with a benchmark at all times. For the implementation in 3D, the comparison sheet provides modeling staff with equally important information for the scaling of the charac-ters. In addition, a **character turnaround** is created: Views of the characters from different angles from the back and front, from ¾- and ¼-turns. Such a turnaround allows the animators to draw the character correctly from all angles and unifies the appearance of the character throughout the production, which often involves the collaboration of many different animators. ∎

Character turnaround of a character design (in this case for a subsequent 3D animation).
Illustration: Michael Meier

Specific Requirements for 3D Animation

The foregoing also applies to the final de-sign of characters in 3D computer animation: What is generally first a two-dimensional de-sign, has to be transferred to the third dimen-sion - a process which is implemented in dig-ital modeling and poses quite a challenge. It requires great skill and ideally the close collaboration with the character designer and other creative professionals. The goal is to retain the vitality and original charm of the initial drafts. The earlier a character design takes into account the requirements of a sub-sequent three-dimensional implementation, the less complications will arise in the model-ing that follows. On the other hand, the chal-lenge of implementing an unusually drawn character design in 3D can lead to innovative design approaches for computer animation that is otherwise often inclined to apply too generic solutions.

It is very helpful and common to draw a char-acter design for 3D animation as a character turnaround from different spatial perspec-tives. This allows the modeler later to stay close to the original ideas of the character designer.

Additional modifications can take place in the CG workflow, when a character is provided with a virtual skeleton in rigging after modeling: Generally, a good rigger will of course try to adapt his work to the character, and not vice versa. Sometimes, however, certain aspects after rigging and animation testing may prove rather impractical and additional adjustments have to be made.

Ultimately, the more technically complex a production, the more essential a precise coordination: A good collaboration of all parties involved is essential in order to achieve a convincing character design for the final result. Just think of photo-realistic characters with highly complex simulations, etc.
Still, the principle should always apply that the artistic vision determines the technical implementation, and not vice versa!

The finished 3D model is often based on the drawn character turnaround, which shows the character in a complete turnaround. After the process of 3D modeling has been completed in computer animation, you actually no longer need a model sheet, since the character is a virtual puppet and can only be manipulated within its skeletal limitations (character rig). Nevertheless, there are usually instructions and guidelines on how to animate the character, which angles are favorable and which to avoid, etc.　■

Turnaround model sheet of a 3D character from "Spycat and the Paper Chase", graduation film by Darren Lim, Derwin Silamaya Suhali, Fung Chun Hong and Soh Yu Xian, Nanyang Technological University 2011.

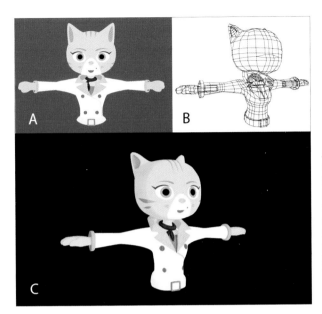

*A 3D animated character is modeled as a **wireframe**. Therefore, the character design has to function in three dimensions from all angles. "Honeycat" from "Spycat and the Paper Chase", graduation film by Darren Lim, Derwin Silamaya Suhali, Fung Chun Hong and Soh Yu Xian, Nanyang Technological University 2011.*

Character Maquettes

In order to enable an illustrator to visualize his character in the third dimension, it is helpful to create a so-called character maquette: a small sculpture of the character that can be turned and viewed from all angles. This helps tremendously in rendering the character correctly, if you are seeking to produce an illusion of a volumetric character in the "flat" medium of 2D animation. For many decades, the creation of character maquettes was common practice with Disney for most of the full-length animation films - at times even with a separate department to do that job. Similarly, creating an "analogous" sculpture can help shape the artist's own artistic vision in the third dimension before a character design in modeling is cast into its final shape for CG. ■

Character maquette as part of a final project (Wang Rui Fan, Digital Animation, School of Art, Design and Media, Nanyang Technological University).

Character Design for Puppet Animation (Stop Motion)

In puppet animation, perhaps the most famous form of stop-motion animation, a real modeled sculpture also becomes the starting point for the puppet. This puppet, which is later usually equipped with interior workings of wire or even an elaborate movable metal skeleton, is also used for filming. Of course, the same rule applies in its most direct form as well: the design of the character must satisfy the requirements of three-dimensionality: After all, the character is supposed to look good from many - if not all - camera angles. For this reason, a design stage with drawings is only of limited value, when it comes to testing the three-dimensional design later.

As shown in the example of the main character as inspector from the puppet film "Whodunnit" by the well-known stop motion animator and designer Kathrin Albers from Hamburg, the design process quickly proceeded to the third dimension after some relatively rough sketches in the beginning.

On the right you see the complete cast of characters from the film "Whodunnit". Here you see the principle of an interesting mixture and good distinguishability of the characters: The characters are based on interesting combinations of basic geometric shapes, which vary significantly in the final result.

Illustrations and design: Kathrin Albers

Here is an example of how such combinations can be transferred from the original drawing to the third dimension.
illustrations: Kathrin Albers

It represents an interesting new version of the famous detective, who is introduced in this chapter in so many different incarnations. This three-dimensional form of the character would also work well as a digital model in computer animation - the design principles to be applied are basically the same. "Whodunnit" is also a film that is shot stereoscopically, so the dimension of spatial depth and plasticity is even more important.

According to Kathrin's experience, problems as well as options usually don't show up until this stage: A character design that is appealing as a drawing can have an unattractive effect in plastic form; just as a drawing, which may appear too conventional or boring at first, can work surprisingly well when transferred to a sculpture. These sketches show, however, that the construction of simple, but highly contrasted combinations of basic shapes can contribute to a successful design.

Kathrin also explores the power of silhouette in her design process. As with 2D designs, this is a good test for the "distinguishability" of the character.
illustrations: Kathrin Albers

Principles of Good Character Design - Style and Overall Design - Character Design as Part of Production Design

It is important to understand that character design is not just about creating pretty drawings of appealing characters. According to the principle of "form follows function", character design has to function well in the conceptual overall context of the film: The characters have to harmonize stylistically, that is, they must come from the same design world. At the same time, they must exhibit sufficient contrast as a cast, in order to be clearly distinguishable and to ensure effective and interesting staging during joint appearances in the film. ■

Three well-distinguishable characters - yet even here, a common stylistic feature: Reduced to simplest graphical shapes, precise basic geometric shapes, simple flat 2D approach. A high degree of stylization!

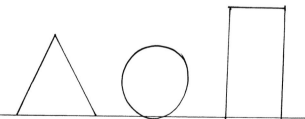

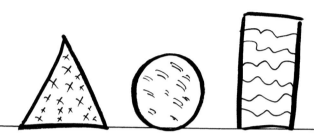

We can also add more features that help to assimilate the characters stylistically: Here it is the wide brush stroke, with which the outlines are drawn, and the addition of graphic texture.

— MORE STYLISTIC SIMILARITIES: OUTLINES & TEXTURES.

— POSING (WITH STRONG **LINES OF ACTION**) COMMUNICATES AN ATTITUDE.

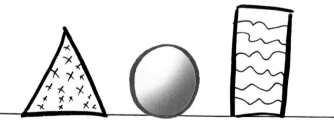

— **STYLISTIC INCONSISTENCY**: A CHARACTER (MIDDLE) RENDERED IN A 3D-VOLUMETRIC STYLE CLEARLY IS AT ODDS WITH THE MORE GRAPHIC CHARACTER DESIGNS OF THE OTHER FIGURES.

Not like this!
We are sticking with the basic geometric shapes, but the guy in the middle does not quite fit into the overall cast. Its 3D volumetric style comes from a different graphic world. Exception: The following story could justify this kind of design approach. If the 3D sphere were defined as an outsider and the story were dealing with a conflict between 2D and 3D, then this design too would be consistent: form follows function!

Character and Environment

It is also important to ensure that the interplay between the characters and the environment of the film, i.e. the background or virtual space, works well. There are basically two possible approaches.

— CHARACTER AND BACKGROUND IN THE SAME LOOK: CAREFUL PLANNING OF THE STAGING MUST ALLOW EASY READABILITY. THE CHARACTER HAS TO BE ABLE TO PERFORM ITS ACTIONS IN THE COURSE OF THE SCENE IN SUCH A WAY THAT IT ALWAYS REMAINS CLEARLY RECOGNIZABLE AGAINST THE BACKGROUND.

Illustration above:
The style of the characters and surroundings/backgrounds are very similar and have the same stylistic features - this unites both as elements of the same world. This approach, however, requires careful staging to ensure that the characters always remain "distinguishable" against the background. This is especially true for 2D production.

Illustration below:

The other approach is the deliberate stylistic contrast between character and background. For a long time, this was an economic necessity for 2D film, since only static backgrounds could be painstakingly painted. The advantage of this method is the good separability and distinguishability of the characters against the background. The obvious disadvantage lies in the stylistic discrepancy between the acting characters and their surroundings. However, this "breach" has been artistically accepted for a long time in the world of traditional 2D animation film. As with all design decisions in a production, a consistent and convincing implementation is particularly important.

— CHARACTER AND BACKGROUND IN STRONGLY DIFFERING
  STYLES: EVEN WITH STRONG OVERLAPPING OF FIGURE
  AND BACKGROUND, THE CLARITY IS GUARANTEED.
  IT IS NECESSARY, NEVERTHELESS, TO ESTABLISH
  SIMILARITIES IN THE DESIGNS OF THE FIGURES AND
  BACKGROUNDS, IN ORDER TO AVOID A STYLISTIC BREAK.

  IN THIS CASE, STYLISTIC CONSISTENCY IS ACHIEVED
  BY APPLYING THE GENERAL CONCEPT OF STRONG
  STYLIZATION AND SIMPLIFICATION OF CHARACTER AND ENVIROMENT.

This is where the style of the UPA Studio in the 50s and 60s came in and broke with the commercially established tradition: An overriding design concept combined stylized characters with equally strongly stylized backgrounds and created a stylistic unity.

In commercial 3D films, a mix of the two approaches is usually used: Using photo-realistic rendering, "cartoony" characters are unified with equally detailed and mostly realistically structured environments. The use of cinematographic stylistic devices (depth of field, cinematography and lighting), which is more closely related to live-action film, facilitates effective staging. The character designer's design must also meet this concept. ∎

The semi-realistic character designs shown here could be used both, for implementation in 2D (drawn) as well as in stylized 3D computer animation. For a 3D version, character designers and modelers would need to work together closely.
illustrations: Michael Meier

* UPA was an innovative animation studio in the United States with a revolutionary impact in the 40s and 50s: It established modern art and graphic design to be used for commercial animation. This often involved the technique of limited animation.

Appeal

One of the classic **principles of animation** is that the characters of an animation film have **appeal**. Appeal should not be understood as the drawing of "cute" characters, (a misconception popularized by the illustrations of cute anthropomorphic cartoon animals frequently shown in reference books). Rather, it is about designing appealing characters. If a design is consistent, even characters commonly regarded as "ugly" or threatening, can have a lot of appeal. Good examples of this are the characters of Tim Burton, which -at least initially - ran counter to the usual Disney stereotype of beauty or aesthetics (and thus the established mainstream-market). However, they are in themselves a graphically completely coherent expression of an artistic vision and therefore have an enormous "appeal". Ironically in this case, the taste of the commercial masses changed completely over time, and now the creations of Burton are part of the mainstream, which is certainly due not least to the graphic consistency, the appeal of the characters. ∎

I am also a very handsome guy....

Principles of Animation
The traditional principles of animation were first developed by the animators of Disney Studios in the 1930s, combining the analysis of live-action film and experimental artistic interpretation. Since then, they have been continuously expanded and refined, but have remained applicable and valid in their original form to this day. However, this applies primarily to Disney's school of "caricatured realism". The principals of motion dynamics in particular, work very well for stylistically very different or even experimental/abstract animations. Chapter 2 deals with these principles in detail.

How do you Design Characters With Appeal?

Interestingly, deliberate and purposeful design is often perceived as "appealing" by the viewer: Animation requires shapes that can be animated in such a way, so that their complexity does not complicate a convincing animation. Thus, an economy of shapes, resulting from an economy of production means, can lead to a very "appealing" design: One might visualize characters composed of simple geometric shapes, and combine them in an interesting manner. ■

— CHARACTER DESIGN, WHICH IS BASED ON THE HIGHLY VARIED AND CONTRAST-RICH COMBINATION OF SIMPLE AND BASIC GEOMETRIC SHAPES.

Illustration above:
In the same way, you should also be able to trace more complex and realistic characters to a single basic shape or a combination of basic shapes in order to achieve a strong design. With this method, you can also achieve the desired contrast between the individual cast members of an animation film.

The cardinal's design concept Richelieu deliberately avoids any detail to emphasize his mysterious/menacing character.

Composition and Proportion

For a good design, it is crucial to combine basic geometric shapes in an artistically convincing manner. In doing so, the fundamental rules governing good composition come into play: Irregularity and interesting variation of shape and line. Furthermore, contrasts between the shapes within the characters and finally, stylistic means, such as the line of action, which combine contrasting individual elements into a whole.

— WORKS WITH SMALL ADJUSTMENTS EVEN FOR MORE REALISTIC DESIGNS.

SUCH CURVES FORM A DELIGHTFUL CONTRAST TO THE OTHERWISE ANGULAR DESIGN OF THE FIGURE.

Aramis

Athos

Porthos

JAMIC OF D'ARTAGNAN OGRESSIVE, WHICH HIS ROLE IN THE STORY.

The relationships of the characters in a cast should also be intelligently reflected in the design, thereby supporting the effects of the story on the audience and reinforcing narrative clarity. ◼

Left an example of a very well-known cast of characters.

Cast of Characters and Design

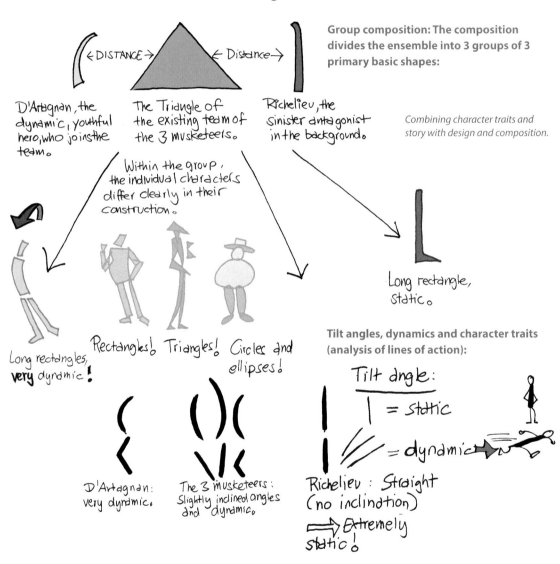

Group composition: The composition divides the ensemble into 3 groups of 3 primary basic shapes:

←DISTANCE→   ← Distance→

D'Artagnan, the dynamic, youthful hero, who joins the team.

The Triangle of the existing team of the 3 musketeers.

Richelieu, the sinister antagonist in the background.

Combining character traits and story with design and composition.

Within the group, the individual characters differ clearly in their construction.

Long rectangle, static.

Long rectangles, **very** dynamic!

Rectangles! Triangles! Circles and ellipses!

Tilt angles, dynamics and character traits (analysis of lines of action):

D'Artagnan: very dynamic.

The 3 musketeers: Slightly inclined angles and dynamic.

Tilt angle:

| = static

| /// = dynamic

Richelieu: Straight (no inclination)

⇒ Extremely static!

The following important objectives are achieved with this type of construction and composition :

■ Clear distinction of the characters (good contrast between each individual character).

■ Concept for an overall design of a group.

■ Statements about character traits and relationship of the individual characters to one another through design and composition.

■ Connecting narration and design - "form follows function".

Weight and Balance, Personality and Action

A common beginner's mistake in character design is to design characters in completely neutral and nondescript poses. Often the figures lack a credible balance and representation of the center of gravity.

— **WRONG**: FIGURES ARE LACKING ANY CLEAR INTERNAL MOTIVATION, ACTION GOAL OR ATTITUDE. BORING COMPOSITION, WRONG PROPORTIONS AND LACK OF CONTRAST IN DESIGN MAKE FOR THE UNAPPEALING OUTCOME.

Arrows indicate the center of gravity.

This can and must be avoided by understanding the attitude and motivation of the character prior to drawing - along with the physical balance and the line of action. In other words: Give your character a purpose!

— **MUCH BETTER**: A CLEAR INTERNAL MOTIVATION DETERMINES THE POSES. CENTER OF GRAVITY AND THE LINES OF ACTION ARE CLEARLY DEFINED.

A character designer is creating a virtual actor. That's why he can not sit back satisfied after a half-way accomplished drawing, but must try to figure out through many sketches, how his character can express and perform the emotions and actions required for the film.

— **NATURALLY** A LIVELY OUTLINE, VARIABLE IN LINE THICKNESS CAN FURTHER ADD TO THE APPEAL (ALTHOUGH IT REQUIRES MORE WORK FOR FINAL PRODUCTION).

Assignment:

Decide on several (at least three) basic stylistic versions for your cast of characters and develop them completely with:

- Clean-up in different line and color versions
- Digital paintings that illustrate 3D volumes and textures
- Model sheets
- Character comparison sheet
- Character turnarounds
- Character maquettes (optional)

Some suggestions in different stylistic versions:

Robin Hood

Unknown jungle hero

Captain Ahab (Moby Dick)

Don Quijote and Sancho Panza

*For a classic 2D design, the shapes should be simplified and stylized, with **outlines** in uniform line thickness.*

Such elaborate textures would have been unthinkable in the past, but are now possible with 3D and 2D hybrid techniques (although still not the easiest way).

A Barbarian

With modern 2D software, outlines can be animated with variable line thickness as well.

Variation with shadow outlines (2D).

In this variation exercise of a classical barbarian, the basic orientation of the character design remains the same: The experimentation is carried out through variations in line thickness and color combinations as well as stylistic options for the background.

What is Production Design for Animation?

In production design, the goal is to create the worlds in which the animated characters move: The surroundings and characters must go together to create the impression of a believable animated universe.

It's about the **look**, the appearance of the film: If a film is set in China or ancient Rome, it should also be designed accordingly - to reflect the look of place and time. The design must create an entire world in which the film is set, thereby uniting the characters and their environment as a credible whole. This requires clear design rules and guidelines, which all parties involved will follow during the production process. Character design is an integral part of production design - since the characters have to fit into the overall concept. A good production designer must be able to work artistically versatile: His designs must construct the film's universe in such a way that it adapts to the content requirements of the film. It is not a matter of placing your own artistic style in the foreground, but of optimally adapting the design to the entire vision of the film.

Briefing

Production design begins with briefing. The director describes his artistic intention for the film to the production designer, who then makes suggestions and starts with the artistic **research.**

Research

As with character design, which is only one aspect of the entire production design, the designer will conduct visual research based on the briefing and create a reference map (also referred to as mood board). This reference map serves as both, orientation and source of inspiration. The collected material should only be used as a starting point or reference. Together with the designer's own artistic style, this evolution should lead to something new in the design process - it cannot, under any circumstances, result in plagiarism or uninspired copies!

Here is a mood board for a student project (artist/director: Yew Ee Venn, 2013/14), which is based on a Chinese tale and is therefore designed in the style of Chinese painting. On the right, a design created for the project, based on the mood board.

Depending on the project and briefing, a research can have very different objectives. That is why it is so important to define the project's artistic direction through briefing.

■ Is it about authenticity and a high aspiration for realism? Then research is needed to document the historical context (architecture, clothing, weapons, etc.) and landscape/geography accurately by means of appropriate pictorial material. Depending on the time period and availability, this may include photos or paintings, drawings and illustrations. With the appropriate budget, this can also lead to on-site research - which of course is hard to beat. Once this documentation is available, it can then serve as the basis for implementing it into different styles - from realistic to very stylized.

■ A somewhat different approach could be to establish a connection between the time and place of action and a corresponding contemporary and culture-specific art:

Concept illustration by Michael Meier for a medieval project with realistic approach: Both the castle and landscape are based on the research of real objects, which were then re-arranged for this image. However, the castle is an idealized combination of various real existing buildings of the High Middle Ages. This style would be suitable for a CG film, which also comes close to the cinematography, visual effects and lighting of a live-action film.

The design of the animated short film "As You Like It" by Hannes Rall applies the action of the Shakespeare play to a Southeast Asian setting. For this, research was conducted into the tradition of Indonesian shadow puppetry play "Wayang Kulit"and the architecture of water temples and palaces in Bali.
Illustration: Lim Wei Ren Darren/Hannes Rall.

- In fantasy films, an amalgam of different cultures and eras is often used for the development of visual design. Since this is not about historical accuracy, original designs, documentary photographs, and art styles of all time periods and cultures can be collected and mixed. It is important, however, that it is all based on a method - an overall artistic vision.
- A different and very "postmodern" concept is the approach to work with "reference to pop culture". Examples are researched, of how a specific classic genre is turned into pop culture of a specific time period or for an entire time span. This is usually the case with genre parodies or tributes, which are largely based on a recognition factor of certain elements familiar to the audience. A good example are parodies of spy films of the 60s and the "swinging sixties" in London. The research will therefore be based on defining typical design elements of these films and the visual culture of the 1960s.

The very successful student production "Spycat and the Paper Chase" (Lim Wei Ren Darren, Fung Chun Hong, Derwin Silamaya Suhali and Soh Yu Xian, Nanyang Technological University, 2011).

An agent parody that works with a lot of references from pop culture: The design elements and color design of the Bond films from the 60s and 70s are used as well as their countless parodies. Retro-futurism of "Steam Punk" is introduced as well: The villain resides in a gigantic airship.
The design of weapons and furnishings is reminiscent of the vision of the 1950s.

This is not about authenticity and " primary sources" , but about the reinterpretation of previous artistic adaptations combined with the resuscitation of a zeitgeist.

It is not without reason that the production design process is also referred to as the visual development of a film project

As a rule, several different versions of this visual implementation are tried out - in the case of large productions, usually with several concept artists, who apply their different styles in the context of the film project. The production designer will "cast" these concept artists like actors so that they are a good fit artistically for the development approaches of the film, i.e. for the briefing. It is always up to him, together with the director, to keep an overview of the big picture and to correct and modify any developing design, even to intervene creatively. Depending on the project, visual development is usually not a completely linear process, but a trial-and-error process, in which the creativity and visual ideas of all participants are always in demand. It is the task of the production designer, in coordination with the director, to specify an **artistic framework**. The artistic intention and the requirements of visual storytelling determine the design. The desired degree of realism in production, on the other hand, strongly influences the extent to which the production design is required to keep the actual authenticity or given complete freedom of artistic expression.

Designs of landscapes for the animation short film "Si Lun-chai" (2014). Production designer: Cheng Yu Chao, director: Hannes Rall.

These designs merged the research of authentic Southeast Asian landscapes with mythically idealized elements. Stylization dominates over realism.

Consider the following example:

An animated "**Viking film**" can look quite **different**, depending on the specifications given for the story and resulting style.

Ill. top right:
A photograph of
Þjóðveldisbærinn in
Iceland, a reconstruction
of the Stöng long house
from the Viking-era. The
medieval building is said to
have constituted the center
of a Viking farm, belonging
to a Viking princess. The
design takes elements of
this building and combines
it with other contemporary
references.

Ill. center right:
Oscar Wergeland, 1909,
"Norsemen Landing in Ice-
land". This illustration is no
longer correct from today's
historical perspective (for ex-
ample, the winged helmet of
the leader), and is therefore
balanced with other sources
for the final design. However,
it shows the more realistic
aspiration in the representa-
tion, which is the basis of the
overall concept.

1.) A story with high **aspirations for realism** - an exciting adventure film from the Viking era. Fixed time and locations: Scandinavia (Norway) and England of the 9th century. Resulting style: Realism.

Research for the Production Design
Primary references:

Historical documents, archaeological finds of original Viking art and crafts, photographs and footage from locations in Norway and England.

Secondary references:

Depictions of the Viking Age in film and art. In order for the story to be communicated credibly, everything must be "correct" or at least appear sufficiently authentic. The focus here, however, is on certain aspirations for realism instead of "pop-cultural" references.

Ill. left:
Knob of a Viking sword

2.) A **parody** of Viking films with **fantasy elements**. Resulting style: implemented as a more stylized animation film - very **cartoony** and **semi-funny**, also known as "caricatured realism".

Research for Production Design
Primary references:
Same as 1.) - however, the results can be implemented much more freely and playfully. In this case, even the research for facts and real scenes of action can be skipped, since it is about an exaggeration of stereotypes. On the other hand, caricatures and stylizations are often most effective when based on reality.

Secondary references:
Representations of Viking clichés in animation, film, contemporary art and illustration, folklore and customs.

Ill. left:
"Vikings" on Shrove Tuesday in Weingarten 2013: The important factor here is the "over the top", deliberately caricaturing a character from the reference material, which corresponds to the parody approach of the film.

Realism does not play a key role here - since authenticity is not the goal. Nevertheless, this style retains a certain sense of realism: vanishing point and three-dimensionality are still used realistically. While the representation of the anatomy is exaggerated, it is still based on reality. The color design is also excessive in comparison to the first example, but still implies a certain lighting mood and therefore daytime.

3.) A highly stylized artistic animation film about Viking legends. References from the "real" world are almost non-existent. Instead, the design is entirely inspired by medieval art, for example by the Bayeux Tapestry, the ornamentation of Viking art and the form language of Nordic runes.

Detail from the Bayeux Tapestry,
ca. 1070.

A characteristic, for example, is the abandoning of any realistic vanishing point perspective, which did not return to Western art until the Renaissance: Therefore, this style reflects the representational forms that were common during the Viking era.

The color scheme and lighting neither define a three-dimensional representation, nor a certain time-related lighting effect. It acts exclusively as a separation for graphically "flat" applied picture planes. This style has the highest abstraction factor.

The need for a consistent design world becomes apparent quickly when the characters and surroundings of the most widely differing concepts 1.) and 3.) are exchanged.

The character in front becomes a foreign body in that particular environment. It does not work, unless it follows a desired narrative concept (as in the classic "fish-out-of-water" story). In other words, if the highly stylized character were from a make-believe world, it would justify the extremely different style.

That means:
The production design should always be implemented in such a way that it optimally supports the **intelligibility** of the story and its **emotional impact** on the viewer.

This production design by Hans Bacher for the feature film project "The Nibelungen" (written and directed by Hannes Rall) achieves iconic effect by limiting colors and shapes, and by focusing on a strong silhouette of the stylized character.
This meets two key objectives for good production design: The protagonist is presented concisely and the coloring results in a dramatic effect.

What does this mean using the specific example of a magical world?

The (production) design should reflect the character of a figure or a whole culture. This should also extend to the environment, home, utensils and objects (props) used in the film.

In a film in which **two cultures** of **magicians** occur, for example, this can be implemented by creating a corresponding environment for one **character** and **culture**, who lives a **very austere** life according to **strict principles**: Buildings are defined by clear geometric shapes, straightforward and with a "clear edge", the architecture reaches for the sky. This design sends a message of purity and spirituality, which is supported by the **color scheme** for this culture: White dominates the scene, clear contrasts prevail, there are hardly any shades of gray or intermediate shades. This approach continues to be consistently applied in the **costume design** and with the appropriate accessories: unadorned, simple robes, clear and pure in color. None of the characters wear jewelry. If you create a design for computer animation, the textures (of fabrics) should suggest the most basic materials.

THE "GOOD", ASCETIC MAGICIANS:
THE STRAIGHT FORWARD CHARACTER OF THESE
PROTAGONISTS IS IMPLEMENTED IN THE APPROPRIATE
PRODUCTION DESIGN FOR THEIR WHOLE CULTURE:
CLEAR LINES, WHITE DOMINATES – NO PLAYFUL SHAPES,
BUT CLARITY AND PURITY INSTEAD (PURISTIC
DESIGN REPRESENTS THE ASCETICISM OF THE
CHARACTERS/WORLD).

DESIGN PRINCIPLE
HORIZONTAL AND
VERTICAL STRAIGHTS
═════ |||
+ CIRCLES + ELLIPSES
○ ○ ○
SYMMETRY +
ORDER

COSTUME, PROPS:
NO JEWELERY,
SIMPLE ROBE =
ASCETIC
CHARACTER.

THE **CHARACTER DESIGN** IS BASED
ON SIMPLE BASIC GEOMETRIC
SHAPES – THIS PRINCIPLE IS CONTINUED
THROUGH THE PRODUCTION DESIGN AS
A WHOLE.

Conversely, a protagonist with an **obscure, shady character, hedonistic, and with a playfully scheming demeanor, will find his visual counterpart** in the design of his surroundings: Round, intricate forms dominate, rich ornamentation decorates furnishings and buildings. Architecture does not have a clear direction in its form language - parts of the buildings reach towards the sky, while others seem to grow into the ground. The design therefore defines the visual equivalent for the ambivalence of the character(s). The **color scheme** supports this effect as well: Gloomy tones predominate, there are more faded nuances and shades of gray of all colors. Similar to the counter-design of the other culture, this approach is continued throughout the **costume design** and design of the **props**. The robes of the characters are richly adorned and decorated. Abundant jewelry and the penchant for jewels communicates the attraction to worldly pleasures and the greed for material goods. Textures would suggest valuable fabrics such as velvet and silk.

THE **GLOOMY, MORALLY SHADY WIZARDS**:
HERE, THE PRODUCTION DESIGN REFLECTS THE CHARACTER OF THE PROTAGONISTS WITH/THROUGH THE INTRICATE, PLAYFUL FORMS OF THEIR SURROUNDINGS, COSTUMES AND ACCESSORIES. NOTHING IS CLEAR AND EASILY RECOGNIZABLE. THE SHAPE ARE BAROQUE AND AMBIVALENT IN THEIR ORIENTATION - WHICH COMMUNICATES THE TURNING TOWARDS MATERIAL THINGS AND EARTHLY DELIGHTS.

DESIGN PRINCIPLE: CURVES

PROPS: THIS CULTURE WORSHIPS JEWELS AND JEWELERY.

THE **FORM LANGUAGE** IS REPEATED/REFLECTED THROUGHOUT PROPS, COSTUMES, ARCHITECTURE AND CHARACTER DESIGN.

ADDING **SUPPORTING CHARACTERS** CAN PROVIDE ADDITIONAL INFORMATION ABOUT THE DEPICTED CULTURE.

ASYMMETRY + CHAOS:
THE SHAPES OF ARCHITECTURE ARE NOT CLEAR IN THEIR ORIENTATION: THEY STRIVE "SKYWARDS" AS WELL AS TO THE GROUND.
(= MORAL AMBIGUITY/CONFLICT)

This design method can be extended both to the production design for surroundings, clothing and accessories of individual characters, as well as to the design of entire groups or cultures - provided that any common character traits have been defined. This approach can be found in the fantasy genre of animation films, - but applies to other genres as well.

As we know from the "real world", larger groups almost always share locally defined cultural similarities, which can be taken into account with the appropriate design. People who live in the same place over a longer period of time will usually develop behavioral and cultural similarities.

Interesting in this context is the approach of signaling an outsider status of a single character within a larger group by using a completely different design.

Consistent implementation of production designs

The preceding examples have illustrated: A good production design should ensure that an established design principle for a film is implemented consistently in all areas of production. **Good movies** have a **consistent design - bad movies** are often characterized by wild, **chaotic styles**, which do not follow any logical rules. In the worst case, even the same characters may look different in different scenes, or specified design rules are ignored for a particular culture in the film. The following applies: Rules can always be broken, but there must be a good content-specific and design reason to do so!

Within a film, single or multiple sequences can, of course, also be designed in **different design styles**, provided there is a **content-related motivation**. Classic examples of this are dream sequences, flashbacks or subjective narrative perspectives. In this case, changing to another design supports the communication of the story.

Example "The Cold Heart"

In my film "The Cold Heart", I followed a holistic approach to production design: it is based on influences of German expressionism, an impression of similar traditional wood and linocuts, and the **excessive** graphic contrast of straights against curves.

Hans Bacher elaborated on this in his blog (2012):
"Several animators from Asia and Europe have worked on the filming of this stylized German fairy tale. Written by WILHELM HAUFF in the nineteenth century, the story tells of a young man whose heart is corrupted by greed. Sounds very much like a very contemporary story, nothing that requires an ordinary look. Stylistically, Hannes decided on a mixture of elements of German expressionism reminiscent of works of painters and woodcutters such as ERNST LUDWIG KIRCHNER, KARL SCHMIDT-ROTTLUFF, EMIL NOLDE, ERNST BARLACH, MAX BECKMANN, OTTO DIX, ERICH HECKEL, KAETHE KOLLWITZ and MAX PECHSTEIN, as well as films such as THE CABINET OF DR. CALIGARI, GOLEM and NOSFERATU.

I myself supported the film with my color design, which was equally inspired by the above painters."

A **style guide** created for the film defined in detail, how these design principles were to be implemented in **all areas** of film production. The environment with landscapes and architecture, the paraphernalia and objects (props) used, the details of character design in terms of contour style. ■

Illustrations from the style guide for "The Cold Heart" by Hannes Rall

Style Guide

A style guide is an indispensable document for the consistent implementation of production design in all areas of animation film production.

In general, this is a highly compartmentalized process. This is why all artists involved have to work from the same information base, from which they create their specific portion for the overall film.

The style guide explains and illustrates in detail and for all areas, what the design principle of the film consists of, and how it is to be implemented: It describes the rules for the design of the film's environment as derived from character design: Landscapes, architecture, props (paraphernalia/items such as furniture, weapons, cutlery, jewelry, etc.), costumes - all the way to visual effects (VFX). The goal is that the basic approach of production design is reflected in every aspect of the film. As an example: In "Mulan" (Bancroft/Cook, 1998), the formal language of Chinese ornamentation is also reflected in the graphic style of VFX, such as fire, explosions and smoke.

Film still from "The Cold Heart" by Hannes Rall

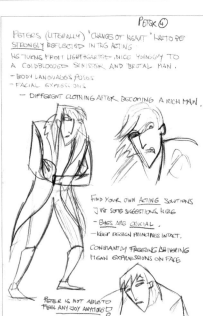

Illustrations from the style guide for "The Cold Heart" by Hannes Rall

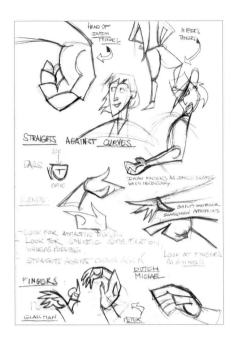

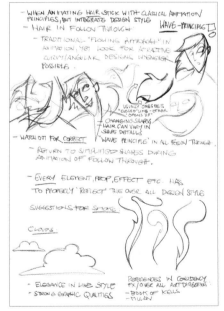

*Illustrations from the
style guide for "The Cold Heart"
by Hannes Rall*

Color Design for the Purpose of Visual Storytelling

Like the mastery of language for a writer, a basic knowledge of color theory is almost indispensable for any production designer. A comprehensive introduction to color theory would go beyond the scope of this chapter and book. However, recommendations for further and in-depth literature are listed in the appendix. Some helpful principles on color composition in general and on color design in (animation) film in particular, will be discussed here.

Good color design is always based on a **principle**, a **design method** decision based on a **concept**: A well-done color composition will never use all possible colors in equal weighting and composition. The color designer makes qualified decisions on which colors to use and which to omit.

Here is the example of a well thought-out color design: The colors are well coordinated, graduated colors dominate in the spectrum yellow-red-blue, green does not occur at all. Red-yellow dominates the fore- and mid-ground; blue for background. Occasional accents of red or blue connect the picture planes visually. The only strong primary color is the red of the collar and loincloth: This attracts attention to the main character. All colors are chosen so that the shapes stand out with sufficient contrast. The red of the suns is reflected on the surface of the planet - the reddish-yellowish tones of the fore- and mid-ground stand out clearly from the background of the night sky. At the same time, the color of the sky is blue with a large red component, so that it blends well with the foreground in spite of the contrast.

This color design version is more problematic - too many primary colors are competing for attention and do not fit together well. The color of the boots is too similar to the ground and does not stand out enough. In contrast to the other color scheme, this one also has an unbroken green, which makes the illustration look more like "candy colors", or very colorful. The pistol and rocket on the right are not as recognizable, since they blend in with the similar color of the night sky. All in all, this color scheme is reminiscent of the typical bright coloring in comic books of the 1970s

It is definitely a less stringent color scheme.

Color drawing of a background from the film project "As You Like It" (Hannes Rall/Lim Wei Ren Darren). Again, the color design is strongly influenced by a concept, which primarily serves the distinguishability of background elements. The key principle is to ensure sufficient contrast between the picture planes and their respective elements. The foreground is dominated by harmonious and warm colors in the red-yellow spectrum, contrasted with saturated green tones. In the background, the principle of aerial perspective is used: the colors are less saturated, lighter and shifted into blue.

The three main variable properties that can be used to create color are **hue**, saturation, and **tone. Harmony** between colors can be produced by **similarity** between these parameters. **Contrast** results from **differences** between hue, saturation and tone of colors. **Sufficient contrast** can be produced already by strong differences in just one of these factors.

The **different lightness** can be used here as an example: If you reduce this illustration to its gray values, you can see that the shapes stand apart from each other strongly enough without any color information. Therefore, as in classical painting, one can start with the shading, that is, the **tonal values**, in order to ensure sufficient contrast.

Hue is defined as the color depth in the area of 4-color printing by the mixing ratio of the color components cyan, magenta, yellow and the black component K as color depth. In the area of video, this corresponds to the color system RGB, which stands for red, green and blue.

In digital image processing programs, the percentage of certain color components can be entered numerically in a very uncomplicated manner: In order to obtain a blue with a high proportion of red, you enter a higher number for magenta; for a yellow with a high proportion of red (closer to orange), you enter a higher proportion of magenta, etc. This makes creating similarities in hue relatively easy: Reddish blues will often harmonize with reddish yellow tones - this can be applied to all color groups. **Saturation** can easily be digitally manipulated as well: When you reduce saturation, intensity and luminosity of a color decreases. The effect of two incompatible colors can be reduced or canceled by reducing the saturation of one (high contrast) or both (low contrast).

Shortcuts in Color Design:

- During coloring, change the image repeatedly into grayscale to check for sufficient contrast.

- Take digital samples of striking color combinations from illustrations and paintings. Use this to create a library of color references, which can be used repeatedly in different combinations

Example from "As You Like It" by Hannes Rall and Darren Lim, 2014

Illustration: "Lighttower", Hans Bacher, 2013

- Digital image processing programs like Photoshop allow for numeric input of color values for CMYK or RGB in their mixing palette. This makes it easy to determine the percentage of a color and to create corresponding colors, for example, over similar red portions.

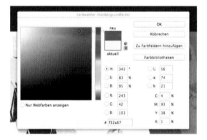

- Do not use "all colors of the rainbow" but use a deliberate color scheme or color concept. A simplified first step: Of the four "main colors" blue, green, yellow, red, use only three. For example, use only yellow, green, and blue tones, instead of a "full" green, use only a turquoise (= green with high proportion of blue (= cyan)).

Design study of Jochen Rall for the film project "As You Like It" (directed by Hannes Rall) It should be noted that overall, only graduated, i.e. no "pure" colors are used. That means that the hues are related, and contrast is achieved mostly through lightness and saturation.

Color concepts can be based on:

- Tonal value/light and shadow
- Color harmony
- Color contrasts
- Complementary contrasts
- Contrasts of warm and cool colors
- Light/dark
- Bright/muted colors
- Dominance of color moods
- Accentuation

An experienced color designer or colorist does not use all these design factors in isolation, but in a well thought-out combination. Added to this is a personal sense of color, which often integrates the above elements intuitively. As always in the world of art, it is, of course, to some extent a matter of taste as well. What may seem too harsh for one person, is absolutely acceptable to another. However, this "total" artistic freedom is put into perspective in the context of any specifications given in a precisely defined briefing, such as for an animation film.

Example 1:

This picture uses an almost monochrome color scheme. Only blue tones are used which can be varied by the ratio of their red and blue parts. Added to this are lightness and saturation as design parameters: This separates the picture planes; a dark foreground stands out with high contrast from the middle plane of the picture. Contrast and saturation decrease in the distance. Such a color scheme can be used to convey mood (blue usually indicates a melancholic mood) or even a time of day (night). For a typical night atmosphere, however, the contrast of the typical city lights (in warm colors) would be missing.

Example 2:
Here is a classic, frequently used means for color design: Strong contrast between cool (blue) and warm colors (yellow). Limiting the only warm accent to the window instantly attracts the viewer's attention. In order to underline this effect and to establish the relationship between the character in the foreground and the person in the window, the couple on the left in the picture was omitted.

Example 3:
Color is used primarily as a dramaturgical design medium. In this illustration, a realistic color scheme was omitted in favor of highlighting specific characters. Restricting the use of red to the "relationship triangle" between the man, woman and child, suggests the importance of the three persons for the plot to the viewer.

Example 4:
Finally, a relatively realistic color scheme that corresponds to a "real" lighting mood in this type of environment. The cool blue separates the dark foreground from the mid-plane of the picture, which is dominated by warm red and yellow tones. This reflects the incident light in the mid-ground. Highlights are added with the incident light rays, which also conveys atmosphere. The "aerial perspective" in the distance lends more depth to the picture. This means that the color contrast is reduced, colors are desaturated and blurred into bluish-green tones.

These concepts are generally also used to define shapes, making them clear and distinguishable: On one hand, colors must significantly differ from one another, but on the other hand, they must also be compatible with each other. In short: the skillful combination of contrast and harmony. For example, you can combine colors harmoniously according to different shapes (or foreground/background) across similar hues, and provide sufficient contrast through varying saturation and lightness. ■

Color study by Hannes Rall for the film project "As You Like It", loosely based on the play by William Shakespeare.

The Dramaturgical Parameter of Color - Color Design and Color Script

What's more, in film, color cannot be viewed in isolation, since it always fulfills a function. If the color design fulfills this function/these functions, it will automatically result in design decisions, which are perceived as aesthetically pleasing.

Such functions, which are usually defined by the narrative intention, are:

- ■ Creating mood
- ■ Time (time of day/year)
- ■ Drawing the viewer's attention
- ■ Representing realism or an emotional statement

- ■ Differentiation of picture planes (fore-/mid-/background)
  - Different color moods (red/blue/yellow)
  - Contrasts: Complementary; warm/cool; light/dark
  - Aerial perspective (colors become gray/bluish, muted, "faded" in the distance)
- ■ Suggesting different narrative levels
  - Flashbacks in different color schemes: sepia, black-white
  - Subjective perspective through vastly different color design
  - Dream sequence through different (e.g., "psychedelic") colors

Color Script

The color script could be called the "dramaturgical map" of a film's color design. Similar to a colored storyboard of the key scenes, the sequence and change of color design are represented in chronological sequence of the film.

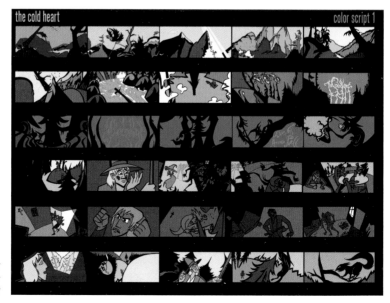

Color Script by Hans Bacher for the film "The Cold Heart" by Hannes Rall

*Color Script by Hans Bacher
for the film "The Cold Heart" by
Hannes Rall*

The **color scheme** must correspond to the **content-related development** of the film. As is generally the case with production design, the design is intended to support and illustrate the **communication** of the story.

Simply put, color is used to support or even create moods: Blue for melancholy; red for battle, anger, aggression; yellow for warmth or comfort.

The designation of colors as "warm" or "cold" implies a relevant connection in terms of content-related significance. Although successful color design for animation film can, of course, be much more complex and subtle, reducing it to the emotional undertone of a scene, represented by a basic color, is a frequently used starting point by renowned color designers. For a feature film, you are able to define many more emotionally motivated color changes - while for a short animated film of about 10 minutes, three different color moods are usually sufficient. The color designer will consult with the film director in order to understand the content and meaning of the emotional aspect of each scene and to be able to assign the appropriate color scheme. Also important are details regarding time of day and season of the film's plot, since the color scheme is probably the most important means for communicating this information. Ideally, the director's artistic and content-related vision and the color designer's composition complement each other in an optimal way, in order to maximize the emotional impact of the film's story on the viewer.

Worksheets of the color script (Hans Bacher).

Once the emotional curve of the film has been defined in the color script by these changing basic colors and moods, individual scenes can be designed with more specific color detail. Transitions between the various color sequences of the film are then designed as follows: Depending on the dramatic intention, transitions can be abrupt or smooth. In order to attract attention or induce terror, a drastic change in color following a cut is ideal; if it deals with a sequence of flashbacks, then gradual color fades work well.

Color script for the opening sequence
of "The Cold Heart"

On the right, the
corresponding development of color
fades for background elements
by Hans Bacher.

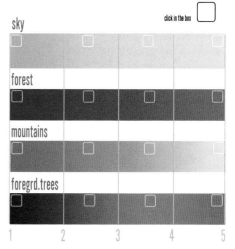

The abstract color concept preceding the final version.

Color Script by Hans Bacher for the
animation "Metamorphoses" by
Hannes Rall (For the documentary
film "Lotte Reiniger - The Dance of
the Shadows", Germany 2012,
Directors: Susanne Marschall, Rada
Bieberstein and Kurt Schneider)

Designs for a cast of "supporting actors" from the animated short film "As You Like It" (Hannes Rall) in different versions. The basic forms of the characters differ greatly, in order to be able to distinguish them well. Character design by Hannes Rall and Lim Wei Ren Darren.

Assignment:

Design the complete production design for one of the public domain characters, which you created in the previous chapter Character Design, i.e., for a jungle hero, Sherlock Holmes, Don Quixote, Robin Hood ... whatever you designed.

Decide on a content-oriented concept (realism, parody, artistic/abstract) and use this as the basis for your research and design decisions.

In the end, you should have a complete "pre-production design package", which should include:

- Research and drawing up of mood boards
- Design of the entire cast as character design and as comparison sheet.
- Model sheets (or 3D models for CG)
- Designs for props and environment/architecture of the film
- 5 to 10 production paintings, which show the final look of the planned production
- Color script of the film

This, of course, also requires the previous development of a storyboard - but you can limit this to an exercise of about 10 to 20 key scenes of the film (for short film).

"I basically treat every design like a stage in the theater."

Hans Bacher (born in Ulm), is one of the world's leading production designers for animation. During his many years of collaboration at Walt Disney Feature Animation he has contributed significantly to the look of such films as "Beauty and the Beast", "Aladdin", "The Lion King" and above all, "Mulan". He has won numerous prestigious awards, including the "Golden Camera" for the animated series "Alfred J. Kwak" (with Harald Siepermann) and the "Annie Award" for the production design in "Mulan". His book "Dream Worlds: Production Design for Animation" (2007) is now considered the standard reference on the topic and has become a worldwide bestseller. Hans is Associate Professor at the School of Art, Design and Media at the Nanyang Technological University of Singapore.

First, a very basic question: What is production design for animation?
What exactly does a production designer do?
It is, as the name implies: You design the production, that is, the look and style of the film. There are productions, in which the production designer works on both, the environmental design, i.e. landscapes, etc., and character design. Then there are productions, where the production designer is only responsible for the environment and where a character designer takes care of all the character designs. That is the case at Disney. There, you usually have two positions.

So in that case, the character designer is actually separate from the production designer. Or do they ever work together?
They definitely work together.

Do they work together all the time?
Yes, it is a very, very close collaboration. And at the very beginning, the very first designs are usually made only by this specific production designer. Anyway, at Disney it is as it was in my case: I started working on productions where there was only one treatment first; a treatment of three, four sentences: This is the project, a possible future project, for which you then develop designs that include rough characters. And only when it's getting

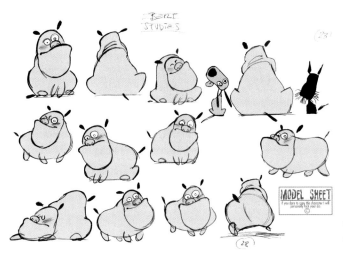

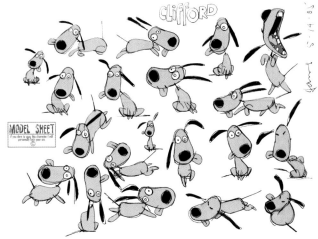

Character design sketches by Hans Bacher.

closer to a decision, when the production is half-way into pre-production, then a character designer is hired, who will concentrate exclusively on the characters. The production designer then focuses on a complete stylistic development that takes on one very specific direction.

In other words, at the time in the beginning, the design should be as diverse as possible. So you are likely to try out several directions within one specific topic.

At the very beginning, for example, when I get a treatment and begin to sketch ideas, they actually reflect my view, my interpretation. As soon as a director adds his ideas to the project, it gets more restricting as you get told: 'Well, we want to take a specific stylistic direction.' Then you have to adapt accordingly.

Suppose there is a theme that is set in ancient China. Would you start out by incorporating a lot of different styles, inspired by art and architecture of this period, in your first draft? How would you proceed?

Yes, I did that in "Mulan" (Bancroft/Cook, 1998). I didn't have a clue about Chinese art at that time. So I first got a few art books and looked at Chinese paintings from the last 400,

500 years. And then, very soon after I was finished with the books, I sat down that same evening and began making the first sketches. Everything was still fresh, I didn't spend a lot of time dealing with it. Interestingly, these sketches had a big impact on the style.

It is probably important to get started when everything is still fresh and begin sketching your impressions, isn't it?

Exactly, while unaffected. Often, these turn out to be the best ideas. It's like making thumbnails, those tiny little sketches. When you enlarge them manually, they always look bad. I load them onto the copier and blow them up 400 percent.

Now the important question: What can go wrong with a production design or really be done wrong? Students or beginners often make mistakes. What are some fundamental mistakes that can actually lead to the failure of a production design?

Of course, there are many things that can happen. The worst thing in my experience is, when the production designer just gets going without understanding the studio's

Strong sketches
(ink with brush on paper) by
Hans Bacher for the feature
film project "Die Nibelungen"
(in preparation), directed by:
Hannes Rall.

background or without knowing which talents will collaborate with the film; when detached from all this information, he sits down and just loosely sketches his ideas on paper. When I know, that I will be working with a studio where there is little talent and only a very small budget, and no time - where the film is supposed be ready in six months or in a very, very short time - if I get there in a case like that, with a production design that would require a Pixar or Disney talent pool, and where I would need five years and an incredible talent like Glen Keane and maybe a background stylist and painter to complete it as a top-notch production - then I should know that this cannot go well! Many production designers present a stylistic look that looks great, but where the concept cannot be implemented in the production. And then you wonder afterwards why the film looks so much worse than the most beautiful production design. So before I begin with my designs, I should know some things: For whom do I work? How big is the budget? Is it worth the effort to go into such details? Or should I offer a style, which is much more reduced, but easier to do. As you said - that's how it is with students. They have an animated feature film in their head, but only 6 months to get it done. This is just as absurd. If I have no means, no time, then I must reduce my designs accordingly.

Exactly, so that it can be done. How would you describe the correlation between the story or theme and the stylistic choices that you make? Do you pay close attention to it, or are you more interested in an atmosphere or a look? How do you define the correlation?

That all depends on the treatments. I have received very few treatments that were written well enough for me to be able to visualize the film completely. The writing style of some writers is more difficult to implement than others. But if I get a short version of a story that is written really well and where you can actually see the characters come alive, and where the environment is also described really well ... The style depends on the time period of the film, whether in the past or the future.

I mean, the story itself can be very, very diverse, it often spans across various areas. And if those are well described, then I can sit down and start immediately. In other words, if there are no complicated environments for which extensive research is required, you can start immediately with thumbnails and the first ideas which you can sketch.

What you mentioned, is indeed an interesting topic: authenticity compared to artistic freedom. After all, sometimes you get a topic that has to be treated very realistically. In that case, you are probably very limited in how much you can contribute from your own artistic vision. And it is probably extremely difficult to artistically move beyond that, because the degree of realism limits your options.

Thank God, this never happened to me. I have only had stories that were artistically very open, except for the specific environment in which they were set, and of course, the corresponding artistic influence associated with it. I would not have been interested in working with realistic stories such as "Atlantis - The Lost Empire" (Trousdale/Wise, 2001).

Color Sketch by Hans Bacher for the feature film project "Die Nibelungen" (in preparation) Director: Hannes Rall. The design concept integrates the influence of expressionist art by painters such as Ernst Ludwig Kirchner.

There's really not very much interesting artistic freedom in this, it really is more about an almost naturalistic depiction, in a sense. There's not much to invent. That's not very exciting.
I agree.

You mentioned research earlier, and again now. This seems to be extremely important to you: If you are working on material that is set, for example, in Asia, then you will actually research Asian art. Later, of course, you will do less research and develop the design, but in any case, you research first to get inspired.
Absolutely. Research takes a very long time: for at least two or three months, you are looking very intensely for only the best reference material, whether photos, illustrations of other artists who have worked in that direction, or art in general, that is, the artistic diversity of the last several hundred years. I don't believe in reinventing the wheel: If the topic was presented before, then I should also refer to it. And if a story is set in a certain culture, then I should become familiar with it.

Anyway, the artists at Disney, who were involved in developing the look or who worked with animation, even went on research trips. We went to France for "Beauty and the Beast" (Trousdale/Wise, 1991) to visit the surroundings, the castles. I think we looked at ten or fifteen castles. For "Hercules" (Clements/Musker, 1997), a whole team traveled to Greece, and I believe we were there for two weeks. For "Kingdom of the Sun" (working title for the later Disney movie "The Emperor's New Groove", director: Mark Dindal, 2000; author's note) they were in South America. The research was actually done on location and they took their own pictures. For "Mulan", a whole team went to China. Unfortunately, I was not able to go at that time.

To this province with the famous mountains?
Everywhere. They were on a two week trip through China. And I missed out on it. You get a completely different impression of the surroundings, the colors, the smells, of the whole world. There are no books or picture and film research that can compare to this. Being there is something completely different.

First studies of color and form by Hans Bacher for the short film project "The Story of the Ghost Ship" (adapted from Wilhelm Hauff), which he is currently working on together with Kathrin Albers and Hannes Rall. Both the coloring and form-based composition draw attention to the most important picture element: the ship. The design integrates influences from authentic references on Arabian art and shipbuilding.

Stylistic color sketch on a Chinese theme by Hans Bacher. The superb color design, which combines a dominant color scheme of subtly composed blue tones with a singular strong accent in orange, stands out in particular. At the same time, the red portion used in all the blue tones achieves overall harmony and stylistic unity.

You also work a lot with digital means, for example with different digital filters and digital brushes. What advice can you give to beginners and students? As a key thought: Relationship between artistic vision and digital tools, how does it go together?

I use only tools that are useful. Anyway, I would never build a topic around a (digital) tool. For example, I use it when I see that I can work ten times faster in Photoshop and when I know how this technique works. If I am up to it, then I am very fast. And the final look is quite comparable to the look I would get if I were to work with tools like watercolor or felt tip pen or any other traditional means. I use digital tools only to achieve certain looks or to implement them more quickly.

You probably already have sketches or an idea about where it should roughly take you. And you use the digital tools more to help you get there.

Of course. I still work completely on paper - at least in the initial phase and for brush drawings etc. prior to coloring.

Combination of traditional ink drawing with digital coloring. © Copyright *Hans Bacher*

If you compare it to how we used to do it, it is indeed much easier with Photoshop: Before the digital era, for example, it was technically much more difficult to create and combine clean color gradients and opaque colors.

The best invention is the undo button. When I worked with felt pen and made a mistake with the airbrush while working, I had to redo all of the work. The use of different digital layers in one image also simplifies the work tremendously.

But there is always the risk that students or other inexperienced artists feel lost and overwhelmed with all these options. That is when it is also helpful to know what you want, and where the artistic journey should take you.

The vision should be there at the beginning. Anyway, you should already have some idea in your head, and roughly know where you want to go. But I have now found, that because technology provides me with so many options that - although I already have a clear picture in my head - I now think, once the design is finished: Well, let me try first, if it would look better to change it to a slightly different color mood. And I try out the other color mood or combine different filters - there are thousands of variations that are possible. It has also happened before, that the results that emerged were better than what I had intended originally.

But you still need the judgment to be able to recognize what is good, and then, for example, not to use the same lens flare (special lens filter in Photoshop, author's note) again.

Endlessly tinkering with things is, of course nonsense too. You should really know when a design is completed.

Now on the subject of stylistic decision. Perhaps you can say something about the importance of balancing details and empty surfaces, that is,

about the compositional-stylistic unity. And on the importance of sufficient contrast.

First on composition. One thing is important in the way I approach a design: I basically treat every design like a stage in a theater. On the stage there is an actor, the actor is in a spotlight, and what the actor, that is, the animation of the main character, the protagonist, does - that is important. My only job is to create the background for this actor, for this animation. If the background is more important, or if the variety in my excessive detail appears to be more important than the animation of the main character, then I have made a mistake. The animation takes center stage, and everything I do, I need to build around the animation. I do this by placing elements in the spotlight, which are important to explain where I am, in what time period this takes place, etc. The more information I need, the more side spotlights I use. Everything else stays off, remains dark or diffuse, unexplained. The best example is "Bambi" (Hand et al, 1942). When Gustaf Tenggren made the very first forest illustrations, he actually painted every single leaf and each branch. Then they "squeezed" a drawing of this animal figure, this deer, into the background and soon realized that the figure got completely lost in it. The background was overloaded with so much detail, that you could not see the animal figure! Along came Tyrus Wong and delivered incredibly atmospheric sketches in pastel, which were strongly influenced by his Chinese heritage, but also by Impressionist painting. When he wanted to depict a meadow, he did not paint every blade of grass - as is done today in CG, where that is commonplace - he actually painted only a green area and two or three blades of grass in the foreground, just to indicate that this is a meadow. And the whole thing was so open, so atmospheric, so poetic, none of which Tenggren's earlier paintings

Jungle study by Hans Bacher: Individual details are very "distinguishable" against the atmospheric/diffuse background.
With increasing depth of the picture plane, color contrast and focus are significantly reduced, contributing to this effect.

could have ever been. And that's why Bambi looks the way it does. It is very minimal in detail, only where detail is really needed it is added to the backgrounds. Everything else is diffused to avoid distraction from the area that needs my attention, which is the area where all the action takes place.

For you as one of the leading color designers, color is a very important topic. In general: What defines a good color design in the area of film and animation for you? How do you apply color in the context of dramaturgy?

Color is comparable to the music in a film, it creates atmosphere. Of course, I can go entirely "over the top", I can exaggerate too much with my selection of color. Then the whole thing looks so awful, as if I had poured all the color into one bucket. That's gaudy or distasteful. You can really go too far. A good example is "The Lion King" (Allers/Minkoff, 1994). When I started working there, there was a background artist whose work was extremely colorful. The director told him: Let's only work with black and white for two weeks, and then we gradually and very carefully introduce color. That's a very good way to approach it. You should first be able to look at the environment or background to be depicted in a reduced version, as if everything were desaturated, in other words, as if the colors were taken out completely. Then, very careful-

Examples of the successful staging of a character that stands out from the background, but at the same time is stylistically integrated. ©
Copyright Hans Bacher

ly, you go in with color. Most of the designs I see for film are much too colorful. There is way too much color in it coming from everywhere. That's why you make a color script. A color script usually starts like the story: very, very calmly, then slowly working up to the dramaturgical apex and culminating in extreme contrast, in harsh color contrasts, like red, black, white - only then to subside again into the normal color world, which can appear quite desaturated in the end.   This means that this entire color development in a color script has to be structured very carefully. It has to be adapted to everything that happens. For example, if I need a romantic color scheme, because there is a romantic scene sequence in my script, then I'll transform the romantic scene with romantic colors; I choose only romantic colors, which definitely would not include green.

For an aggressive scene, for example, an attack like our Huns attack in "Mulan", or other scenes with very brutal action scenes, I use colors that are based less on reality. Such colors should reveal what narratively defines this scene. Anyway, if I illustrate an attack, then I choose colors that represent less the environment, in other words, no realistic colors of landscapes, but I may color the entire landscape red, for example. I set extremely drastic shadows in black and then add white highlights within the spaces. The whole thing looks like a city going up in flames. With this kind of background, I can then really illustrate an attack. In "Mulan", we were unable to use red because the whole thing took place in the snow, but we used quite harsh color contrasts in the sequence of the Huns attack.

The color selection corresponds to the romantic/melancholic mood of the scene. The composition directs the viewer's attention by means of "interpretive" shapes and shadows to the couple ascending the stairs. The horizontal structure of the gray stairs calms the background in order not to disturb this attention.
© Copyright Hans Bacher

An example of the subtle, but focused and contrasting use of color.
© Copyright Hans Bacher

For such scenes, the concept of local color is also omitted. Thus, the skin color is no longer a local skin color, but rather the dominant color mood is applied to all the components in the scene.

Yes, of course. As if the entire scene had been stained. I just add a filter.

I have one last question : Can you name some examples of successful production design in animation, and perhaps also from live-action film?

In the area of animation, I would say: "Bambi". That is an absolute top example. Another very good example is "101 Dalmatians" (Geronimi/ Lusk/Reitherman, 1961), where everything is superbly done, not just the color, but style as well. The background style is adapted to the style of the animation in front. Otherwise "Sleeping Beauty" (Clark/Geronimi/Larson/ Reitherman, 1959). At first, the background looks a little bit overloaded, but Eyvind Earle, the production designer of "Sleeping Beauty", solved this problem brilliantly. He chose an entirely different approach for the color mood, the color design of the environments conpared to the colors he used for the foreground characters. So each character can be perfectly distinguished from the background, absolutely perfect. In live-action: Every movie that Ridley Scott has ever made thus far, each one is a masterpiece. My absolute favorites, apart from Ridley Scott, are all Orson Welles films. There are not many films that I consider fantastic, but those are definitely some of them!

Thanks.

In this color study by Hans Bacher for an animation film project that is not yet completed, the concept of local color is completely abandoned in favor of a predominant, here almost monochrome-modulated, color composition. This lends atmosphere to the scene, since there are no diverging color details to interfere with the overall mood.

The Principles of Animation and their Application

This chapter provides an overview of the various animation techniques. It introduces the principles of animation, which can be applied to all techniques.

Film consists of single images (frames), which are played in rapid succession one after the other, creating the illusion of continuous motion for the viewer. In film, the world standard is 24 frames per second, but experiments with a frame rate of 48 frames per second are being conducted, in order to produce an even more life-like illusion of movement ("The Hobbit" trilogy, directed by Peter Jackson, 2012-2014). Animation refers to the art form that is produced by this cinematic illusion through the sequential exposure of single frames. In this process, the illusion for the animation of non-living objects is achieved through incremental changes of each single frame shot. The objects to be animated are usually "created" by the animator himself (or a team): This can be through drawings (traditional or digital), 2D animation, puppets or objects (stop motion), or digitally modeled characters (3D computer animation).

For the animator, it is both appealing and challenging to have absolute control over the look of each individual frame, as well as over rhythm and speed of the frame sequence, similar to a virtual puppeteer.

*An animator has absolute **control** over every single image in the film, each frame.*

*In virtual **3D animation** on the computer, each single frame is created as a modified version of the **3D model** and can be played back immediately as a test.*

***Single frame exposure** of each small change to the character for **stop motion** or **puppet animation**.*

*In **traditional 2D animation**, animation is done on paper in sequences, using a light box, and the successive drawings are then **scanned** and played back as a **line test**.*

Some techniques:

For **hand-drawn 2D animation** (traditionally on paper or with digital tablet), incrementally modified drawings are sequentially shot. This technique offers the greatest artistic freedom for animation itself, since it does not impose limitations due to any physically or virtually defined object. These rest, however, in the drawing ability of the animator: Some tasks (such as perspective animation of an extremely detailed texture) exceed the capabilities of even the most talented animator.

Since traditional 2D animation was the dominant technology in mainstream animation until the onset of the digital age, the number of outstanding examples here is numerous, first and foremost in the area of mainstream, all Disney feature films, such as "Snow White and the Seven Dwarfs" (Hand, 1937) or "Sleeping Beauty" (Clark/Geronimi/Larson/Reithermann, 1959). In artistic short film, some outstanding examples are "Moonbird" by John and Faith Hubley (1959) and "Hill Farm" (1989) by Mark Baker.

Example for hand-drawn 2D animation from "The Cold Heart" by Hannes Rall

In **stop motion**, real objects (e.g., movable puppets) are animated, in other words, they are changed little by little by the animator and filmed with a camera after each change. The use of this technique, although identical in principle, can result in stylistically completely different films: The "Wallace & Gromit" films (Park, 1990-2008), are based on a comedic caricature approach and use puppets with a flexible rig. "Dimensions of Dialogue" (Švankmajer, 1982) uses clay animation to express visually disturbing political and philosophical allegories in experimental form.

Example from the student's work "Dr. Avis' Dream" by Wang Rui Fan, School of Art, Design and Media, Nanyang Technological University, 2010: "Classic" stop motion, here puppet animation in a carefully and very detailed physically constructed set.

Cutout animation uses the same technique as stop motion, however, the animated objects are flat and are moved on a flat plane. This is possible both with real objects (similar to traditional stop motion) and with digital/virtual objects. Stop motion techniques often achieve a look that is more related to the drawn 2D animation, since it is graphical and "flat" in appearance. However, the conceptual approach resembles more traditional stop motion than 3D computer animation, regardless of the means of production. A well-known classic example is "The Adventures of Prince Achmed" (1926) by the German animation pioneer Lotte Reiniger.

One of today's masters of digital cutout animation is the Swiss animator Isabelle Favez ("Heart of Winter", 2011).

Image from "Si Lunchai" (2013), Director: Hannes Rall, digital cut-out, animation: Darren Lim, character design: Cheng Yu Chao. This film combines Lotte Reiniger's tradition of silhouette film with influences of modernism and Southeast Asian shadow puppetry "Wayang Kulit".

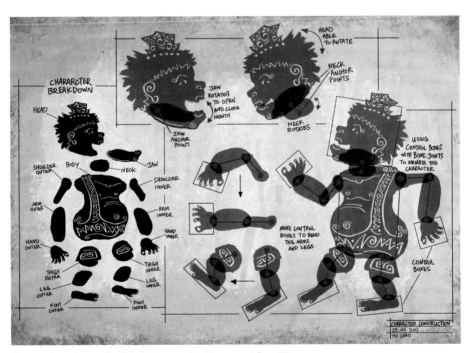

Construction scheme of a digital cut-out animation puppet from "Si Lunchai", design: Cheng Yu Chao.
A digital or physical cut-out animation puppet must be constructed with movable joints so that it can be changed to match the movements: The more complex and versatile these movements are, the more of these joints have to be inserted.

Hybrid forms between drawn animation, traditional painting, cut-out animation and stop motion:

- **Sand animation** uses sand as a medium for animation, which is filmed on a glass plate lit from underneath. The freedom of manipulation in this medium makes this technique the most comparable to drawn animation. Ferenc Cakó from Hungary ("Ab Ovo", 1987) and Caroline Leaf from Canada ("The Metamorphosis of Mr. Samsa", 1977) are masters of this technique.
- In a similar manner, **plasticine on a light box** can also be shot in various colors. However, this medium is more difficult to manipulate and therefore often uses a cross-dissolve technique and three- to six-frame animation. A master and pioneer of this technique is Ishu Patel from India/Canada. ("Afterlife", 1978).
- **Animated painting** is the **animation of painting on glass**, which is related to the above-mentioned techniques and an extremely difficult and elaborate technique, if you want to achieve a certain degree of realism. An outstanding artist in this style is Aleksandr Petrov ("The Old Man and the Sea", 1999).

Painting and Drawing as a Process:
Other animators are less interested in the creation of an imaginary, yet credible world, but instead integrate the artificiality of their process as a conscious stylistic device by filming the incremental development of their large-format drawings or paintings during the development process. William Kentridge from South Africa ("Ubu Tells the Truth", 1996-97) and Jochen Kuhn from Germany ("Neulich 1", 1998) should be mentioned. They intentionally cross over into the field of "classical" fine art and exhibit their works also in the traditional settings of galleries.

In the case of **3D computer animation**, a virtual puppet is usually created on the computer (= **modeling**), equipped with an animatable virtual skeleton (= rigging) and then animated like in the other techniques. Since the animator manipulates a virtual puppet step by step, this technique is actually more related to stop motion than drawn animation. All the more so, since, as a rule, his creative freedom is restricted by the limitations of his character, which are defined by modeling and, above all, rigging. The Pixar Studios, headed by John Lasseter, are inextricably linked to the rise of this technique as the world's dominating mainstream animation technology. Two of the most outstanding examples of this technique are "The Incredibles" (Bird, 2004) and the short film "The Lost Thing" (Ruhemann/Tan, 2010).

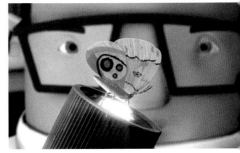

Example of a 3D computer animation: "Color Theory" (2011) by Davier Yoon, School of Art, Design and Media, Nanyang Technological University, Singapore.

Example of pixilation from "Big Bio" by Eileen Reynolds (2011).

Pixilation presents an exceptional situation, a special form of stop motion: Here, the actions of real actors are not simply filmed, but as in stop motion, single frame shots are manipulated. This creates interesting alienation effects (such as time lapse shots), resulting in a surreal and artistically appealing atmosphere. Pixilation also allows a simple form of visual effects, for example, by directly linking time separated images or omitting certain drawings of a movement.

Live-action film has to rely much more on the circumstances of live-action sets, looks, the abilities of "live" actors and so forth. In animation film, everything is controlled by the creative power of the director and his team: He creates his own world, which has to submit completely to the rhythm of the director as the leading conductor!

Convergence and Mixed Forms of Traditional and Digital Techniques

While the visual language in the early and developing years of digital animation was predominantly aimed at completely replacing traditional aesthetics with a new hyper-perfect and hyper-realistic visual language, an alternative trend has now emerged:

The integration of the organic quality of traditional animation techniques in 3D computer animation. This includes, for example, the element of human "imperfection" as an intentional means of artistic expression. Conversely, the computer is increasingly used as a means of preserving and supporting the aesthetics of formerly purely traditional forms of animation: Good examples are the calculation of inbetweens for extremely complex painting, or the computer-assisted planning of inbetweens for stop motion, which was previously not possible.

Formal eclecticism of a new era

It is particularly the new young generation of animators that combines traditional and digital techniques in a completely unbiased and unconventional manner.

This often results in artistically very exciting and attractive films: For example, a 3D computer-animated character is placed in a traditionally drawn environment, a stop-motion character interacts with real actors in a virtually modeled environment, traditional hand-drawn animation is digitally edited and combined with digitally painted backgrounds. The possibilities are almost infinite and will certainly increase in the future.

"The Hunt": Combination of hand-drawn 2D animation and digital compositing with After Effects, student work by Jegannath, M. Sufjan and Eunice Ong (Singapore 2012).

"Innocent Memory", student film by Nguyen Thi Nam Phuong, drawn animation (paper), with camera animation (traditional), Toon Boom, After Effects compositing (Singapore 2012).

The first step is always the hardest, or: How do I learn to animate?

The "bouncing ball" exercise or: What does a bouncing ball have to do with good animation?

Almost every textbook about animation, almost every course that provides an introduction into the basics, begins with the "bouncing ball". There are good reasons why this example is so popular: It is an excellent method to understand many principles of animation using a simple object: A ball is easy to draw and can also be modeled quickly for 3D animation or downloaded as an existing model. The bouncing ball is squashed on the ground upon impact, and stretches as it bounces back up. When it reaches the apex of the curve it follows, the bouncing ball returns to its original shape. It is important that the volume of the object remains the same. This principle can be applied to all kinds of objects and when applied properly, it can credibly convey the material properties of an object: A poorly inflated soccer ball changes its shape more than a golf ball consisting of solid, unyielding material (which basically does not change shape). This corresponds to the animation principle of squash and stretch.

It is extremely important for students to understand that the bouncing ball example is about the underlying principles of animation - not the ball itself. Unfortunately, this exercise is often taught or applied incorrectly. A simple copying or just a slight variation of the presented method does not lead to a deeper understanding. The exercise must therefore be executed and explained in such a way that the student can comprehend the concept and later transfer it to completely different objects or characters to be animated.

So here is the frequently seen bouncing ball, presented somewhat differently and its significance explained for other applications. The point of the matter is, that the bouncing ball can be used to explain many basic principles of animation.

THE BOUNCING BALL

A SIMPLE METHOD TO DEMONSTRATE MANY PRINCIPLES OF ANIMATION AND PRACTICE THEM.

TIMING (= NUMBER OF DRAWINGS)
THE BALL SLOWS DOWN (CLOSER SPACINGS) AT THE PEAK OF THE CURVE, BECAUSE GRAVITY AFFECTS IT.

SPACING: DISTANCES BETWEEN DRAWINGS DECREASE WHEN NEARING THE APEX AND THEN INCREASE AGAIN.
MORE DRAWINGS IN DECREASING / INCREASING DISTANCE.
THE COMBINATION OF TIMING (NUMBER OF DRAWINGS) AND SPACING (DISTANCE BETWEEN DRAWINGS) CREATES ACCELERATION AND DECELERATION.
TIMING = HOW MANY DRAWINGS — SHOT WITH HOW MANY FRAMES (→ 1s, 2s or more?)
SPACING = SPATIAL POSITION / DISTANCE BETWEEN DRAWINGS.

EFFECT:
ILLUSION OF WEIGHT CREATED THROUGH TIMING AND SPACING AND THE ASSOCIATED ACCELERATION DECELERATION (SLOW OUT/SLOW IN).

"SQUASH" AND "STRETCH":
CHANGE OF SHAPE THROUGH PHYSICAL IMPACT. (HITTING THE GROUND).

THE EXTENT OF SQUASH AND STRETCH MAKES STATEMENTS ABOUT THE STRENGTH OF FORCES ACTING ON THE BALL AND ITS MATERIAL TEXTURE: A BADLY INFLATED FOOTBALL DEFORMS VERY STRONGLY, FOR EXAMPLE, A GOLF BALL OR A CANNONBALL DO NOT DEFORM AT ALL—THEY RATHER IMPACT THE GROUND THEY ARE HITTING.

SOLIDDRAWING: VOLUMES MUST REMAIN CONSISTENT.

ARCS

MOST ORGANIC MOVEMENTS UNFOLD AS ARCS — NOT AS A STRAIGHT LINE FROM A TO B. THE DECREASING HEIGHT OF THE ARCS HERE DEMONSTRATES THE DECREASING MOMENTUM AND THEREFORE ADDS THE IMPRESSION OF WEIGHT.

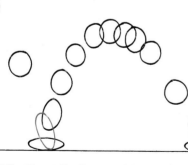

The aim is therefore to understand the bouncing ball as an easily comprehensible and implementable example, that allows students to develop a basic understanding of the major animation principles of motion mechanics, as well as artistic/aesthetic principles. A simple copying and repeating of the model shown above may be a good place to start - but then the learning process must continue by applying the acquired knowledge of the principles to other examples.

ANTICIPATION: THE STRETCHED DRAWING OF THE BALL PREPARES THE EYE OF THE VIEWER FOR THE IMMEDIATELY FOLLOWING SQUASHED DRAWING: VISUAL CONTRAST CREATES ANTICIPATION.

EXAGGERATION:
FROM A PURELY PHYSICAL POINT OF VIEW, THERE IS NO REASON TO INSERT ANOTHER DRAWING IN STRETCHED SHAPE BECAUSE THE BALL SHOULD NOT BE DECELERATED: BUT IT WORKS BRILLIANTLY AS A VISUAL TRICK, AN EXAGGERATION OF REALITY. IT IS RATHER FELT THAN SEEN.

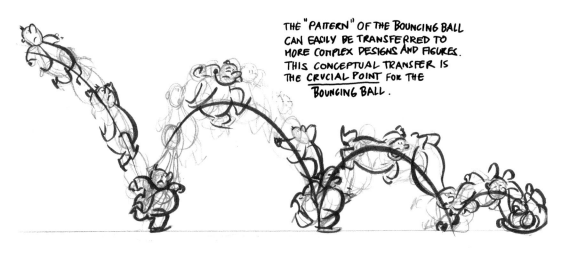

THE "PATTERN" OF THE BOUNCING BALL
CAN EASILY BE TRANSFERRED TO
MORE COMPLEX DESIGNS AND FIGURES.
THIS CONCEPTUAL TRANSFER IS
THE CRUCIAL POINT FOR THE
BOUNCING BALL.

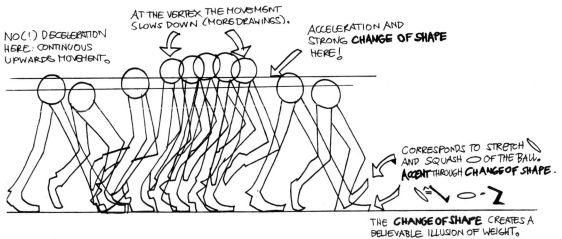

NO(!) DECELERATION
HERE: CONTINUOUS
UPWARDS MOVEMENT.

AT THE VERTEX THE MOVEMENT
SLOWS DOWN (MORE DRAWINGS).

ACCELERATION AND
STRONG CHANGE OF SHAPE
HERE!

CORRESPONDS TO STRETCH
AND SQUASH OF THE BALL.
ACCENT THROUGH CHANGE OF SHAPE.

THE CHANGE OF SHAPE CREATES A
BELIEVABLE ILLUSION OF WEIGHT.

Assignment:

Make up your own version of the bouncing ball exercise:

- Try to animate a ball of a certain weight and a certain material, e.g. a ping-pong ball, a football/soccer ball or a cannonball.
- Replace the ball with another shape or figure and try to implement the acquired principles, e.g. with a leaping frog, a jumping cricket or an animated dice.
- Analyze the animation to see if you can identify the principles of the bouncing ball, e.g. the deceleration at the apex of a motion.

BASIC PRINCIPLES OF ANIMATION

Below is an explanation of the terms of the animation principles as they were first developed by Disney Studios in the 1930s. They are based on the basic aesthetic idea that animation should represent an exaggerated, caricatured version of "reality" - an aesthetics and mechanics of motion, which renders the acting characters believable, thus eliciting the empathy of the audience. They are certainly a good start to understanding motion-mechanical principles, in order to be able to apply them to animation. However, anyone interested in implementing very experimental and abstract animation may deviate completely from some of these principles - since they would not be intending to achieve "credibility". But it can also be very interesting to apply these classical animation rules to free experimental and abstract forms - for this, there are many excellent examples as in the films of Oskar Fischinger or Michel Gagné ("Sensology", 2010).

These rules were, of course, subject to a continuous evolutionary process over many decades and have been further refined. Much of it, however, has remained valid throughout the decades and is still up-to-date. It is interesting to notice that these rules, which are mainly derived from the tradition of hand-drawn animation, are now an integral part of the stylistic repertoire of modern computer animation. This was made possible by the further development of software, allowing for such effects like squash and stretch to be implemented in computer animation. It is based, for example, on much more complex and flexible rigging of models. From a technical point of view, we are in a golden age for computer animation, which can easily handle very cartoony animation as well. (The infinite and simple flexibility of drawn animation still stands unrivaled though.)

The classic "12 Basic Principles of Animation", written and published by the famous Disney animators Frank Thomas and Ollie Johnston (1995) are as follows:

- **Squash and Stretch**
- **Anticipation**
- **Staging**
- **Straight Ahead Action and Pose to Pose**
- **Follow Through and Overlapping Action**
- **Slow In and Slow Out**
- **Arcs**
- **Secondary Action**
- **Timing**
- **Exaggeration**
- **Solid Drawing**
- **Appeal**

How can a student or beginner best understand these principles? And more importantly: How can he/she implement them sensibly for his/her own animations?

Reform and Expansion of the „Basic Principles of Animation": Hierarchy of Basic Animation Rules

In general, the following applies: It is important to learn the rules to be able to break them later. Animation is a living art form that must be subject to constant change and refinement in order to progress! What works as a test and looks convincing is "right", even if it violates the rules.

Nevertheless, I believe that particularly beginners (child prodigies and geniuses excluded) would be well advised to try to learn these rules. They are also good guidelines to get started. It is important, however, not to simply copy examples, but to understand the underlying concepts and to implement them in one's own work!

As an instructor in the area of classical animation, I have always looked for ways to make basic rules as comprehensible as possible for my students and to establish them in a logical consistency.

I have also expanded the list of "principles" to include new components that I consider essential: for example, the principle of change of shape, which was introduced by Richard Williams.

1.) Timing
2.) Spacing
3.) Slow In und Slow Out
4.) Straight Ahead and Pose-to-Pose Animation
5.) Overlapping Action, Follow Through
6.) Secondary Action
7.) Anticipation
8.) Squash and Stretch
9.) Arcs
10.) Solid Drawing
11.) Exaggeration
12.) Weight
13.) Appeal and Strong Poses
14.) Staging
15.) Change of Shape
16.) Counteraction

The individual principles in this chapter are explained in this order. In addition, I would like to add that there is a sort of hierarchy among the important principles of animation - simply put: Some are extremely important on a general scale, others cover more partial aspects of animation. As Grim Natwick once put it so aptly: *"It is all in the timing and the spacing"* (in: Williams, 2002).

Therefore: Timing and spacing makes or breaks everything. You can certainly find good examples among animated films, in which most of the other principles have been neglected - and where the animation works beautifully nonetheless.

If the timing (and the story) is right, then even a movie with (real) coins as protagonists can work great - even without any squashing and stretching, exaggerated drawing etc.!

What does that mean? I think that the "classical" rules, those which have always remained relevant, can not be lumped together, but should be assigned to different groups according to topic, and that they should be taught in a certain chronological order. For example, animation techniques (e.g., **timing**), which must be mastered first in order to implement certain artistic concepts convincingly (e.g., **staging**).

Working Methodology
▨ Straight Ahead Action and Pose to Pose

Animation techniques:

1.) **Timing and its various aspects**
1.1) Spacing
1.2.) Slow In and Slow Out
1.3.) Overlapping Action, Follow Through, important aspect: Waves
1.4) Secondary Action
1.5) Anticipation

2.) **Shaping and Design**
2.1) Squash and Stretch
2.2) Arcs
2.3.) Solid Drawing
2.4.) Change of Shape
2.5) Exaggeration – an exception, since here, the right timing is an important component!
2.6.) Counteraction

3.) **Design/artistic concepts** (which can only be achieved by combining the above-mentioned techniques):
3.1.) Weight
3.2) Staging (this also includes knowledge of composition and film language, see also chapter 1.1 "Script and Storyboarding")
3.3) Appeal

In my opinion, it is also important to understand that these concepts should not necessarily be treated in isolation, since they often have to be used together: Anticipation can only be demonstrated convincingly, if you use timing and spacing correctly, just as squash and stretch or a general change of shape.
▨

All concepts are subsequently explained with reference to drawings - but they can also be applied to any other animation technique, since the principles basically remain the same. The individual chapters which follow will focus on any differences, particularities and relevant work process of the various animation techniques.

1.) Timing

Actually, timing is the most important over-riding principle, since it affects almost all other principles directly, more specifically, the other principles are supported or fulfilled by correct timing. Timing defines, how long a motion will last "on screen" based on the number of drawings (or frames**).**

> More drawings
> = longer action
> Less drawings
> = shorter action

Rhythm and contrast in timing

Contrast in timing is critical for good animation. As in music, the change between fast and slow, intense and subtle, "loud" and "soft" is crucial: Never-ending fast actions in sequence are tiring, and you lose the viewer's attention - a quick extreme action after a slow and subtle movement has a much greater impact. A film, in which all the characters move at the same pace and in the same manner for the entire time, is unspeakably boring.

Stylistic means, such as monotony and uniformity of movement can certainly be introduced deliberately to support the story - but of course only, if this is intended. Very often, however, such uniform movements are created unintentionally, because not enough thought was put into the spatial distribution of inbetweens and the graphic expression of key frames. For 3D computer animation each single frame of film is different, that means animation on "ones". In other animation techniques, exposing the same image twice on film will often suffice to create a believable illusion of fluid movement. This approach is called animation on "twos". For very fast actions, you usually need to animate each single frame, i.e. on "ones". (even in traditionally drawn animation). This is because a lot of change takes place in an extremely short time span. Therefore, you have to illustrate this short period of time as detailed as possible, using animation on ones (24 drawings per second).

— ANIMATE **FAST MOVEMENTS** ON **ONES**!

IN SOME ACTIONS, THERE IS SO MUCH CHANGE IN A VERY SHORT PERIOD OF TIME THAT THEY DEFINITELY HAVE TO BE ANIMATED ON **ONES**. OTHERWISE ESSENTIAL STAGES OF THE MOVEMENT WOULD NOT BE VISUALIZED AND THE MOVEMENT AS A WHOLE NOT READABLE FOR THE VIEWER.

THESE ESSENTIAL PHASES OF THE MOMENT WOULD BE LACKING COMPLETELY WHEN ANIMATING THE SAME ACTION ON **TWOS**!

▦ How do I create a contrast between fast and slow?

▦ Are my movements slow, elegant and flowing, or jerky, abrupt and brisk?

▦ How do I switch?

▦ Where and how long do I place holds?

How do I figure out the correct timing for my animation?

One answer could be: Experience that comes with time. This means, to animate, test, correct, until the length "feels" right. Over time, you will be able to estimate the appropriate time it takes (measured in frames) for frequently occurring actions as you draw from the experiences you have gained. On the other hand, I am sometimes very surprised at the fact that students in the age of video cameras in mobile phones do not quickly "shoot" reference material of a movement they need, in order to get an approximate feeling for more complex timing.

With the help of a friend you can shoot it and play it back for your future animation, analyzing it later as a digital file. Of course, such reference must be dealt with correctly - it can only serve as a reference and must be exaggerated for the animation in timing and expression (see also exaggeration). But: It is a good starting point, especially for anatomically complicated animations!

The work of an animator is often most creative and interesting without any references - in that case, he is able to achieve complete creative freedom. The decision also depends largely on the required level of realism for an animation: The more stylized and abstract an animation should be, the less you will work with life action references.

A very common mistake for beginners in timing is, that too many actions are shown in too short a time. Most beginners are not really aware of the fact that in animation film in general, many frames or drawings have to be created. This unawareness leaves them thinking that an action is already adequately represented in time, because the inexperienced animator has already animated "so many" frames (as seen subjectively).

You have to keep in mind that (in the case of animation on ones), one frame represents only one 24th of a second, and that the viewer must see an action or a pose for a reasonable amount of time, in order to perceive it at all.

TO ENSURE THE VITALITY, THE
STATIC MAIN POSE IS COMBINED
WITH MOVEMENT OR MOVING
ELEMENTS : THE HAIR FOLLOWS
THROUGH / KEEPS MOVING, EYES
CAN BLINK . THIS MEANS
CREATING (ONE FORM OF)
A **MOVING HOLD**.

IF THIS POSE IS HELD FOR LESS THAN
6 FRAMES, IT WILL NOT BE PERCEIVED
AS A HOLD I.E. A RESTING POINT, BUT
RATHER AS A JERK IN THE MOVEMENT.
TO ACHIEVE THE IMPRESSION OF A
TRUE **HOLD** A POSE SHOULD USUALLY
BE HELD FOR A MINIMUM OF
10 FRAMES.

A good gauge for a hold is that it should not be less than 10 frames in length: Otherwise it is perceived as an irritation in a continuous movement (jerking) rather than a resting point.

NATURALLY, **INBETWEENS**, NEED TO BE ADDED HERE TO MAKE THE MOVEMENT WORK PROPERLY. HOWEVER, THE NUMBER (TIMING) AND POSITIONS (SPACING) NEED TO BE CONSIDERED CAREFULLY. THEY DETERMINE THE FINAL APPEARANCE OF THE WALK.

COMPARE WITH THE BOUNCING BALL.
WRONG
RIGHT

WRONG   RIGHT

IT IS WRONG TO ADD TOO MANY INBETWEENS IN THE MIDDLE OF AN UPWARD DYNAMIC: THIS LEADS TO A LOSS OF MOMENTUM. (TOO MANY DRAWINGS = SLOW).

For certain important movement patterns, such as walking, there are some good basic rules, which can of course be varied according to artistic taste. A beginner's mistake, which should be avoided at all cost, is a "pause" in a continuous movement (such as a typical walk), or even to slow down at the wrong point: This will always look wrong, since it interrupts motion dynamics.

Assignment:

■ Use these drawings and add in-betweens to create a convincing animation. See also instructions for constructing a walk cycle on page 201.

The most common timing errors and how to avoid them.

Very often beginners are underestimating the length of time, in which a particular pose or movement has to be shown in order for it to be sufficiently understood by the audience. They are often tempted to show expressive drawings of individual poses only briefly and assume that they are nevertheless perceived; but you need at least 10 frames, so that a very specific posture or expression can actually be read properly.

As a first step, the drawings, which are essential for the understanding of the action (storytelling drawings) should be tested very roughly with regard to correct timing: How long do we have to see a pose, action, or movement, so that it can be understood? For this purpose, we film these first drawings, each with the appropriate number of frames for length. Of course, we still lack the inbetweens, which we basically include in the frame number for the storytelling drawings. Although this first test is still quite inaccurate, it provides us an excellent indication for rough timing: From this point forward, you can continue working and refining, since you have established a solid foundation - provided that the test worked.

HOLDS AS A METHOD FOR EXTREMELY **LIMITED ANIMATION,** ANIMATICS AND LINE TESTING.

) = LINES OF ACTION

8 FR.

24 FR.

24 FR.

14 FR.

18 FR.

2 FR.

These poses can of course be combined with mouth movements.
⇒ A common method for limited animation.

IS AMAZING HOW WELL THE USE OF EXTREMELY DIFFERENT (KEY) POSES OR XTREMES ONLY CAN WORK, WITHOUT USING ANY INBETWEENS! UT THIS DOES ONLY FUNCTION PROPERLY WITH CORRECTLY APPLIED TIMING AND DR A MORE CARTOONY/STYLIZED ANIMATION AND DESIGN STYLE. THIS METHOD IS LSO OFTEN USED TO CREATE AN ANIMATIC OR TO DETERMINE THE ROUGH TIMING IN A LINETEST/EXPERIMENTAL ANIMATION.

We now know how long we have to show the particular pose so that it can be properly "read", but it seems that another problem has emerged now: The pose does not change, it is standing still for a certain period of time. Although everyone can grasp the meaning, the character seems lifeless, since no changes take place - an unsolvable problem?

The moving hold

At this point, a brilliant discovery from the classic principles of animation comes into play: the moving hold. In short, this basically means keeping the main pose (within the timing that works), but changing it subtly to avoid the impression of lifelessness. This technique is especially important for animation in a more realistic style, particularly for computer animation, which is actually not very forgiving of a complete standstill of a character (not even for two single frames). There are several techniques that you can use to achieve a moving hold, the classic one is as follows: You design a more extreme version of the original storytelling frame or key frame. In doing so, you remain relatively close to the original design, but make the physical

TO MAKE THE ANTICIPATION APPEAR LONGER, THE CORRESPONDING DRAWING CAN SIMPLY BE EXPOSED WITH MORE FRAMES:

＝E.G. 14 FRAMES THIS IS CALLED A HOLD.

THIS WORKS WELL FOR HIGHLY STYLIZED DIGITAL OR TRADITIONAL 2D ANIMATION.

WHEN DOING MORE COMPLEX 2D ANIMATIONS WITH A MORE REALISTIC LOOK AND GENERALLY WITH 3D COMPUTER ANIMATION SUCH A SOLUTION WILL NOT WORK BECAUSE A STATIC POSE OF THE FIGURE APPEARS LIFELESS WHEN HELD FOR SEVERAL FRAMES. THE "ILLUSION OF LIFE" IS DESTROYED. THE SOLUTION TO THIS PROBLEM IS OFFERED BY APPLYING THE METHOD OF THE MOVING HOLD.

A MOVING HOLD CAN BE ACHIEVED BY "PUSHING" THE POSE OF A STATIC HOLD WITH AN ADDITIONAL DRAWING (THAT IS SLIGHTLY MORE EXTREME, YET VERY CLOSE/SIMILAR TO THE PRECEDING DRAWING AND THE INSERTING INBETWEEN DRAWINGS THAT DIMINISH IN SPACING TOWARDS THE "PUSHED" DRAWING. (THE SAME WORKS FOR COMPUTER ANIMATION BY CREATING INBETWEENS/INTERPOLATIONS) FOLLOWING THE SAME PRINCIPLE).

IF YOU WANT TO CREATE A MOVING HOLD WITH A TOTAL LENGTH OF 18 FRAMES, YOU START BY CREATING THE STARTING POSE AND THE FINAL POSE OF THE MOVING HOLD AND THEN THE CORRESPONDING INBETWEENS: 7 IF ANIMATION IS DONE ON 1s, 16, IF ANIMATING ON 2s.

— TOTAL LENGTH (ON 2s) = 18 FRAMES. KEY FRAMES ① AND ⑨ AND 7 INBETWEENS.

① 2 3 4 5 6 7 ⑨

A SUBTLE CHANGE IN POSTURE (PLUS IBs) RESULTS IN THE MOVING HOLD.

features more distinct, more extreme or theatrically more expressive. Just how drastic such a change can or should be, depends again on the degree of realism and style of animation.

Next are the inbetweens, which go between the two new extremes. The total for your timing is the same as originally tested - only now you have a "living" character instead of a lifeless hold.

sert ① and ②

This effect can be further enhanced (and the vitality of the pose increased) by adding elements of **overlapping action** and **follow through**.
(Hair, clothing in continuous movement).
Such elements must be animated according to their materiality and weight (⟹ timing and spacing) to create a believable "illusion of life".

Blink and you'll miss it!

REMARK:
A SIMPLIFIED VARIATION OF A MOVING HOLD LEAVES THE FIGURE UNCHANGED AND ADDS ONLY SUCH ELEMENTS. IN EXTREME CASES (E.G. FOR BUDGET REASONS) ONE CAN GO AS FAR AS TO ONLY USE A BLINKING OF THE FIGURE TO CREATE AN "ANIMATED" IMPRESSION. HOWEVER THIS EXTREMELY LIMITED TYPE OF ANIMATION CAN ONLY WORK WITH STYLISTIC CORRESPONDENCE = GRAPHICALLY STRONGLY STYLIZED ANIMATION AND IN 2D ONLY!

There are other methods to achieve a "moving hold", such as by using a loop, or follow-through and overlapping action. The best animation is often achieved by the fact that these stylistic devices are synchronized and combined very subtly, which is often essential for feature quality animation. Any good animator will get more sophisticated combinations as he gains more experience.

Gap and contrast in lines of action
One of the best ways to achieve a "snappy" or lively animation is the combined use of frames with strongly contrasting lines of action with a gap between the anticipation and the execution of a fast action.

HERE IS THE CLASSIC:

For the impact of great dynamics, it is important to follow up the slow anticipation with a distinctly different animation frame (e.g., change of action lines from convex to concave)! There must be a gap between the last anticipation frame and the first frame of the actual action, in order to achieve the desired dynamics, i.e., inbetweens will not be used here.

A WORD ABOUT SPEEDLINES:

Especially with beginners, I often see that they try to use speedlines to add dynamics to their animation. But good animation does not need speedlines, in order to create credible dynamics. By applying speedlines the wrong way they achieve the opposite of the desired effect.

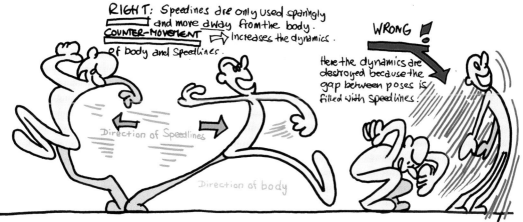

RIGHT: Speedlines are only used sparingly and more away from the body. Increases the dynamics.

COUNTER-MOVEMENT of body and Speedlines.

WRONG !

Here the dynamics are destroyed because the gap between poses is filled with speedlines!

Direction of Speedlines

Direction of body

*Speed lines are a **stylistic device** of **comics**! In animation, the impression of speed must be achieved solely by **timing** and **spacing** of the frames. Speed lines can be added as an **additional** graphic stylistic device, but must be animated properly and cannot "clog up" the gap between the frames, otherwise the dynamics will be destroyed!*

If you use an inbetween, it must be drawn and placed in such a way that the dynamics are retained, i.e. show a distinct contrast to the anticipation frame. It has to be a spatially well-placed and well-designed inbetween - a purely "mechanical" inbetween is not helpful here and would destroy the desired effect.

MOTION BLUR:

*The more **modern** (and, of course, more **cinematic**) **equivalent** of speed lines is the use of **motion blur**. Here too, the stylistic means should fit the design concept of the animation. "Smear" animation (see below) and speed lines are used more in stylized 2D animation, motion blur is used more in 3D and realistic animation and stop motion.*

ADDITIONALLY / ALTERNATIVELY THE STYLISTIC MEANS OF MOTION BLUR CAN STILL BE USED (MOST CONVINCINGLY IN COMPUTER ANIMATION, 2D WOULD OFTEN REVERT TO CREATE AN APPROXIMATION: A "SMEAR" AS AN INBETWEEN). IN ANY CASE THIS MUST BE APPLIED IN A WAY THE CONSIDERS THE GENERAL ART DIRECTION: GOOD FOR REALISTIC 3D ANIMATION, RATHER INAPPROPRIATE FOR VERY STYLIZED, GRAPHIC 2D ANIMATION. (BETTER TO USE GRAPHICALLY CLEARLY CONTOURED DRAWINGS).

SMEARS

Fast transition with one inbetween between two key frames, which are held longer (2 holds). Works also with "moving holds".

ANTICIPATION
Hold or moving hold
held for 18 frames.
SMEAR: 1 or 2 images.

Next Pose:
As hold or moving
hold held for
e.g. 24 frames.

Strong change
of shape is important
to achieve the
dynamics!

ATTENTION !!

Smear inbetween
1 or 2 images
(drawings)

A STYLISTIC TOOL OFTEN USED FOR HIGHLY STYLIZED AND LIMITED ANIMATION IS THE **SMEAR**: A GRAPHICALLY STRONGLY DISTORTED INBETWEEN, WHICH PROVIDES THE FAST TRANSITION BETWEEN LONGER HELD KEY FRAMES OR MAIN POSES. SINCE THIS CAN RESULT IN VERY DYNAMIC AND SHARPLY ACCENTUATED ANIMATION, THIS ALSO IS AN OPTION FOR HIGH-CONTRAST (SNAPPY) TIMING EVEN WITH FULL ANIMATION.

Time to Think, or: Action and Reaction

Apart from certain exceptions, most movements require a certain physical or motivational anticipation time (see also Anticipation). If I yell at someone, it usually takes at least a fraction of a second of anticipation, before the other person responds.

This is because the information has to be processed before the person can respond. What appears as an immediate reaction in the macrocosm of superficial observation, often turns out to be single-frame delays in the microcosm of animation. This principle is also consistent with the need not to overwhelm the viewer by showing too many actions at the same time. As a rule, attention should be drawn to a key action. In other words: Show them one after the other! (In doing so, you have to let actions overlap elegantly - see chapter on Overlapping Action/Follow Through).

First (1), the "wake-up call" is shown. The sleepy student reacts with delay, more specifically, he anticipates (2) his reaction in (3). While the student returns from the "fright stage" to a more neutral position (4) - (5), the teacher, on the other hand, anticipates (4) his reaction (5) to the outcome of the action.

These are, of course, only the extremes or breakdowns of this animation.

Assignment:

- Take these drawings and create a full animation (complete with inbetweens)! **Vary** the extremes and breakdowns to get the best timing.

2.) Spacing

Spacing refers to the spatial arrangement of inbetweens between the key frames of an animation: It helps to define the dynamics of movement. "Uneven" spacing of the inbetweens is crucial for a convincing effect. If the drawings are evenly spaced, they appear mechanical and unnatural.

RIGHT   Key Frames

WRONG!   Key Frames

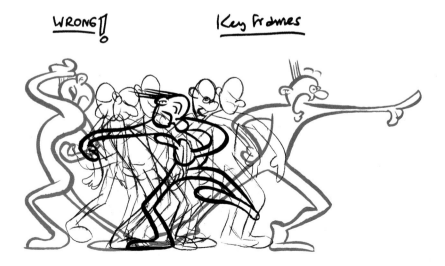

3.) Slow In und Slow Out (deceleration/acceleration)

This means that movements generally accelerate initially (gradual wider spacing of drawings) and slow down again (gradual narrower spacing of drawings), before they come to a standstill or go into a key pose or key frame. (Of course there are exceptions to the rule.)

SLOW IN / SLOW OUT

DECELERATION / ACCELERATION

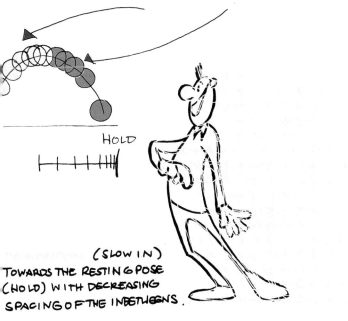

HOLD

(SLOW IN)
TOWARDS THE RESTING POSE
(HOLD) WITH DECREASING
SPACING OF THE INBETWEENS.

ALSO KNOWN AS **CUSHIONING**
(FROM "CUSHION" =
PILLOW = CUSHIONED)

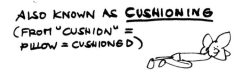

TRANSITION TO
THE NEXT POSE.

HOLD   HOLD

→ ACCELERATION WHILE
MOVING AWAY FROM THE
RESTING POSE. INCREASING
SPACING OF INBETWEENS!

4.) Straight Ahead and Pose-to-Pose Animation

Straight ahead animation simply means "re-inventing" one drawing after the other. This ensures great spontaneity during animation, so that even the animator is "pleasantly surprised". In commercial animation, however, the straight ahead method is only possible as part of a scene made from sketches (thumbnails), or one that has been carefully planned.

Straight ahead animation leads to a constant flow of movements without coming to a real "standstill" - everything changes constantly. This results in very flowing movements, since the animation does not move "into" and then again "out" of previously set extremes. However, if used incorrectly, there is a risk that the scene will lose its temporal structure and that important story points will not be communicated, since not enough emphasis was placed on the appropriate expressive key frames.

Pose-to-pose animation primarily defines the most **expressive key frames or extremes**, which provide structure to the scene and make it predictable. Once the extremes have been defined, the inbetweens are inserted. This method, which allows for extremely good planning and structuring of the animation, also carries a possible disadvantage, as it lacks spontaneity and unexpected developments.

In my experience, it is much **easier** for **beginners** to start with **pose-to-pose** animation: The more spontaneous process of straight-ahead animation requires some experience with timing, spacing, etc. to achieve good results. Once the initial success is established, an advanced beginner can also experiment with straight-ahead animation. **"The Best of Both Worlds":** Often, both methods are combined in order to achieve optimal results. Extremes, for example, which were defined in the first pass, can be revised in subsequent passes in order to introduce new ideas and different timing. Or certain aspects of a character, which are essential for structuring and planning a scene, are animated "pose-to-pose" - while other elements are added in straight ahead animation, as they may be more suitable for this.

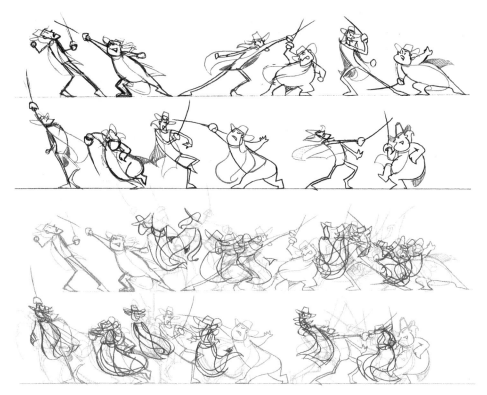

Certain types of animation are better suited for straight ahead animation: When each new frame requires a drastic change of shape, such as VFX animation. A fire takes on a drastically different shape in each new drawing, which does not "go" to a certain extreme. Instead, it is a permanently changing continuum of movement. The same applies to water, clouds, smoke etc.

5.) Overlapping Action and Follow Through

With the techniques mentioned so far, I can now show my character in sufficiently long "held" poses, while slow in and slow out allows me to arrive with the correct timing from pose A to pose B. But is movement really that simple? And what can I do about the problem that my character appears absolutely lifeless when I show it without any change for several drawings? (Note: This can be acceptable with highly stylized 2D animation or a desired stylistic device, but it is completely unacceptable for 3D computer animation.) This is where overlapping action and follow through are used to achieve the above-described moving hold. ▪

COMIC: EVERYTHING HAPPENS AT ONCE.

Comics lack the temporal element: The reader himself can decide on the reading duration of each panel. Therefore, more details can be displayed simultaneously, that is, in one image. A time period is condensed into one image. This could work the same way in a storyboard!

ANIMATION: ONE THING AFTER THE OTHER PLUS OVERLAPPING ACTION AND FOLLOW THROUGH.

THE MAIN POSE (HEAD, BODY, LEFT ARM) IS ESTABLISHED FIRST.

HAND ARRIVES SLIGHTLY DELAYED

COUNTER MOVEMENT CREATES ACCENT

ELEMENTS OF FOLLOW THROUGH AND OVERLAPPING ACTION FURTHER VITALIZE THE ANIMATION.

THE CURL FOLLOWS THROUGH AFTER THE HEAD HAS ALREADY ARRIVED. IT UNFOLDS AS A "WAVE-MOVEMENT" WITH A DECREASING RADIUS OF MOTION.

*An **animation**, on the other hand, runs for a **specified time**: A good animator must therefore ensure that important actions are seen **long enough** in order to be perceived by the viewer. Therefore, they can not compete: This can be achieved by showing important actions **one at a time**. For a life-like and credible appearance, you should also work with **overlapping action** and **follow through**.*

MOVING HOLD: (AS A VARIATION OF OVERLAPPING ACTION):
- RIGHT HAND SPREADS OUT SLOTLY.
- THE MOUTH OPENS A LITTLE BIT WIDER.

*A wink directs the viewer's attention to the character's **line of sight** ...*

*... **then** the light bulb appears. The light bulb appears last and remains visible as a loop for at least 18 frames.*

5a) Wave Principle

The basic principle of wave action is similarly important to animation as the principle of the bouncing ball. This principle can and must be applied to many different movements of flexible objects, if you want to achieve a credible impression. (As always, you can certainly deviate from this as a deliberate artistic measure, but it is crucial to understand the possibilities of this technique.) At the same time, I have learned that it is one of the hardest-to-learn basic rules for beginners: We are talking about a non-linear movement pattern, which requires out-of-the-box thinking at key points. Purely mechanical inbetweens (which should basically be avoided) do not work at all here. Waves have to be used quite often for ele-

ments of a character in follow through and in overlapping action, such as a windblown coat, or hair, for an animal's tail, etc. It is often best to animate "straight ahead" (within a roughly established time structure) and to insert waves only in a later animation pass, after the movements of the main object (body) have already been implemented.

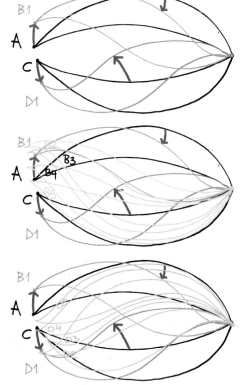

AN EQUALLY FREQUENT USE OF THE WAVE PRINCIPLE : HAIR, FLAGS ETC. DRIFTING IN THE WIND. HERE , OF COURSE, THE INBETWEENS ARE MISSING TO COMPLETE THE ANIMATED LOOP / CYCLE (AFTER 4 FOLLOWS 1). DEPENDING ON THE DESIRED SPEED OF MOVEMENT (TIMING) THEY NEED TO BE ADDED WITH THE REQUISITE SLOW IN / SLOW OUT TOWARDS KEY FRAMES .

6.) Secondary Action

A secondary action supports or even counteracts the primary action of a character. It is important that this secondary action does not dominate or drown out the primary movement: It must be noticeable, but must remain secondary. This could be, for example, wiping away a tear with the arm (secondary action,) while a character

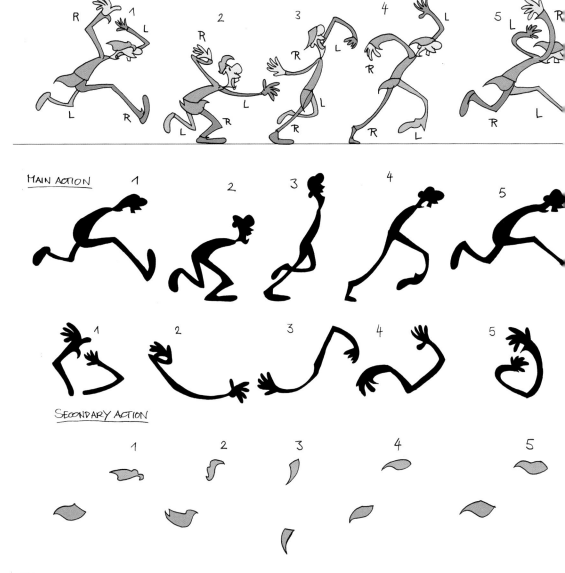

MAIN ACTION

SECONDARY ACTION

is walking away (main action). This secondary action is intended to give more depth to the performance through additional information, but can not dominate or drown out the primary movement.

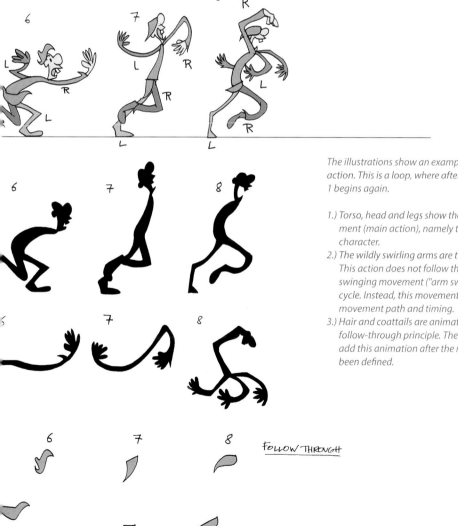

The illustrations show an example of secondary action. This is a loop, where after drawing 8, drawing 1 begins again.

1.) Torso, head and legs show the primary movement (main action), namely the running of the character.
2.) The wildly swirling arms are the secondary action: This action does not follow the classic balancing swinging movement ("arm swing") of a running cycle. Instead, this movement follows its own movement path and timing.
3.) Hair and coattails are animated according to the follow-through principle. The Animator would add this animation after the main animation has been defined.

7.) Anticipation - Preparation (Anticipation of Movements)

If you will, this principle is another aspect of timing: As a rule, any action or movement is preceded by a preparatory smaller action. Even this rule was originally discovered while observing material from live-action film, and then adapted (often intentionally exaggerated) for animation.

WITHOUT ANTICIPATION

WITH ANTICIPATION

A **BREAKDOWN** PLACED PRECISELY IN THE MIDDLE IS UNNATURAL AND STIFF.

WITH THE **CORRECT PREPARATION**, THE BODY AXES CHANGE. THIS IS FLEXIBLE **AND** NATURAL. ADDING OVERLAPPING ACTION (HAIR, NECKTIE) ENHANCES THIS EFFECT FURTHER.

HERE, THE ANTICIPATION POSE ALSO COMMUNICATES THE WEIGHT OF THE CHARACTER: THE ARM CARRIES THE WEIGHT TO SUPPORT THE STANDING UP.

Anticipation of movement is also a helpful trick to attract the viewer's attention to actions that would otherwise be over quickly (in very few single frames), making sure that they can be perceived at all. The anticipation of the action to follow can/must be held longer than the actual action (= use more frames as spacing narrows). Thus, the viewer will automatically anticipate that "something is about to happen" and perceive the actual primary action sufficiently, despite its extreme brevity (1 or 2 frames).

On the opposite page an example based on Homer's Odyssey: Upon returning home, Odysseus points his famous bow to the not-so-happy suitors, who are competing for his wife Penelope. The anticipation together with the reactions, helps to make the arrow shot noticeable - also, keep in mind the importance of timing here!

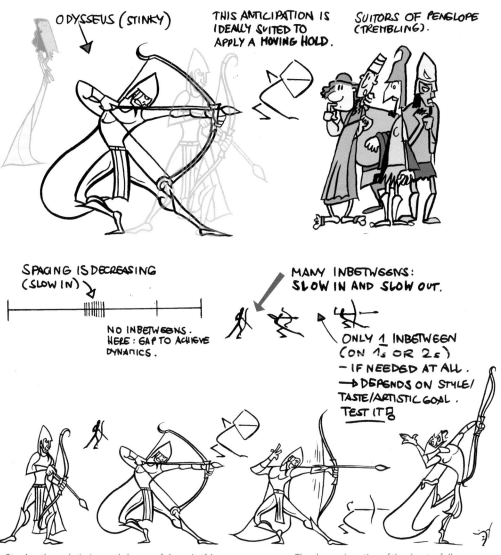

ODYSSEUS (STINKY)

THIS ANTICIPATION IS IDEALLY SUITED TO APPLY A MOVING HOLD.

SUITORS OF PENELOPE (TREMBLING).

SPACING IS DECREASING (SLOW IN)

NO INBETWEENS. HERE: GAP TO ACHIEVE DYNAMICS.

MANY INBETWEENS: SLOW IN AND SLOW OUT.

ONLY 1 INBETWEEN (ON 1s OR 2s) — IF NEEDED AT ALL. → DEPENDS ON STYLE/ TASTE/ARTISTIC GOAL. TEST IT

Staging through timing and change of shape in **this** scene: The only elements changing are those needed to perceive the **arrow shot**.

The change/reaction of the shooter follows *later*, in order not to divert the attention!

Assignment:

▓ Complete the animation by using the extremes to draw inbetweens. Pay particular attention to the correct **timing** (number) and **spacing** (position) of the inbetweens!

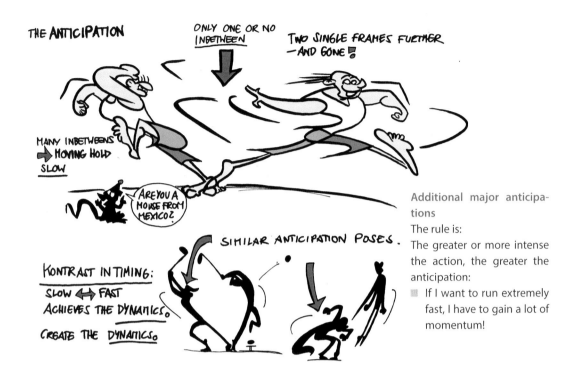

THE ANTICIPATION

ONLY ONE OR NO INBETWEEN

TWO SINGLE FRAMES FURTHER — AND GONE!

MANY INBETWEENS → MOVING HOLD SLOW

ARE YOU A MOUSE FROM MEXICO?

KONTRAST IN TIMING:
SLOW ⟷ FAST
ACHIEVES THE DYNAMICS,
CREATE THE DYNAMICS.

SIMILAR ANTICIPATION POSES.

Additional major anticipations

The rule is:

The greater or more intense the action, the greater the anticipation:

▓ If I want to run extremely fast, I have to gain a lot of momentum!

PSYCHOLOGICAL ANTICIPATION

PHYSICAL ANTICIPATION

▓ If I want to lift a very heavy object, I have to "gather" my strength and prepare the upward motion physically (possibly mentally as well...). Here it becomes apparent how the repeated effort of anticipation can contribute to conveying the illusion of weight for the animation!

Paying close attention to stark contrasts in change of shape is an essential component and absolutely necessary: convex changes to concave (in lines of action) etc. These opposites are enormously important for lively animation - the more cartoony, the better!

Subtle Anticipation
Working with very subtle anticipation can greatly enrich animation as well: a wink, slightly raising/lowering the head, a slight turn of the body. The action and its preparation should always be expressed in a reasonable relationship. The same applies to timing, spacing and change of shape!

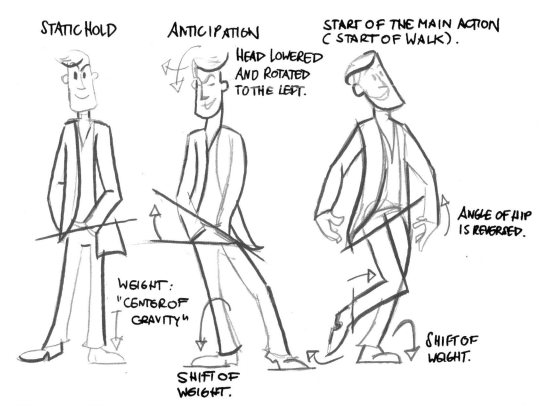

STATIC HOLD

ANTICIPATION

START OF THE MAIN ACTION
(START OF WALK).

HEAD LOWERED
AND ROTATED
TO THE LEFT.

ANGLE OF HIP
IS REVERSED.

WEIGHT:
"CENTER OF
GRAVITY"

SHIFT OF
WEIGHT.

SHIFT OF
WEIGHT.

OFTENTIMES **ANTICIPATION** IS ALSO USED MORE SUBTLY TO PREPARE THE START OF A BIGGER MOVEMENT WITH A SLIGHT COUNTER-MOVEMENT. THIS PROVES A USEFUL METHOD TO ANIMATE OUT OF A STATIC POSE INTO A BEGINNING MOVEMENT, E.G. WHEN STARTING A WALK. THIS OFTEN STARTS WITH A SUBTLE COUNTER-MOVEMENT AND A SHIFT OF WEIGHT TO "FREE" THE STARTING LEG FROM WEIGHT AND ALLOWING IT TO MOVE FORWARD.

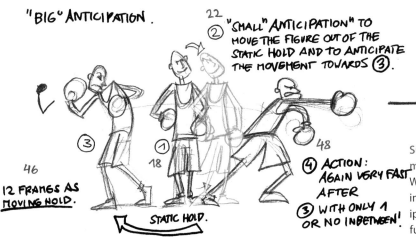

"BIG" ANTICIPATION.

22
② "SMALL" ANTICIPATION" TO MOVE THE FIGURE OUT OF THE STATIC HOLD AND TO ANTICIPATE THE MOVEMENT TOWARDS ③.

③
①
18

46

12 FRAMES AS MOVING HOLD.

STATIC HOLD.

48
④ ACTION: AGAIN VERY FAST AFTER ③ WITH ONLY 1 OR NO INBETWEEN!

Subtle anticipation of a major anticipation
When it comes to introducing a very pronounced anticipation itself, it is often helpful to open it with a smaller anticipatory movement.

OBVIOUSLY, THE INBETWEENS ARE STILL MISSING HERE, SHOWN ARE ONLY THE KEY FRAMES (NUMBER ② COULD ALMOST BE SEEN AS A BREAKDOWN). THE POSSIBLE TIMING IS INDICATED IN NUMBERS IN RED.

Accentuating movements through anticipation
One rather sophisticated trick is to integrate an anticipation into a continuous movement in order to highlight a certain aspect: For this, appropriate spacing is combined with the principle of overlapping action (i.e. different timing for different body parts). The counteraction of the hand within the forward movement of the arm anticipates the final "finger pointing": The hand anticipates until shortly before the final extreme, then reaching the final position with only one inbetween.

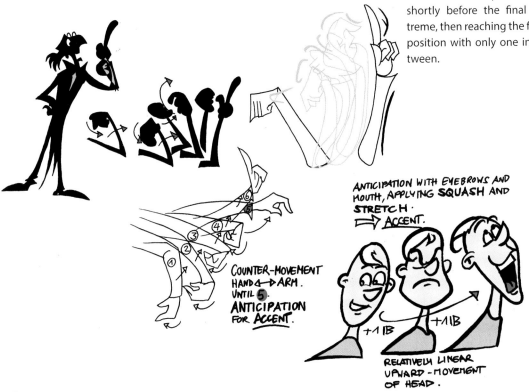

ANTICIPATION WITH EYEBROWS AND MOUTH, APPLYING SQUASH AND STRETCH.
⟹ ACCENT.

COUNTER-MOVEMENT HAND⟷ARM. UNTIL ⑤. ANTICIPATION FOR ACCENT.

+1 IB   +1 IB

RELATIVELY LINEAR UPWARD-MOVEMENT OF HEAD.

8.) Squash and Stretch

Squash and stretch describes the physically induced deformations of objects when forces act on them: A classic example is the bouncing ball. The following rule applies: The more naturalistic an animation should be, the less squash and stretch should be applied.

"NORMAL" SQUASH STRETCH

SQUASH AND STRETCH ALSO PLAY AN IMPORTANT ROLE IN DIALOGUE ANIMATION: THE ANATOMY OF THE FACE ALLOWS AMAZING FLEXIBILITY.

NATURALLY THE EXTENT SHOULD BE ADJUSTED TO THE STYLE: ALMOST EVERYTHING "GOES" FOR HIGHLY STYLIZED/NON-REALISTIC ANIMATION: SQUASH AND STRETCH CAN BE OVERLY EXAGGERATED.

THE MORE REALISTIC THE FIGURE DESIGN IS, THE MORE SUBTLY SQUASH AND STRETCH SHOULD BE APPLIED.

Movement along a straight line: very unusual, e.g. for a desired "stiff" exercise-type of march.

9.) Arcs

Most movements do not run along (imaginary) straight lines, but along curved or arc-like paths of movement: the arcs.

Movements along straight lines are stiff/mechanical/robotic - most naturally organic movements follow an arc.

Natural walking movement: Arms and legs move along curves (arcs).

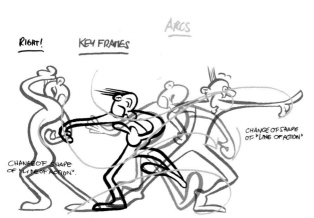

The illustration on the left shows the different paths of movement of the individual body elements:

You can clearly see the arc-shaped character, which lends elegance, expression and a certain genuineness to the animation (with the exaggeration typical to animation). These movement arcs are achieved by establishing a movement hierarchy to obtain flexibility: the delayed transfer of movement through joints.

Flexibility by delayed transfer of force through joints: In the case of rigid "rods" (i.e., lower arm/upper arm), which are connected by joints, a delayed force transfer of the primary movement takes place through the joint. In other words: When the upper arm moves in one direction, the forearm first moves into the opposite direction before following the direction of the primary movement. Flexibility and arcs can be achieved with this delayed movement dynamics.

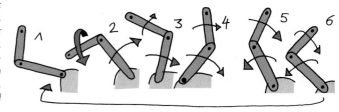

*Another good example of this principle: The foot follows the shinbone's direction of movement with delay and first moves into the **opposite direction**.*

10.) Solid Drawing

Solid drawing refers to the fact that animated objects should always retain their original overall volume when undergoing any deformation. For example, what is added in length, has to be removed in width. Although it sounds simple in theory, it is extremely difficult to implement and requires the highest level of mastery in drawing. The degree of difficulty increases significantly with the complexity of the objects/characters. In computer animation, this is carried out by the computer, which calculates the necessary deformations based on pre-defined volumes.

If the drawings are not "solid", then the (un-intentional) change in volume will dominate the intended change of shape in the illustration of movement: This means that in extreme cases, the viewer can no longer recognize the movement, the actual animation, but is totally distracted by the sloppy shape change of fluctuating volume.

THIS IS CLEARLY SHOWN IN THE FOLLOWING ILLUSTRATION:

SOLID DRAWING

THE VOLUME REMAINS THE SAME FOR EACH DEFORMATION

IN FIGURES THAT ARE CONSTRUCTED FROM RELATIVELY SIMPLE BASIC SHAPES, IT IS EASY TO CONTROL THE SOLID DRAWING.

THIS WOULD PROBABLY STILL FUNCTION AS A "WILDLY EX-PERIMENTAL" ANIMATION – BUT THE SHAPE CHANGE OF THE FIGURE WITH CHANGING VOLUME PREVENTS A "REALISTIC" MOVEMENT SUPPOSITION.

WITHOUT CONSIDERING THE PRINCIPLES OF **SOLID DRAWING** THIS COULD, FOR EXAMPLE, LOOK LIKE THIS :

INTERESTING FROM A PURELY DESIGN POINT OF VIEW – BUT THE FIGURE CANNOT BE RECOGNIZED ANYMORE – IT IS "OFF MODEL".

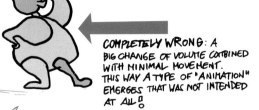

COMPLETELY WRONG: A BIG CHANGE OF VOLUME COMBINED WITH MINIMAL MOVEMENT. THIS WAY A TYPE OF "ANIMATION" EMERGES THAT WAS NOT INTENDED AT ALL.

OF COURSE I MIGHT HAVE AN ARTISTIC CONCEPT FOR WHICH I WANT TO DELIBERATELY NE-GLECT THE RULES OF SOLID DRAWING.
BUT IF I WANT TO PAY ATTEN-TION TO THEM, THEN THIS IS DEFINITELY THE WRONG WAY.

THE CHANGE OF VOLUME(S) MUST NOT BE STRONGER THAN THE MOTION I WANT TO SHOW

WITH THE SAME CAMERA PERSPECTIVE THE EYES MUST NOT "WANDER" WITHIN THE INNER SHAPE.

ATTENTION IS TO BE GIVEN TO THE WING FLAP, BUT IS DEFLECTED BY THE STRONG (UNINTENTIONAL) SHAPE CHANGE.

ALMOST IMPOSSIBLE TO DRAW BY HAND: AN ANTLER FROM DIFFERENT PERSPECTIVES/ CAMERA ANGLES. THEREFORE 3D COMPUTER-ANIMATION IS THE BEST SOLUTION TO ANIMATE SUCH COMPLEX DESIGNS DIMENSIONALLY.

CA: 3D MODEL CREATED ONLY ONCE. VIRTUAL CAMERA "SHOOTS" FROM EVERY ANGLE/ PERSPECTIVE.

For "Bambi" (Hand et al., 1942) a plaster model had to be created and filmed. The animators then traced the antler from the footage, in the perspective they needed!

A common mistake:

The shape changes too much, with volume and/or line thickness of the outer line varying greatly. These changes prevent or interfere with the originally intended, clear communi-cation of the character's movement: Varying the line width of the outlines can be a desired artistic effect, but this effect should never be so pronounced that it interferes with the ac-tual animation!

In an artistic animation, it can be quite attrac-tive to change the contour lines from one draw-ing to the next in thickness and expansion, i.e., deviating from the very strict rules of solid drawing: This is always an artistic judgment call. However, this change or deviation should never be so drastic that the actual movement of the character is no longer recognizable.

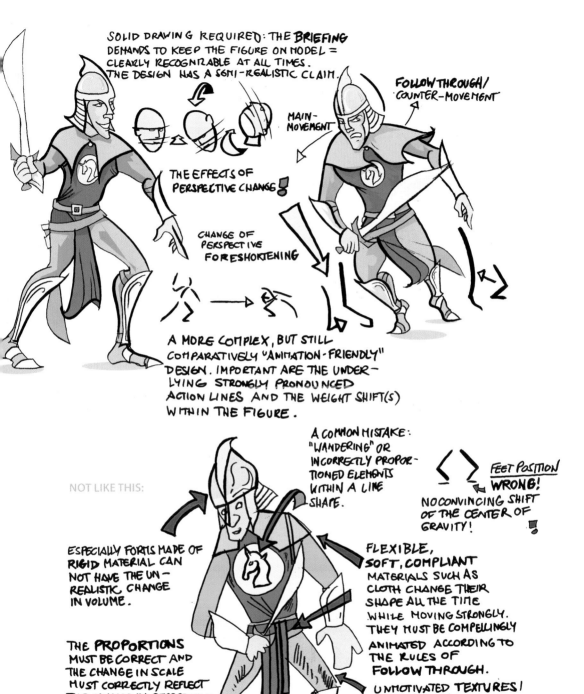

SOLID DRAWING REQUIRED: THE **BRIEFING** DEMANDS TO KEEP THE FIGURE ON MODEL = CLEARLY RECOGNIZABLE AT ALL TIMES. THE DESIGN HAS A SEMI-REALISTIC CLAIM.

MAIN-MOVEMENT

FOLLOW THROUGH / COUNTER-MOVEMENT

THE EFFECTS OF PERSPECTIVE CHANGE

CHANGE OF PERSPECTIVE FORESHORTENING

A MORE COMPLEX, BUT STILL COMPARATIVELY "ANIMATION-FRIENDLY" DESIGN. IMPORTANT ARE THE UNDER-LYING STRONGLY PRONOUNCED ACTION LINES AND THE WEIGHT SHIFT(S) WITHIN THE FIGURE.

NOT LIKE THIS:

A COMMON MISTAKE: "WANDERING" OR INCORRECTLY PROPOR-TIONED ELEMENTS WITHIN A LINE SHAPE.

FEET POSITION **WRONG!** NO CONVINCING SHIFT OF THE CENTER OF GRAVITY!

ESPECIALLY FOR TS MADE OF RIGID MATERIAL CAN NOT HAVE THE UN-REALISTIC CHANGE IN VOLUME.

FLEXIBLE, SOFT, COMPLIANT MATERIALS SUCH AS CLOTH CHANGE THEIR SHAPE ALL THE TIME WHILE MOVING STRONGLY. THEY MUST BE COMPELLINGLY ANIMATED ACCORDING TO THE RULES OF FOLLOW THROUGH.

THE **PROPORTIONS** MUST BE CORRECT AND THE CHANGE IN SCALE MUST CORRECTLY REFLECT THE CHANGE IN PERSPECTIVE.

UNMOTIVATED TEXTURES / HATCHING HAVE NO PLACE IN ANIMATION. ALL LINES MUST DEFINE AND ILLUSTRATE THE MOVEMENT THROUGH CHANGE OF SHAPE.

NO DEFINITION OF FORM, LACK OF USING "STRAIGHTS" AGAINST "CURVES".

RIGHT

WEIGHT

11.) Exaggeration

It is a well-known phenomenon that simply "tracing" live action images (known as rotoscoping) does not work as a foundation for animation: The result may seem relatively realistic, but completely lacks the desired momentum and liveliness, especially in cartoony animation. The same applies to the digital version of rotoscoping - motion capture. For this reason, extremes are almost always edited, even with live-action concepts, and the animation is adapted in order to achieve satisfactory results.

Exaggeration is an overriding artistic concept that must be applied to all animation techniques, more specifically, that can only be achieved by applying these techniques correctly:

- extreme expressive poses,
- more pronounced squash and stretch,
- stronger contrasts in timing: fast versus slow,
- wider spacing versus very closely "placed" frames.

Also important to know (applies especially to traditional 2D animation): The more complex a design, the more difficult it is to create extreme animation, in other words, to be able to deform and change the animation freely.

EXAGGERATION OF **TIMING**
AN EXAMPLE:

18 Frames

2 Fr.

12 Fr.

1 Fr.

16 Fr.

"Snappy timing": only extremes ("pose-to-pose") no or few in-betweens

EXAGGERATION

Version with little exaggeration, relatively close to live-action film - "realistic" design, subtle expression.

*Typical cartoon version: high degree of stylization, **extreme** exaggeration, extreme use of **squash** and **stretch** - only possible like this in cartoons.*

TIMING
(1s)

TO LITTLE CHANGE OF SHAPE ACCORDING TO PRINCIPLES OF ANIMATION.

Here also: Little "change of shape."

A relatively "normal" or standard walk cycle comparatively similar to "real life". While there are typical animation elements present (follow through, overlapping action, squash and stretch) - they only exist in moderate form.
The change-of-shape element is not very pronounced and would undermine the impact of credibly illustrated shift in weight.

This animation uses significantly **more** exaggeration: The character is very cartoony in design. The poses are much more extreme, there are more pronounced changes in shape. The lines of action are emphasized, and the upper body of the character shifts heavily to the right and left in perspective.

STRAIGHT ⟷ BENT.

As a rule, animation must be "larger than life", i.e., surpass reality in order to succeed artistically. In general, the following rule applies:

▥ The more stylized (cartoony) a project is, the more exaggeration can be achieved.

▥ The more "life-like" an animation has to be, the less exaggeration (especially for the animation of digital characters, which are used as visual effects in a live-action movie, for example, where they interact with real actors).

The classic "Tex Avery popping eyes."

Exceptions prove the rule:
It may also be artistically attractive to apply extreme exaggeration to a realistic design. Thanks to digital production techniques, this is now also possible with real actors (classic example of the film "The Mask" [Russell, 1994] with Jim Carrey).

12.) Weight - How do I show weight in animation?

A drawn or virtual character has no real weight, of course: Therefore, the credible illusion of weight must be produced when this is the artistic intention. This is mainly the case with commercial or linear narrative animation, in order to lend a certain "life-like" aspect to the artificial actors. However, this is generally not about naturalism, but about credibility, for which - ironically - the stylistic means of exaggeration (see previous section) is required. In order to leave a "weighty impression", an animator must skillfully combine the previously learned techniques of timing, spacing, squash and stretch, follow through, overlapping action and change of shape.

"UP" AND "DOWN" TIMING AND SPACING FOR:

HEAVY CHARACTER/FIGURE

Fewer drawings with decreased spacing in "up stage", since a heavy character is pulled down strongly by gravitational force.

More drawings in "down-stage" ("recoil" stage), since a heavy character needs more time and strength to overcome gravity.

LIGHT CHARACTER/FIGURE

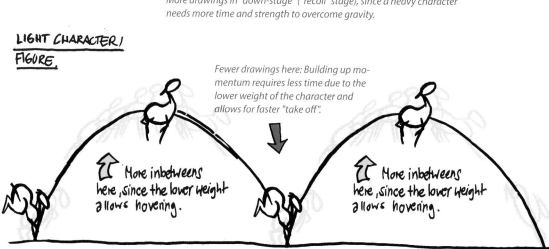

Fewer drawings here: Building up momentum requires less time due to the lower weight of the character and allows for faster "take off".

More inbetweens here, since the lower weight allows hovering.

More inbetweens here, since the lower weight allows hovering.

TIMING

A heavy character usually moves more slowly (=many inbetweens), because it takes time and effort to overcome the effects of gravity.

A light figure can move faster because it takes less time and effort to get going.

NO INBETWEEN OR ONLY ONE WITH A STRONG CHANGE OF SHAPE COMPARED TO THE CONTACT.

STRONG CHANGE IN THE "GRAPH" IN 3D COMPUTER-ANIMATION - NO GRADUAL TRANSITION.

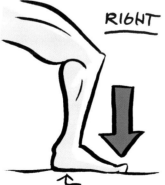

RIGHT

DUE TO THE WEIGHT THE UNDERLINE OF THE FOOT IS FLATTENED -TURNING IT ALMOST INTO A FLAT/STRAIGHT LINE.

WRONG

THIS DRAWING LOOKS AS IF THERE IS NO WEIGHT ON THE FOOT AT ALL.

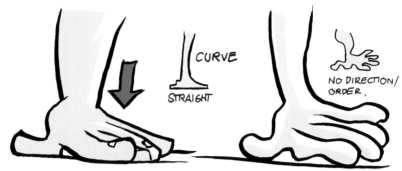

DUE TO THE WEIGHT LOAD A SQUASH
EFFECT IS CREATED ON THE UNDERSIDE
OF THE FINGERS.

AGAIN: NO LOAD EFFECT
CAN BE DETECTED.
FINGERS IN UNDEFINED
ROUND SHAPES.

NATURAL
EFFECT: FLEXIBLE MASS DEFORMS
WITH THE WEIGHT AND BACK
PRESSURE OF A HARD SURFACE.

ABSTRACT/
UNREALISTIC
SEEMS STIFFER.

NO DEFORMATION
DUE TO WEIGHT AND
RESISTANCE BECAUSE
OF THE RIGID
SURFACE.

A very important factor for a convincing illusion of weight is also the representation of weight shift during movement. This is especially true for movements that require overcoming gravity - for example, getting up from a resting position. Having knowledge of the anatomy and real movement sequence helps to represent the process correctly.

The underlying principle is usually a gradual shifting of weight: Only when an arm or a leg is relieved of its weight, is it free to change position and then to bear weight on it again (see illustrations). The more complex such a movement, the more useful it is to record a reference

WEIGHT SHIFT

① Here I sit and nothing else I can do?

② Or can I? But how to get up from here?

③

④ Now the right leg is free to move. The left arm is carrying the weight.

First the weight needs to be shifted, so that it can support the upward movement.

SUBSEQUENTLY **WEIGHT SHIFT** TO THE LEFT LEG.

PRINCIPLE OF SUCCESSIVE **WEIGHT SHIFT**

⑤ Now the actual getting up occurs. The right arm follows through.

⑥ Now I can get up, can't I?

This is how a mechanical middle position looks that does not reflect perspective and weight shift.

video of a life action. This should really only serve as a reference and must be implemented in the style of the animation. An animator should always continue figure drawing: With the exercises described in the previous chapter, such sequences can always be practiced with a live model: This will allow an experienced animator to have a complete catalog of anatomically correct options of weight shifting in his head, which he can retrieve as needed.

WRONG

FINAL POSITION

THIS IS HOW IT'S DONE:

13.) Appeal and Strong Poses

Appeal means that the quality of the animation design or character design should have a positive effect on the audience.

This is not the same as a "sweet" or "cute" look - the design must be convincing and coherent for the relevant style. Depending on the style, this can look quite different: Lilo from "Lilo and Stitch" (DeBlois/Sanders, 2002) and Jack Skellington from "Nightmare Before Christmas" (Selick, 1993) are both examples of characters with great appeal. All careful planning of timing and spacing can be completely destroyed, if the shaping, the design of the characters, does not support the animation in each drawing. The change of shape and the quality of key frames or key poses is crucial:

- Do they have tension, appeal, expressiveness?
- Can I make strong, continuous lines of action?
  (Tip: They should always be the basis of strong poses.)
- Can my pose be "distinguished" as a silhouette?
- How do I get from pose A to pose B, does the change of shape support the timing and accentuate it correctly?
- Is the drawing solid and "on model" (match the design of the character)?
- Am I choosing the right perspective for 3D animation to show the character in the best way possible?

EXPRESSIVE POSES

WHICH ALSO WORK WELL AS SILHOUETTES.

CAN BE REDUCED TO STRONG LINES OF ACTION.

RIGHT!

NOT LIKE THAT!

No perspective / scale in hands.

- **SHAPES** LACK CONTRAST.
- LACKING OR BADLY DEFINED **LINES OF ACTION.**
- **NO FLOW** OR CONTINUOUS RHYTHM IN THE FIGURE.
- **UNCLEAR** DEFINITION OF CENTER(S) OF GRAVITY.
- FIGURE NOT IN **BALANCE**
- "CROOKED" AXIS WITHOUT COUNTER WEIGHT → FIGURE WILL FALL OVER.

No counter weight ↗ ✗ RIGHT:

RIGHT!

WRONG ANGLES OF BODY AXES. RIGHT:

SHAPE OF FOOT DOESN'T DEMONSTRATE THE WEIGHT. RIGHT:

STRAIGHT

COUNTER WEIGHT CATCHES THE WEIGHT.

INCORRECT   CORRECT   INCORRECT   CORRECT

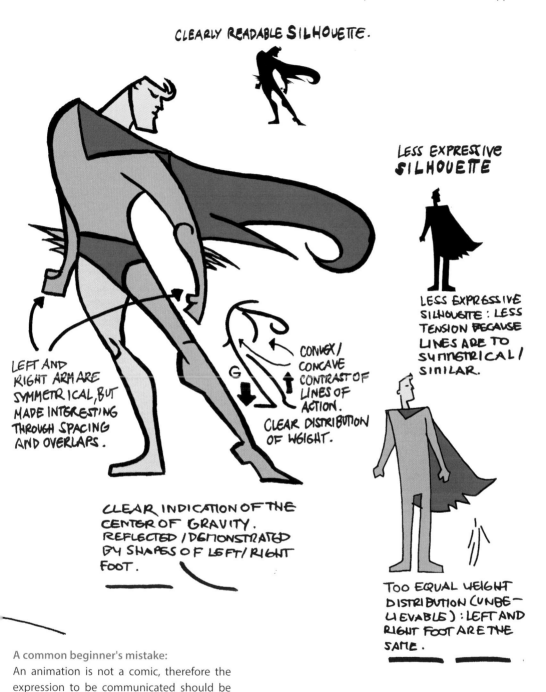

CLEARLY READABLE SILHOUETTE.

LESS EXPRESSIVE SILHOUETTE

LESS EXPRESSIVE SILHOUETTE : LESS TENSION BECAUSE LINES ARE TO SYMMETRICAL / SIMILAR.

LEFT AND RIGHT ARM ARE SYMMETRICAL, BUT MADE INTERESTING THROUGH SPACING AND OVERLAPS.

CONVEX / CONCAVE CONTRAST OF LINES OF ACTION.
CLEAR DISTRIBUTION OF WEIGHT.

CLEAR INDICATION OF THE CENTER OF GRAVITY. REFLECTED / DEMONSTRATED BY SHAPES OF LEFT / RIGHT FOOT.

TOO EQUAL WEIGHT DISTRIBUTION (UNBELIEVABLE) : LEFT AND RIGHT FOOT ARE THE SAME.

A common beginner's mistake:
An animation is not a comic, therefore the expression to be communicated should be communicated through acting/the action of the character- not with the usual comic-style means, such as speech- or thought bubbles. It conveys a weak animation, which does not rely on the movement of the character for expression!

14.) Staging

Staging is about using all design elements so that the action is optimally staged in such a way that the viewer can understand it! Composition, poses, appeal and, last but not least, timing must be designed in such a way, that the attention of the audience is directed in terms of visual storytelling:

▓ The background must not conflict with the acting characters in front.

▓ Important actions may not compete for the attention of the audience.
▓ A distinction must be made between primary and secondary action.

Most importantly:
The (animation) filmmaker has to decide what should be narrated with each shot. It is only when he has made that decision, that staging can be structured coherently. ▓

STAGING: SKILFULLY "SET IN SCENE", IN ORDER TO COMMUNICATE THE STORY IN THE BEST WAY POSSIBLE.

EMPTY STAGE IN FRONT OF WHICH THE CHARACTER CAN ACT WITHOUT CONFLICT WITH THE BACKGROUND AND WITHIN THE INTENDED AREA.

GOOD **STAGING** DIRECTS THE **ATTENTION** IN SERVICE OF **STORY**.

Composition
- *positioning*
- *strong/clear poses*
- *can I "distinguish" the silhouette?*
- *contrast*
- *scaling*
- *density of detail*
- *tonal values/lighting*

Timing
- *overlapping action, follow through*
- *secondary action*
- *balance of fast and slow movements*

One character dominates the scene with its action: If both actors were acting with equal intensity, it would confuse the viewer. Maximum action - minimal action.

THERE SHOULD BE COMPELLING GRAPHIC COMBINATIONS.

RESTRAINED ACTION, JUST ENOUGH TO KEEP THE CHARACTER "ALIVE".

FOR GOOD STAGING WITHIN THE SCENE, CONSIDER THE PRINCIPLE OF ACTION - REACTION : FIRST THE FIGURE ACTS IN A STRONGER MANNER IN THE REACTION THE OTHER FIGURE ACTS STRONGER - THE FIRST ONE'S ACTIONS ARE VERY RESTRAINED . THIS PRINCIPLE APPLIES VICE VERSA .

STRONG ACTION

MINIMAL ACTION : A BLINK MAY SUFFICE. YOU CAN ALSO USE A MOVING HOLD.

ONLY ONE CHARACTER ACTS STRONGLY AT THE SAME TIME → CONTRAST IN ACTING SUPPORTS STAGING .

Assignment:

Exercise for staging of interaction/action/reaction.

▦ Use all characters (Odysseus, Penelope, suitor) and animate the following scene: Odysseus standing with a bow, positions himself to shoot, then shoots. Penelope reacts, suitors react.

▦ Use **all the resources** at your disposal to produce good timing: composition, timing, spacing, change of shape.

▦ **Story:** Think of something funny - what happens to the suitors?

15.) Change of Shape

As we have seen in previous examples, it is very important for the dynamics and accentuation of animation to work with strong shape changes:

▦ Bent to stretched
▦ Concave to convex... etc.:

These shape changes can be applied abruptly (without inbetweens) in order to emphasize features - or gradually as extremes with appropriate inbetweens.

▦ For example, the moment of bearing or relieving weight almost always involves a strong change in shape (from stretched leg to bent leg and vice versa).
▦ In order to achieve a very dynamic movement, the first drawing of this movement must be very contrasting (such as convex instead of concave) to the preceding drawing.   ▦

DYNAMIC THROUGH SHAPE CHANGE.

WEIGHT + WEIGHTSHIFT DEMONSTRATED THROUGH CHANGE OF SHAPE.

STRONG
CHANGE OF SHAPE
WITHOUT ADDITIONAL
INBETWEEN.

ACCENT THROUGH SHAPE CHANGE AND COUNTER-MOVEMENT.

16.) Counteraction

While counteraction is not one of the classically defined animation principles, it merits a closer look. Counteractions are usually perceived by the viewer as appealing and should therefore be an important design element of sophisticated animation. Basically, they are derived from the other principles: anticipation and overlapping action or follow through, i.e., the time-delayed action of connected objects (e.g., head and hair). The principle of counteraction is not an invention of animators, but can also be observed in nature:

- The right arm moves forward, right leg backward to maintain balance. (The counteraction is therefore also an important principle to show weight.)
- Before standing up from a sitting position, a counteraction in anticipation is first carried out. This is to gain momentum, in other words, to gather strength in order to be able to get up.
- Differences in weight and texture lead to counteractions:

The head moves in one direction - the hair is first "blown" in the other direction caused by wind resistance, before it belatedly follows the movement direction of the head (follow though).

From a purely formal point of view, counteractions ensure that the dynamics of movements intensify, while the effects of movements in the same direction tend to cancel out or weaken. For this reason, an animator can also use this design element to increase the dynamics or effect of his animation - even in abstract form.

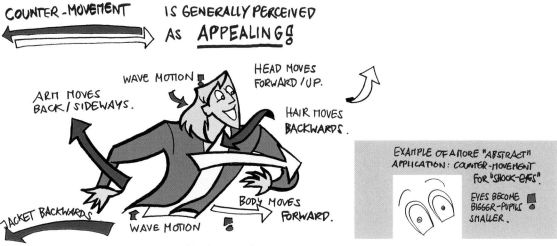

COUNTER-MOVEMENT IS GENERALLY PERCEIVED AS APPEALING!

WAVE MOTION
HEAD MOVES FORWARD / UP.
ARM MOVES BACK / SIDEWAYS.
HAIR MOVES BACKWARDS.
JACKET BACKWARDS
WAVE MOTION
BODY MOVES FORWARD.

EXAMPLE OF A MORE "ABSTRACT" APPLICATION: COUNTER-MOVEMENT FOR "SHOCK-EYES".
EYES BECOME BIGGER-PUPILS SMALLER.

COUNTER-MOVEMENT IS NATURAL AND DERIVED FROM OBSERVATION (FOR EXAMPLE THE DELAYED TRANSMISSION OF FORCE THROUGH JOINTS, OVERLAPPING ACTION, FOLLOW THROUGH).

Example of use: Walk Cycles

A big challenge for the animator is that these animation principles cannot be used in isolation, but they must almost always be applied in combination. This is why it is important to understand these fundamentals first, so that then they can be applied in a constantly refined form. Walking is a very good example to demonstrate the application of multiple animation principles at the same time, but also because this rhythmic form of movement can be designed as a loop or cycle (with a limited number of drawings that can be repeated).

If you observe the walking, running or pacing of a person in real life, you quickly realize that no two persons in the world have exactly the same gait: There are infinite number of ways to move on two feet.

Therefore, it is immensely important for an animator to avoid any mechanical copying of patterns for walk cycles from text books, but to seek inspiration by observing and exaggerating real life. There are basically no limitations to the inventiveness and exaggeration - just how far you take this depends solely on the required degree of realism for the animation.

On the other hand, it is essential for the beginner to understand and learn that all walking movements are based on a system. You can explore endless variations within that system. If you work without a system, you will not be able to obtain a credible impression of walking, running and racing, because the necessary rhythmic repetition is missing.

The following drawings show how you can build such a system and then vary it as well. Perhaps this could be compared to a jazz musician, who first learns the scales and then uses this foundation for free improvisations.

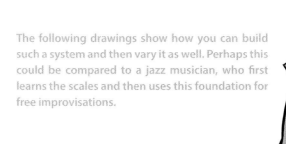

Illustration: Hannes Rall

CONSTRUCTING A WALK CYCLE:

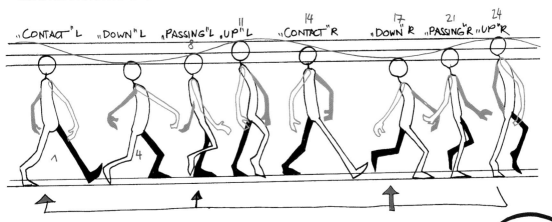

"CONTACT" L   "DOWN" L   "PASSING" L "UP" L   "CONTACT" R   "DOWN" R   "PASSING" R "UP" R

Up-and-down drawings can be seen as applications of stretch and squash - to what extent this is implemented, depends on the desired degree of realism in the animation.

"Inverted" 4 clearly distinguishable in the silhouette. In the passing drawing, you should make sure that the drawing remains distinguishable, for example, in the form of an inverted 4.

In general, the swinging movement of the arms is most pronounced in the down drawing.

I WANT TO LEARN HOW TO WALK.

IT MAKES SENSE TO FIRST SKETCH OUT THE **BASIC STRUCTURE** OF A WALK WITH THE ABOVE SPECIFIED **CONTACT, DOWN, PASSING** AND **UP** POSITIONS AND THEN TRY IT OUT IN A **LINE TEST**. THIS WAY YOU CAN SEE EARLY ON WHETHER THE ROUGH TIMING WORKS. THE INDIVIDUAL DRAWINGS ARE RECORDED WITH THE CORRESPONDING NUMBER OF FRAMES TO ACHIEVE THE DESIRED WALK TEMPO (OR TO TRY OUT WHICH SPEED WORKS BEST FOR YOUR PURPOSES).

EXAMPLE: IF YOU WANT TO SET A STEP EVERY 1/2 SEC. THIS CORRESPONDS TO 12 FRAMES: IN THIS CASE YOU CAN EXPOSE **CONTACT, DOWN, PASSING** AND **UP** WITH 3 FRAMES FOR BOTH SIDES (LEFT AND RIGHT LEG.) KEEP IN MIND: THIS IS ONLY TO DETERMINE THE TIMING — LATER ON INBETWEENS MUST BE ADDED ACCORDINGLY! A WALK CYCLE NEVER LOOKS FLUID ENOUGH WHEN RECORDED / ANIMATED ON 3s. 2s ARE THE MINIMUM — ONES EVEN BETTER.

I FIND IT USEFUL TO ALREADY DETERMINE THE ROUGH STRUCTURE OF THE **ARM MOVEMENT** AT THIS STAGE — THIS IS VERY HELPFUL TO UNDERSTAND THE **GENERAL** EXPRESSION OF THE WALK. BEGINNERS SHOULD BE MINDFUL THOUGH TO PROPERLY WORK OUT THE LEG CYCLE FIRST — OTHERWISE THEY MIGHT EASILY GET CONFUSED.

THE **FUNDAMENTAL ADVANTAGE** OF THIS METHOD IS TO BE ABLE TO TEST THE BASIC STRUCTURE OF THE WALK CYCLE BEFORE HAVING TO ADD ALL THE INBETWEENS (TIME SAVING — ALTERNATIVES CAN BE TESTED QUICKLY). IN ADDITION THIS APPROACH ALLOWS THE STRUCTURED PLANNING OF A **WALK CYCLE**.

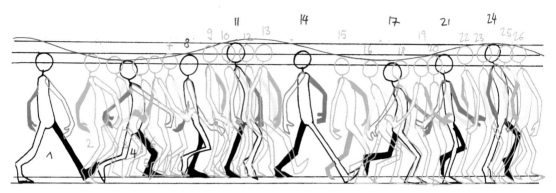

IF YOU ARE SATISFIED WITH THE BASIC STRUCTURE AND HAVE
DEFINED A ROUGH TIMING, INSERT THE INBETWEENS. THE
METHOD OF ACCELERATION AND DECELERATION, AS KNOWN
FROM THE BOUNCING BALL EXERCISE, CAN BE FOLLOWED.
AS ALREADY SHOWN, IT IS IMPORTANT NO TO BRAKE IN
THE MIDDLE OF DOWNWARDS OR UPWARD MOVEMENTS
BY USING TOO MANY INBETWEENS.
USUALLY (EXCEPTIONS CONFIRM THE RULE) THE MOVEMENT
SLOWS DOWN (= MORE INBETWEENS) AT THE APEX AND
DURING THE DOWN/RECOIL PHASE, AS MOMENTUM NEEDS
TO BE GATHERED TO OVERCOME GRAVITY.

FREQUENT BEGINNER'S MISTAKES:

CONFUSING LEFT/RIGHT ARM/LEG DURING THE
CONSTRUCTION OF THE WALK CYCLE. → AVOID
BY USING DIFFERENT COLORS FOR LEFT/RIGHT
ARM/LEG.

REVERSED
MOVEMENTS FOR
BALANCE.

VERY IMPORTANT

WALKS ARE **RHYTHMIC** MOVEMENTS: WHEN WALKING OR
RUNNING ONE LEG/ARM REPEATS EXACTLY THE
MOVEMENT OF THE OTHER LEG/ARM. OR IT VARIES
IN A **MIRROR-LIKE** MANNER.

THE **TIMING** AND **SPACING** OF THE LEFT/RIGHT
LEG/ARM IS ABSOLUTELY **IDENTICAL**. IF YOU
DO NOT FOLLOW THIS IMPORTANT RULE, THE
WALK CYCLE DOES NOT WORK – YOU MIGHT GET
A LIMP OR AN IRREGULAR GEAR.

„CONTACT" L   „DOWN" L   „PASSING" L „UP" L   „CONTACT" R   „DOWN" R „PASSING" R „UP" R

THE **FOLLOW THROUGH** OF HAIR AND CLOAK SHOULD BE ADDED, ONLY IF
THE STRUCTURE OF THE ANIMATION IS OTHERWISE COMPLETE.
AS THE NAME SUGGESTS, THESE ELEMENTS FOLLOW THE MOVEMENT
OF THE BODY AND MUST BE ADAPTED ACCORDINGLY. IN THIS
CASE, **STRAIGHT AHEAD ANIMATION** CAN BE USED, SINCE THESE
LOOSE SHAPES VARY GREATLY FROM DRAWING TO DRAWING
→ THEY FOLLOW THE PRINCIPLE OF THE **WAVE MOVEMENT**.

HOWEVER, IN ORDER TO CONTROL THE ANIMATION IN SERVICE
OF ACHIEVING A PERFECT LOOPING MOTION, IT MAKES SENSE
TO PLAN ALSO THIS MO VEMENT FIRST WITH COARSE **KEY FRAMES**.

FOR ALL STEPS IT IS NECESSARY TO TEST THE INBETWEENS
AND TO **CORRECT** THEM IF NECESSARY, UNTIL THE WALK
MATCHES YOUR OWN IDEA.

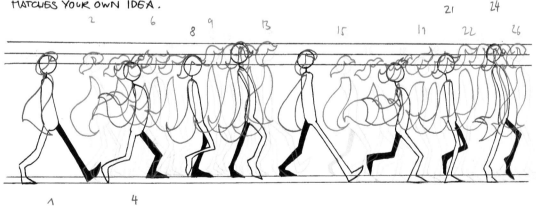

LOOPS oR CYCLES = ENDLESSLY REPEATABLE ANIMATION-
LOOPS, SINCE THE LAST DRAWING (OR INTERPOLATION IN CG)
PRECEDES THE FIRST ONE.
IN THE EXAMPLES SHOWN, DRAWING 10 IS TO BE FOLLOWED
BY DRAWING 1. THIS WORKS NATURALLY (DEPENDING
ON THE DESIRED MOVEMENT) WITH ANY REQUIRED
NUMBER OF DRAWINGS / INTERPOLATIONS.

THE PURPOSE OF LOOPS OR CYCLES IS TO GET AS
MUCH ANIMATION TIME AS POSSIBLE WITH AS
FEW DRAWINGS / INTERPOLATIONS REQUIRED.
THE MORE INTERESTING THE LOOP APPEARS,
THE LESS NOTICEABLE THE REPETITIVE EFFECT
WILL BE.

What is a Cycle or Loop?

A cycle or loop makes it possible to animate an endlessly repeatable movement using a limited number of drawings:

- A cycle consists of the drawings 1 to 10, for example.
- The animation is designed so that drawing 10 is followed by drawing 1
  again and can be played indefinitely "in a cycle".

REPOSITIONING IN WALK CYCLES

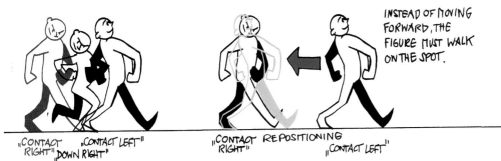

INSTEAD OF MOVING FORWARD, THE FIGURE MUST WALK ON THE SPOT.

„CONTACT RIGHT" „CONTACT LEFT" „DOWN RIGHT"

„CONTACT RIGHT" REPOSITIONING „CONTACT LEFT"

Instead of moving out of the image format, the figure has to walk in place. For this, every step has to be repositioned (see below). First, you should (especially as a beginner) animate the walk cycle completely and then adjust the position. It is best to perform this repositioning between the "down" and "contact" drawings. Apply the same principle for right and left!

IN ORDER TO MAKE THE ILLUSTRATION CLEARER, THE PHASES **CONTACT RIGHT** AND **DOWN RIGHT** ARE HERE DRAWN APART FURTHER THAN IT WOULD BE CONVENIENT IN PRACTICE. YOU SHOULD ALREADY PLACE AFTER

 CONTACT RIGHT   DOWN RIGHT SLIGHTLY BACKWARDS

TOWARDS THE LEFT. THEN ACCORDING TO THIS SCHEME REPOSITION **PASSING LEFT** AND **UP LEFT**. IN THE END **CONTACT LEFT** SHOULD END UP IN EXACTLY THE SAME POSITION AS **CONTACT RIGHT**.

REPOSITIONING

„CONTACT RIGHT" „DOWN RIGHT" „UP LEFT" „CONTACT LEFT" „PASSING LEFT"

For walk cycles, the illusion of a movement is generated by the fact that the character walks virtually in place while the background rolls past in a continuous horizontal pan. To make my character actually walk in place, I have to reposition the individual drawings of the walk cycle - otherwise my character would walk out of frame.

RIGHT

ABRUPT CHANGE WITH
UNEVENLY SPACED INBETWEENS.

WRONG

SLOW, GRADUAL TRANSITION.

*Correct: Transition to the moment
of **bearing weight** ("down" drawing) without many inbetweens and
with large change of shape (con-
trast/accent). The only inbetween
already close to "down" drawing.*

*Weight bears down on sole
of foot - the shape/line must
show that!*

***No** slow weight shift as
shown above.*

*No curvy shape on the
bottom of the foot, since it is
bearing weight!*

TO AVOID THAT ARM MOVEMENTS APPEAR STIFF, THE PRINCIPLE OF
OVERLAPPING ACTION AND **DELAYED TRANSMISSION OF
FORCE THROUGH JOINTS** ARE IMPLEMENTED:

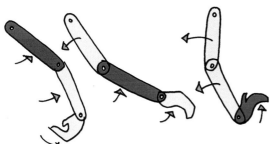

THE UPPER ARM, FOREARM
AND HAND REACH THEIR
OUTER POSITION ON THE RIGHT
(RED) **ONE AFTER THE OTHER.**
FLEXIBILITY RESULTS FROM
OPPOSING MOVEMENTS.

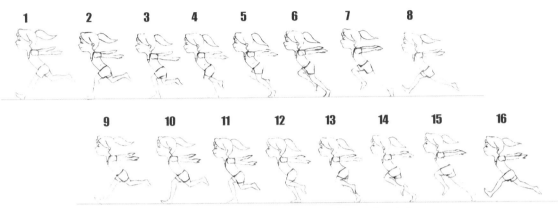

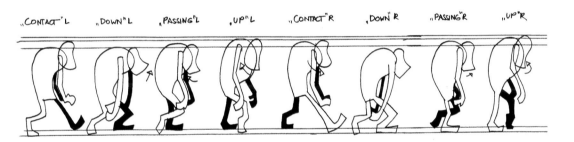

Run cycle animated on ones. A run cycle works basically just like a walk cycle. In most cases, however, it is essential to animate a run cycle on ones, in order to make the distinct changes of shape visible within a short time. All drawings of the animation are shown; drawing 16 is followed again by drawing 1.

Student work by Patricia Teo (2014) at the School of Art, Design and Media, Nanyang Technological University.

Assignment:

■ Complete and refine the "outline" of a walk cycle shown here with the right timing, spacing, (inbetweens) and overlapping action/follow through of hair and clothing for the character shown on the left.

Posture is extremely important for the expression of a walk cycle. It is usually maintained in its basic form and only slightly varied. It is defined by physical conditions (anatomy, weight) and psychological motivation. Emotional states such as aggression, joy, exuberance will certainly be expressed in the gait.

OF COURSE THE POSE OF THE BODY THROUGHOUT A WALK IS ALSO DETERMINED TO KEEP IT IN BALANCE - OTHERWISE THE CHARACTER WOULD FALL OVER . WALKING COULD ALSO BE DEFINED AS "CONTROLLED FALLING". THROUGH A CONTINU-OUS SHIFT OF WEIGHT, MOMENTS OF FALLING ARE ALWAYS COMPENSATED FOR BY REGAINING BALANCE.

FALLING   FALLING

THE ARMS KEEP THE BODY IN BALANCE.

WEIGHT IS "CAUGHT".

Once you understand the principle of variation within a given system, the real fun begins: Inventing innovative and stylized walk cycles. Such walk cycles can be fictitious or even exaggerated versions of "real" observed walk cycles.

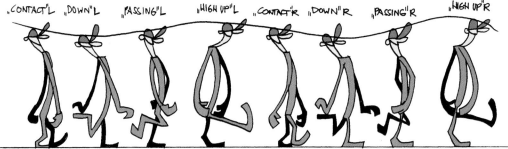

„CONTACT"L   „DOWN"L   „PASSING"L   „HIGH UP"L   „CONTACT"R   „DOWN"R   „PASSING"R   „HIGH UP"R

IN THE EXAMPLE SHOWN BELOW THE PRINCIPLE OF COUNTERACTION OF ARMS AND LEGS IS IGNORED : THE CHARACTER IS SO FAT THAT THE ARM HAS TO MOVE ALONG WITH THE CORRESPONDING LEG.

An example of a highly stylized run cycle: Jumping/ running featuring all the inbetweens.
Animation: Hannes Rall for the animated short film "Turnstunde" (Gym Lesson) (2008).

Summary:
The most common beginner's mistakes and how to avoid them

Timing and reference
The following phrase also applies to animation: "Practice makes perfect". Knowing how much time a particular movement takes, comes only with time and experience, and after much trial and error. On the other hand, it is easier than ever before to find references for certain movements or to record them quickly, to save them as video clips and to analyze them in single frames. I am often surprised that students continue to get the timing totally wrong for a particular action, instead of simply recording the action as a video to get a sense of timing.

Poses lacking expression
If you work with the pose-to-pose method, it is important to find poses that best illustrate the momentary expression and the sequence of the action. These poses must have appeal, line of action and credible balance.

Too many actions are shown in too short a time:
Beginners often falsely assume that several expressive poses can make a great animation, if you simply film them one after the other with one frame or two frames each. This does not work at all, since the individual frame is then only visible for a fraction of a second. The key frames must be shot with the right timing and with the appropriate number of inbetweens. A hold or moving hold must be visible for at least 10 frames, otherwise it will be perceived by the viewer as a break in a continuous movement. In general, beginners underestimate the amount of time it takes for a particular action or posture to be understood by the audience.

THIS DOESN'T WORK! (FRAME NUMBERS)

1 1 1 1 1 1
2 2 2 2 2 2

CORRECT TIMING (E.G.) FOR THE HOLDS:

18   12   16   14   12   18

TO TRANSFORM THIS INTO A **MOVING HOLD** INBETWEENS
NEED TO BE ADDED CLOSE TO THE "FINAL HOLD" 18 ≙
AN ENTIRELY STATIC HOLD IS CHANGED TO A VERY
SUBTLE MOVEMENT = MOVING HOLD.

AFTER TRANSFORMING THE **HOLDS** INTO **MOVING HOLDS**
THE REGULAR **INBETWEENS** CAN BE ADDED. (INBETWEEN = IB).

+ +6 IBs   + 7 IBs   +7 IBs   +8 IBs   +4 IBs

Lack of Contrast in Timing and Spacing

Animation needs rhythm just as music does - fast actions have to alternate with slow actions. Drawings of frenetic action must be interspersed with resting periods. For this, timing (how many frames) and spacing (position and spacing of frames) must be irregular. To do this, the basic rules of animation (e.g. slow in and slow out) must be applied skillfully.

Some helpful basic rules

In general, the following applies:

The content of the story and style of animation must match. Therefore: The style of the design and the style of the animation must be the same.

For example:

Naturalistic design = full animation, closer to reality.

Stylized design = also works with limited animation. The style of the movements can be designed creatively, or be fictitious. Few or no references of live-action film necessary.

Staging/Acting/Poses:
- What do I want to communicate?
- Which drawings/poses best tell my story?
- From the overall concept to minute details (not vice versa!)

Assignment:

Film analysis "frame by frame":

I regularly make the following suggestion in my classes, which results in incredulous amazement of my students:

Analyze animation und live-action film frame by frame. When I see a fascinating animation and a great scene from a live-action film, I try to figure out how that is done. I can only do this, if I analyze the relevant sequence frame-by-frame. These days it is easier than ever to have access to the material and to analyze it using software. This usually works with any film program, such as Quicktime or Premiere.

- Choose five outstanding animated or acted (live-action film) sequences, and analyze them frame-by-frame. Make sketches of key frames and relevant notes on how the artistic effect was achieved through the use of timing, spacing and staging (composition).
- Then create your own 10 to 30 second animation sequence, in which you apply some of the methods discovered in the analysis to your own animation. Write down in detail, which analysis technique you used for which part of your own animation.

Traditional 2D Animation

What makes hand-drawn 2D animation so special, is that each single frame is uniquely created by the animator. This applies to both, the traditional mode of production with pencil and light box and the modern version with a digital drawing tablet. Artistic freedom is therefore virtually infinite and is limited only by imagination and/or artistic skills.

General Information

Advantages

With hand-drawn animation, the animator is completely free in designing each frame of the film. In the case of 3D computer animation and stop motion, predefined virtual or real puppets are simply modified frame-by-frame. However, it is not really possible to radically alter the basic form of the virtual or real puppets.

With hand-drawn animation, on the other hand, the animator can draw a completely new shape with each frame, or radically change a character at his own discretion. He is limited only by his own ability to apply this graphically in a convincing manner: There are no technical obstacles.

Radical camera movements can be created as well as dramatic changes of the background. The most extreme squash and stretch of characters can be drawn with only a few strokes just as well as interestingly designed transformations (metamorphoses) of the characters.

The technological threshold for implementation is extremely low or absent, so that the animator's imagination and drawing ability are the only prerequisites for a successful outcome.

For these reasons, hand-drawn 2D animation remains a relevant and completely independent art form to this day. In my opinion, this is especially true for artistic approaches that distance themselves from realism and gravitate towards more abstracted and experimental styles. These days, the field of hyperrealism is largely occupied by 3D computer animation. Although computer animation is increasingly developing methods to approach the free manipulability of characters, it is still far from the spontaneous organic expressiveness of hand-drawn animation.

Which brings us to another important aspect: Hand-drawn animation is the most personal form of expression for an animator, especially when it comes to individual projects or short films. We see the artistic handwriting directly on the screen (especially if there is no clean-up by an assistant). In the case of 3D computer animation, on the other hand, the layer of technical implementation, i.e. the modeling in the software always interferes with the original artistic vision. This can often lead to an inorganic "plastic look" that clings to the characters, a weakness that it has not been able to overcome completely thus far. Which is why it can not yet hold a candle to hand-drawn animation film with regard to organic appearance and artistic individuality.

However, it must be added, that there are increasingly intelligent hybrid forms of formerly separate animation techniques on the rise: These hybrids combine the advantages of various animation techniques in a skillful approach.

COMPLEX

Disadvantages and Solutions

The most obvious drawback of the artistically satisfying technique of traditional hand-drawn 2D animation is the incredible effort, with which it has to be done: Each single frame (or every second frame, in the case of two-frame animation) has to be completely redrawn (full animation) - that is, 24 animations per second in the case of single frame animation; in two-frame animation, it is still 12 drawings per second.

Depending on the complexity of the characters, this can be very difficult: Any change in perspective has to be drawn individually. This makes implementing complex patterns, textures in characters, etc. incredibly labor-intensive and difficult, at times nearly impossible: You have to have both - unlimited time and perfect drawing skills, in order to achieve something satisfying. A design as in the drawing **above** can only be reproduced in its complexity as a 3D computer animation or stop motion. For these techniques, details and textures are virtually or actually "built", i.e., they exist: any perspective change is either simply calculated (computer) or physically existent (using a puppet in stop motion technique).

STYLIZED

Basically, it is helpful and necessary to stylize and simplify the characters (**left**), in order to keep the workload feasible: After all, each individual additional line must also be drawn! While modern digital imaging software allows for relatively comfortable additional shading - greater simplification still remains an important rule for hand-drawn 2D animation.

It is precisely this pressure for reduction that can also serve as a creative stimulus. Instead of sprawling (and often unnecessary) details, elegance and purism can be graphically implemented through stylization and abstraction.

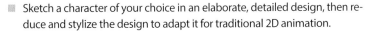

Assignment:

■ Sketch a character of your choice in an elaborate, detailed design, then reduce and stylize the design to adapt it for traditional 2D animation.

Separation of characters and background in traditional 2D animation

In the early days of animation film, a method was developed for drawing backgrounds only once and combining them with the drawings of characters on transparent "cels" on several planes. The reason for this, of course, was to save time and labor. Instead of having to redraw the background of a scene for each frame, only the drawings of the characters (on the cels) were exchanged. A moving background was achieved by moving the camera on the vertical and horizontal axes - camera zooms were also possible, of course.

Top left: The animation of the character on transparent cels.
Top right: Detailed background with animation punch holes.
Center right: Transparent cel with character against the background.
Bottom right: The background can be "moved" horizontally while the cel remains in the same place. This results in the illusion of the character's locomotion during a walk cycle - although he actually walks on the spot.

This separation between characters and background is mainly found in traditional commercial animation productions of full-length feature films and classic Hollywood short films. There are also other methods for creative short films and increasingly for independent feature film productions: In some cases (abstracted) backgrounds are always redrawn, every animation takes place on "one layer" of paper - or the background can also be animated when divided into different digital planes. Nowadays, more and more hybrids of all these techniques are possible and are being used - the variety is enormous. In my own films, for example, the background becomes an active part of the animation with significant changes in shape and perspective.

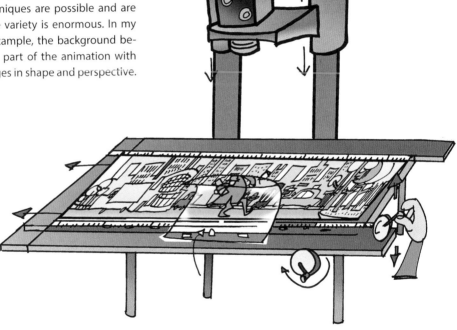

Today, these classic animation stands are basically obsolete and have been replaced - and considerably expanded - with digital programs. Since the dependence for mechanical devices has become non-existent, extreme camera movements and zooms for sufficient resolution of digital images are now possible in an almost unrestricted manner.

Classic animation stand ("rostrum"-camera) - today almost completely replaced by digital methods (computer). The animation stand could be moved horizontally (by cranking), the camera moved vertically. In modern software, there are almost unlimited camera movements possible now.

Animation cels and traditional coloring are "out"

In production, the original cels for the animation film were replaced by separate digital planes for characters and backgrounds. This has the enormous advantage that the cels are no longer "dust collectors", which used to be a problem in the past, and many planes can now be combined without any loss of quality. In the same way, there are no more physical colored cels, but the clean-ups are either scanned or animated directly in the program (see section "Digital Traditional"). Coloring is always done on the computer, since it works much faster and easier than physical color: One click is enough to fill properly outlined surfaces with color. Some modern programs now offer functional automation options and the possibility to to fill areas defined by intermittently broken outlines properly with color as well. If the artistic concept requires the implementation of complex ornamentation and countless de-

tails, while at the same time maintaining the "flat" 2D appearance, the method of digital cutout animation should be chosen instead of the traditional 2D animation technology: It is basically a two-dimensional form of the three-dimensional stop-motion technique. "Flat" two-dimensional models of characters are created and equipped with a virtual skeleton connected by joints. These characters are then changed in the shot "frame-by-frame". Using this technique drastically reduces the possibility of changing the characters, but it retains the rich detail of the designs without any problem. After all, not every frame needs to be redrawn. The animation software Toon Boom described later in this chapter is well suited for this technique.

Example of digital cutout technique from the film "Si Lunchai" by Hannes Rall (2014).

Tools

Old School

Light box

You need a light box to make the drawings transparent on several layers of paper: For example, you place two key frames on top of each other, and then place a blank sheet of paper on top to draw the breakdown between the key frames. Then you draw the in-between(s) between the first key frame and the breakdown - and so on.

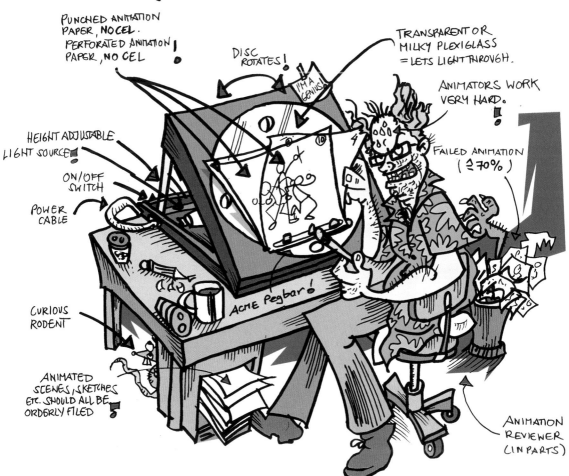

Animation peg bar (ACME Pegbar)
A peg bar is needed to keep your animated drawings perfectly aligned - the format should not move, but remain in place. After all, the only movements should be the ones drawn by the animator - the paper itself must not move. The industry standard here is the ACME Pegbar, which should be used. It requires certain punch holes in the paper.

— POSE-TO-POSE ANIMATION ON THE LIGHTBOX

Keyframe ① in red.   Keyframe ⑩ in green.   Breakdown 4 in blue.

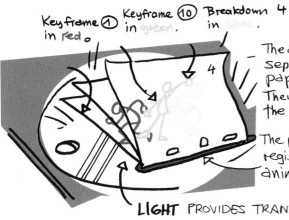

The animation drawings are created on separate sheets of punched animation paper layered on top of each other. They are held in the correct position on the animation light desk by the pegbar.

The pegbar ensures the correct registration/positioning of all animation drawings.

LIGHT PROVIDES TRANSPARENCY.

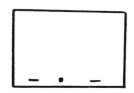

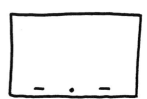

I position my first key frame (N¹.①) on the peg bar on the light desk.

On top follows my second key frame (⑩).

On top goes an empty sheet of pegged / punched animation paper.

On this sheet I draw the breakdown drawing (the important "middle" inbetween) - referencing the two key frames that shine through.

THEN

I leave my first key frame in place (①).

But I replace my second key frame (⑩) (I put it aside) with the breakdown drawing (4).

Now I add another empty sheet of punched paper...

and on there I draw my inbetween with the number 3. I decide how close it is to number 4. (SPACING). If I am given an inbetween chart, I have to follow its indication:

① 2 3 4

AND SO ON AND SO ON....!
BY THE WAY...

ALL DRAWINGS MUST BE ON **SEPARATE SHEETS** BECAUSE THEY REPRESENT THE FILM FRAMES IN SEQUENCE - **THIS DOES NOT** WORK AS ANIMATION.
(ALL DRAWINGS ON ONE SHEET).

Paper, hole punch and field guides

You can either purchase pre-punched paper for the standard ACME Pegbar at (still) existing suppliers for animation supplies, or you can buy a special ACME Pegbar hole punch yourself. An animation hole punch of good quality is usually quite expensive. The current price is approximately 600 US dollars. A very important tool for the layout of scenes to be animated are so-called field guides (available on the Internet at no charge, while physical versions are available from a retailer). They show the (standardized) distance between the animation peg bar and the field of view (aspect ratio) for certain paper formats. These refer to American size formats (e.g., 11 inches). It is helpful to follow these field guides, since most 2D animation software uses them as default settings. However, the position of the field of view in the software can also be adjusted later with relatively little effort. What is important though, is that there is always sufficient drawing (at a proportional ratio) for the selected field size: Therefore you should always (!!) draw the field size when planning the keys and breakdowns of scenes. (Place as a reference under the light box, or draw at least the keys directly "with frame" - both works.)

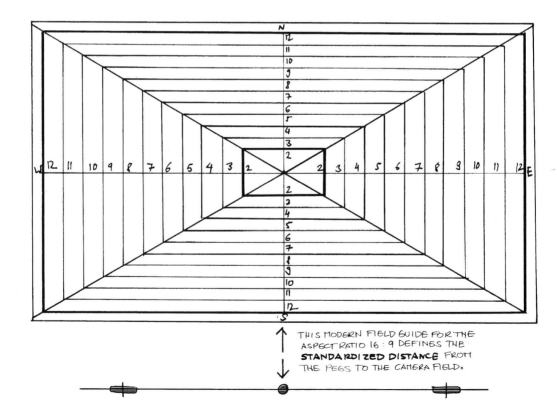

THIS MODERN FIELD GUIDE FOR THE ASPECT RATIO 16 : 9 DEFINES THE **STANDARDIZED DISTANCE** FROM THE PEGS TO THE CAMERA FIELD.

Pencils etc.

As a rule, the choice of the right drawing tool tends to be secondary - after all, it's the result that counts. And the final look is determined by the cleaned up version anyway. However, pencil and eraser are appropriate tools for the traditional way of working - since animation work is characterized by continuous improvement and revision/redrawing. A pencil that is easy to erase and glides smoothly over paper is, of course, the tool of choice. I personally prefer to draw with HB pencils - but individual preferences can certainly vary.

Pencils that are too hard are not recommended since they are difficult to see (when shooting or scanning the drawings) and because they can tear the paper when you press down harder. Using colored pencils can be useful for various purposes, especially when it comes to distinguishing complex elements in a drawing.

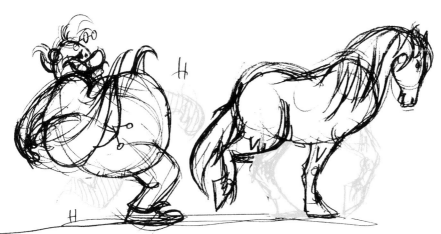

A very common beginner's mistake is confusing the left leg for the right leg (or arm) in walk cycles. Using different colors can help avoid this mix-up.

Line tester

The main technical tool in traditional 2D animation is the line tester, which is a simple system that allows you to scan or shoot the drawings on video in order to then experiment with the right timing.

There is now an infinite variety of easy-to-use, fully digital and/or camera-based line test systems on the market.

Every 2D software (see the following pages) has manageable line test systems that can test scanned or digitally imported drawings very easily during production.

Digital Traditional: Software for Traditional 2D Animation

There is a rapidly evolving and constantly changing market for animation software for traditional (or hybrid) 2D animation. Any mention of names would only provide a snapshot, and it is recommended that you always stay up to date in blogs and forums.

At the time of publication of this book there are two somewhat differently positioned, but each very well-functioning and proven programs that are worth mentioning:

TV Paint

This software is particularly well-suited for the animator, who still draws on paper and then scans the drawings. The program's work flow is well designed for this, and the scanning feature for importing drawings is superbly integrated. It is a pixel-based program that is particularly well-suited for painterly styles and refined contour variations.

Toon Boom

Toon Boom consists of a software product family, which is available in individual modules (for example, line test) all the way to the relatively expensive professional version "Toon Boom Harmony". It is a vector-based program that is best suited for flat colors and sharply defined outlines (although other looks can be achieved as well).

While TV Paint is actually designed for the (partially) digitally working traditional (2D) animator, the spectrum at Toon Boom is much broader: "traditionally" hand-drawn animation is only one option at Toon Boom. There are also functions for digital cutout animation that work very well and are easy to use. Previously created 2D models of characters are equipped with a movable skeleton (rig), which can then be animated frame-by-frame just as in the stop motion technique.

Importing scanned animation drawings is also possible with Toon Boom, but somewhat more complicated than with TV Paint. All scanned drawings must be vectorized afterwards. The vectorization module works very well indeed, and with some practice, you can almost always achieve the desired look of the contour line. However, Toon Boom primarily relies on a completely paperless workflow for "traditional" 2D animation, in which each frame (or second frame) is redrawn.

Digital drawing tablet

2D animation software such as Toon Boom or TV Paint allows you to draw on a virtual light box by using a drawing tablet. The physical overlaying of key frames for the purpose of drawing inbetweens is replaced by onion skinning, in which the two (or more) drawings needed for reference remain translucent. The drawings created are imported directly into the program and have to be saved.

The work process is basically the same as on paper - except that you are drawing on a digital drawing tablet rather than a traditional light box. Paper is also no longer required, of course.

A key advantage is the extensive selection for digital line variations. Likewise, the tablet or animation software offers many options for smoothing the stroke automatically - which can be regarded as an advantage or a disadvantage, but you definitely have the choice!

Working Methods - A System for 2D Animation

Animation is an art form that requires an exceptionally high degree of planning and control: After all, it is about creating every single frame of the film from scratch. This can be both, exciting and challenging: Systematic planning is indispensable, a system, in which one step builds on the other, A is followed by B.

It is particularly important never to loose sight - metaphorically speaking - to see the forest despite the trees - to have a clear vision of the overall concept at all times. In doing so, it is crucial to always begin working from a basic and rough design to the minute details, and never vice versa. A good example of this is blocking or rough estimation of timing, which is common to all forms of animation and is worked up before any movements are animated in detail.

The million dollar question: "Ones" or "twos"?

It is a matter of conviction among traditional animators whether to (always) animate on ones or twos. I already touched on the topic in the chapter "The Principles of Animation", but here are some additional notes:

While eminent experts insist that animation on ones is always better, I would like to qualify this point of view: It depends on the circumstances. The more "realistic" and "smooth" the desired look of the animation, the more you will favor ones. If characters are more abstracted and stylized, then a two-frame animation will work perfectly fine.

In principle it is remains good advice to animate on ones for very fast movements: In such movements, the shape changes very rapidly in a very short time; if you only animate every second frame, you may "miss" important shape changes in the inbetween drawings.

Let's not forget that many of Disney's classical masterpieces were animated "only" on twos as well. The audience will hardly perceive the difference, at most, they may "sense" it.

However, a clear line of distinction must be drawn between two-frame (12 drawings per second) and three-frame animation (4 drawings per second): the three-frame animation, often used in cheap TV animation or with graphically very complex animes (Japanese animation), completely destroys the illusion of smooth movement. You need to be aware of this, if you decide to animate sparingly. It will no longer achieve the renowned "illusion of life"!

1.) Briefing

In terms of where the animator's work begins and what his starting point is, that depends entirely on the medium and type of production:

In 2D animation, the animator receives the storyboard, layout, and dialogue - that is called the "animation handout". As a rule, the animation director will also brief the animator on the expectations for the scene.

For independent productions, such as an artistic short film, several roles - author, director and animator(s) - are often combined in one. That means, the animator may have drawn the storyboard himself and prepared the layout as well. Depending on the size of the team, however, task-specific assignments are also common.

Here is an example of the drawings I created as the director for an animation handout for my film "The Cold Heart": The characters' range of movement during the scene is already precisely defined. This is because the movements of the actors in the scene had to be combined with the background using a continuous tracking shot.

In addition, the graphic design of the scene was an essential part of the emotional expression for me - so it could not be changed too much.

Example of components of an animation handout: Layouts showing background, and background combined with characters, and a dialog sheet. From the film "The Cold Heart" (2013) by Hannes Rall.

2.) Thumbnails and planning with the X-sheet (exposure sheet)

Not mandatory (some animators start directly with the "original size"), but it is often very helpful to explore a scene first with thumbnails. In doing so, you can quickly and easily test variations in the animation, think about how you want to create movements in the scene. The deliberate sketchiness and spontaneity of these fast scribbles often lead to great vitality and determination in expression, which could never be achieved with "accurate" drawing. Many of the most famous animators were and are known to use this method to think through as many variations of a scene as possible before selecting one or more options in the animation.

The X-sheet, short for exposure sheet, serves as an excellent foundation for such visual simulation: All shot frames are vertically listed in a table - drawings can then be entered in parallel listing on the different levels with the appropriate timing.

The X-sheet is absolutely crucial for syncing already existing dialogue (always pre-recorded for animation) or music: First, the sound breakdown must be entered frame-by-frame. After all, you have to know exactly where the beats are located or when which letter is spoken, in order to be able to animate spot-on in sync.

You can use the thumbnails to roughly plan your timing as well. The constant revisions and improvements are typical for almost every form of animation - they are the very first steps for approximation, as the final timing will be arrived at later in the process.

X-sheet with thumbnails

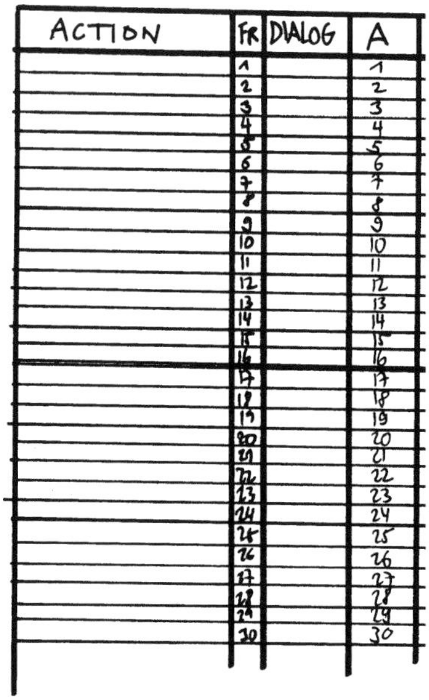

X-sheet for single-frame animation

Numbering drawings

In the classical animation studio method, drawings are numbered to reflect timing.

Example:

1.) In **single-frame** animation, the first drawing is number 1, the second drawing is number 2, the third drawing is number 3 etc.

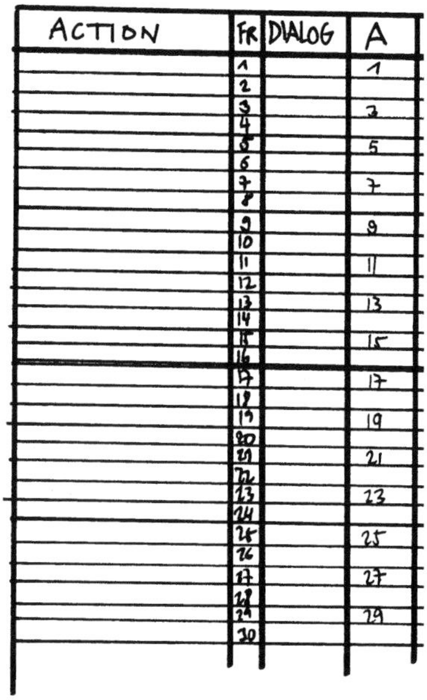

X-sheet for two-frame animation

2.) In **two-frame** animation, the first drawing is number 1, the second drawing is number 3 (!!), the third drawing is number 5, etc.

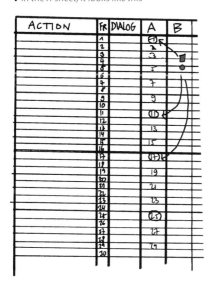

In the X-sheet, it looks like this

The major advantage of this method is the simple option of combining animation on ones and twos, or adding additional (single-frame) drawings:

If in example 2.), I want to insert a drawing (single-frame) between the second (number 3) and third drawing (number 5), I simply designate the number **4** to the drawing. (In this case, drawing number 3 will only be single-frame, but this is usually the animator's intention.)

Key frame numbers (and only those!) are circled (on both, the drawing and the X-sheet).

Assignment:

Design and animate a scene based on existing music. Use the X-Sheet as the basis for working out timing. First, you do a sound breakdown: Count the music into frames and add the beats and the dramatic arcs in the music to a column of the X-sheet, which you label "sound". (You can either use a software program that allows unlimited addition of such columns, or you can use an easily accessible template from the Internet, for analog or digital use). Number all your drawings accordingly and test the animation repeatedly with the line tester.

3.) Animation Roughs

It is never about the single drawing, it is always about the flow of the drawings in the sequence! Always start with very abstract, rough shapes (sketchy designs), omitting details. A good method is to simply "blow up" - either digitally or with a copier - the mostly spontaneous and expressive thumbnails to the size needed, and use them directly as keys.

Thumbnails: Thumbnail sketches, which can often serve as a starting point for rough animation.

Always remember concepts, such as line of action and change of shape. What works with a rough concept will also work after adding details - but rarely in reverse!

Assignment:

 Think of a scene with two interacting characters and try them out in different versions, using thumbnails. Make sure that it is a scene with strong visual communication in the poses: Contrasting poses and characters is important. For example, a dispute or a fight would work well.

Strong poses alone are not enough: You need **inbetweens!**

A widespread rookie mistake is the assumption that drawing (supposedly) expressive key frames is enough: Don't forget that each single drawing represents only a fraction of a second:

1/24 of a second for **single-frame** animation ("on ones")

1/12 of a second for **two-frame** animation ("on twos")

Therefore, sufficient drawings have to be drawn in order to make the action clearly intelligible to the viewer. That is, key frames and transitions must last **long enough** to be **understood**. This can only be achieved by more drawings.

Additional note:
Here too, exceptions prove the rule: Certain "snappy" cartoon actions are characterized by the minimal use of inbetweens between key frames. See section "The Principles of Animation" under "timing", page 157.
For this, moving holds (see section "The Principles of Animation") are used for key frames; and sufficient inbetweens to make the transitions readable.

Key frames and sufficient inbetweens

A first test of the key frames and breakdowns with the line tester is very helpful. (This method is also described in more detail in "The Principles of Animation", page 161.)

TIP: For beginners, it is helpful to record reference material (nowadays very easy to do with cameras in mobile phones) and to analyze it frame-by-frame after converting it to a Quick-Time Movie, for example. Alternatively, using a digital stopwatch is an excellent way to determine the length of a particular action (e.g., "standing up from the chair").

With increasing practice, the animator will gain the necessary experience that will allow him to become less dependent on reference material. (Although it may always remain an important tool for more complex actions/acting).

4.) Testing and improving

If there are a very large number of movements, it is advantageous to construct these in a modular design, i.e., in multiple passes: First, you should be developing an artistic vision of movement through sketches - such as: what overall impression do I want to achieve in the physical and emotional expression of the character?

LINES OF ACTION IN THE TORSO REMAIN LARGELY UNCHANGED DURING THE WALK-CYCLE.

LINE OF ACTION

MINIMAL ARM SWING

LITTLE "UP AND DOWN"

LINE OF ACTION

LINE OF ACTION

HANDS DELAYED.

ARM SWING

These three different approaches for a "glum" walk cycle show the general attitude and certain movement characteristics that are maintained throughout the entire walk cycle. They include, for example, the extent of the arm swing, how high the legs lift, etc. Of course, animation is almost always an experimentally shaped development process, so that changes can always occur in the course of testing. Some seemingly promising idea often does not work in animation!

FOOT SHUFFLES ALONG THE GROUND.

Afterwards you can implement the details of the animation step-by-step during several passes:
First, legs with torso - test to see if timing works (and possibly revise, until it does!)

Then the head and swinging movement of the arms, re-testing and correcting.

Finally, overlapping action, such as loose clothing, hair - here again, testing and correcting until everything works in unison!

Assignment:

■ Now, animate the entire scene that you started with thumbnails: Add breakdowns and inbetweens after testing your poses (key frames). If necessary, follow the principle of repeated passes. Test as much as necessary after each step and continue only, if you think the outcome of the tests was successful!

Rough animation (above) and clean-up below.
Drawings by Hannes Rall, from his film "The Cold Heart" (2013).

5.) Styles and clean-up

In the traditional work-sharing process of the Disney tradition, it is the task of the assistant or specialized department to clean-up the exactly timed, but rough drawings of the animator. This process uses the rules of solid drawing ("The Principles of Animation", page 183). The goal is to have the character look the same and anatomically correct from every perspective, as defined in the model sheet.

A thin outline was generally used for this purpose, a style that is still used in traditional Disney-style productions. The process of clean-up, i.e., the reinterpretation of the original animation drawings, often results in a loss of the initial expressiveness of the original drawings. This is because the clean-up assistant usually has to make a selection from several lines of the animation rough and does not always understand exactly the artistic intention of the animator with each individual drawing. It is rare that the animator is satisfied with the clean-up of his original drawings. The famous Disney animator Milt Kahl (Jacob 2014) was notorious for being extremely dissatisfied with the work of his assistants. The Xerox process of the Disney studios, which has been used since the film "101 Dalmatians" (Geronimi / Luske, 1961) and copies the animators' drawings directly onto films, has been a welcomed feature for animators. (These drawings still required a certain minimum standard, in order to be used in this form for film.) As Andreas Deja explains in his blog "Deja View" (2014), Disney films, which were made with this process, show a surprising number of sketchy and "unfinished" animation drawings. According to him, this is to the animator's benefit. Deja describes this as "seeing an animator's personal handwriting motion". Even if the animator himself performs the entire process from the first sketch to the clean-up drawing, it is usually impossible to retain the vitality of the animation roughs in a "cleaned-up" version. In this respect, the version of "Beauty and the Beast" (Kirk/Trousdale 1991), which showed the original pencil drawings by Glen Keane instead of the cleaned up version, became famous. The stylistic spectrum for the final look of the lines of hand-drawn animation film has long-since been dramatically expanded through artistic and technical development: In addition to the approach of using more "unfinished" animations directly without clean-up, these include outlines in different line intensities that "pulsate" on the screen, the complete elimination of outlines, or experimental/abstract approaches that completely abandon any figural representation.

Examples of different 2D styles. Clockwise from top left:
Picture from the film "The Beach Boy" (2016), oil pastel on black cardboard, directed by: Hannes Rall, artist: Turine Tran;
Picture from the film "The Beach Boy", digital brush technique with CACANi software, artists: Ng Yuwen Yvonne (animation) and Low Zi Rong (CACANi clean-up);
Picture from "Red", animated on paper and digitally colored, director and artist: Nur Aisyah Binte Suhaimi;
Frame sequence from the animation for the documentary "Lotte Reiniger: The Dance of Shadows" (2012), animated on paper and digitally colored, artists: Hannes Rall and Hans Bacher, directed by: Rada Bieberstein, Susanne Marschall and Kurt Schneider.

Assignment:

▮ Complete your scene once you are satisfied with the timing of your animation and after all of the frames have been completed as rough animation. Draw the clean-up versions of your roughs (using the desired line style) and color the scene.

Interview with Andreas Deja

"That scene and that character - that's me!"

Andreas Deja is undoubtedly one of the best character animators in the field of traditional 2D animation, the hand-drawn animation. Andreas became known for the outstanding animation of original characters during his many years at Walt Disney Feature Animation (since 1980). These include memorable characters such as the "villains" Gaston, Jafar and Scar from "Beauty and the Beast" (1991), "Aladdin" (1992) and "The Lion King" (1994), as well as the little girl Lilo from "Lilo & Stitch" (2002).

Andreas' strengths include his creative skills in the design of animation characters, his acting skills, his ability to transform, as well as his knowledge of the techniques of the "old masters" - the "Nine Old Men" - at Disney. Andreas has just written a book about these Disney legends and is working on his first independent animation short film: "Mushka", another traditional 2D animation film - what else!

Andreas, in your estimation, what makes 2D or hand-drawn animation an independent art form to this day as compared to computer animation? Where do you see the difference or special quality?

To put it in a nutshell: In 2D animation it's all about drawing, and drawing is not only about what to draw, but also about what you leave out. A 2D animator is actually an editor, who says: This line is important here, but over there, I will leave out a lot. In computer-generated animation you show everything. It is total realism. You show every fold in the fabric, every texture and all sorts of things. It's more like "in real life", while 2D animation, I believe, is more about fantasy, inspiring or stimulating your imagination.

And more likely to create a world of its own?

Exactly. The worlds created during the 60 years of the 2D era are so divergent! And when I look at all these 3D things, whether feature film or shorts

- sooner or later they all press the "realism button".

The preparatory work is always beautiful, they are designed graphically and with pastel or watercolors, but in the end - this button is pressed again and somehow everything looks the same. And I wonder why? Because with 3D, you can actually do anything. Of course, there are commercial reasons. 3D movies are all very accessible, most look similar to live-action video games with which children have grown up.

In 2D animations, the direct transfer of the handwriting is an important aspect, isn't it? What do you think about that?

You can actually see the artist's handwriting on the screen. Even a non-professional can see that there are dif-

ferent approaches in Disney films, different temperaments, different drawing styles. The artist's expression is on the screen. That is not the case with CG films. Most CG animators move all the characters in a scene, they don't specialize in one particular character.

Exactly, this has changed quite drastically to that effect.

I once asked a producer from Pixar studios, how they handle character design, who is responsible for the development of character in the movie, the character arc - I was told that this was not the animator, but the director who says to the animators: This is how the character should act. So with regard to CG-animators lending ex-

Sketch by Andreas Deja for his independent animation film project "Mushka", the story of a friendship between a girl and a tiger in Siberia. © Copyright Andreas Deja

Additional sketches for "Mushka", which show Andreas' mastery in the drawing of animals.

pression to the character, it is quite restricted. During my time with Disney, I was always responsible for my characters like Jafar - good or bad, I am responsible, Scar, good or bad, I was responsible for the character.

This leads to actually owning the character! In CG this is less so, because there is a "fix-up group", who changes your animation again, goes over follow through again and even changes some minor things in terms of acting. As an artist, I find that a little odd. If my character has to be reworked again, then I own it and execute the changes. In 2D, it looks like this: I do the rough animation, the clean-ups are done by assistants - but I have always checked the work of the clean-up crew. Whether it was Jafar or Roger Rabbit, I wanted to see all the clean-up keys, every single key drawing! In the end, I had to sign off on the key drawings. I made sure that I was able to say in the end: That scene and that character - that's me!"

Relinquishing any responsibility for the character arc is one very distinct difference.

After all, it is actually a lot of fun to get into your own character, to develop it during the course of the film - in consultation with the director, of course, and with all the story people. If I'm not responsible for it, then it's somehow a different thing. I have also never understood that 3D animators are not well-known at all. Who are the star animators at Pixar or Dreamworks, Blue Sky?

Yes, there are a few that are relatively well-known. I can think of Kristof Serrand of Dreamworks, for example, who originally started in 2D animation, though. But getting back to the development of a character: Character design for animation is also teamwork. Namely in the sense that a character designer does not work in an open space and the character is fixed for all times, but that the character has to work for the animation. I know that you are always very interested in developing and refining your characters so they can work in the animation. Maybe you can tell a bit about your experiences, or what the actual process looks like.

At Disney, it had been the rule for decades that the animator was not only responsible for the character's behavior and development, but also for the design. However, when I started working on a film such as "Aladdin" or "The Lion King", there were already storyboards that I could look at, but the characters were not yet visually specified. Graphically speaking, they were mostly roughs and lacked refinement. There were visual development people who had already worked out designs, I could look at those, but I had to provide the finishing touches, and the other animators had to do the same, of course. Tony Bancroft, who drew Pumba (the warthog in "The Lion King", author's note), studied real boars to make his character believable. Glen Keane - with the beast from "Beauty and the Beast" - had many different ways in which he could have developed the beast. In the end it, was a "Glen-Keane beast". And Scar became an "Andreas-Deja lion" ("The Lion King").

In your blog you mention the collaboration with the famous British illustrator Gerald Scarfe, in "Hercules" (Clements, Musker 1997). This was an extremely graphic approach, at first. You describe in your blog, how it evolved. But how was it in this specific case? Did the development take place already in the dialogue or how did it happen?

Gerald Scarfe and I were both a bit frustrated, because we did not make any progress with the character of Hercules. All the other characters were already graphically defined, like these three "Fates" and these monsters, the Cyclops. Meg, the female protagonist as well.

It was easier to use Scarfe's style, because the character was a bit more angular, in personality too. When I saw Gerald Scarfe's draft for Hercules, I realized that the representation was either quite realistic or too cartoony. Gerald Scarfe could not make the character fit in his own style. In the end, we sat down in a meeting and scribbled until the character was reasonably defined and used those sketches for the final design.

Do you use any animation tests at that point?
They come in later.

So you would develop the design first, to the point where you think that it works for you, and then...
... you discuss it with the directors, who have to okay it, of course, and then you start with test animations. First you want to see whether the character can be drawn three-dimensionally. If it does not quite work out one hundred percent in a few places, then this is the time where we can still make changes.

But from here on, this is actually more fine tuning?
Exactly.

Getting back to 2D animation: Interestingly, almost all universities or educational institutions for animation still have their students start their education with hand-drawn animation. Where do

An immensely dynamic study of a jumping tiger from "Mushka".
© Copyright Andreas Deja

you see the major advantages, if you actually learn how to animate by still hand-drawing animation, instead of sitting down at the machine right away?

Yes, I agree that it is better to learn animation with 2D, at least initially, because it is somehow taken up easier. You have more light-bulb moments than if you immediately start working with a CG model: Because when you draw something, you have to learn to control proportions; observation skills are so important when you have to draw an animal, a horse, a lion or an elephant. It is necessary that you first go to the zoo and really take time to do studies with this animal - it is all incredibly important preparatory work, which will then benefit your work later. I do not know if these 3D artists are doing this - observing, constantly taking in new impressions.

Well, I think this may vary, but I just always notice that our students really

enjoy drawing as well. I think this goes back to exactly what you said, that this experience in drawing is much more immediate as compared to starting out by working with a digital puppet. You are first confronted with some graphs and curves, software and controllers - it lacks immediacy and the results are probably not as forthcoming.

I agree with that. If I may talk briefly about hands, because they represent a problem in CG animation. There are actually no fantastic CG hands yet. There is somehow always something strange, for example, there is a bump somewhere on the hand that does not belong there. This organic, expressive element a hand has to offer - I have not seen it yet in CG. As a 2D artist, you also have had lots of practice with figure drawing, and at some point you learned how to draw hands as well. You also know the expressive power of a hand: Not just how a hand works mechanically, but also what is emotionally feasible. Because you took time to observe that. And you also have an informed opinion, about what makes for a good hand and a bad hand. And I do not see that in most 3D hands.

I believe it is also easier to establish a totality of impressions in drawings rather than in CG; because there, they are always adjusting and tweaking something. I think this often leads to the problem similar to the principle of easily distinguishable silhouettes, which sometimes is overlooked and then it does not work very well.

Since you mentioned figure drawing: To what extent is figure drawing for animation actually different from what is taught in the traditional, academic figure drawing?

Traditional academic drawing is really different, because movement is not added, the poses are more static. Those who are mainly interested in animation will be frustrated with these one-to-two-hour positions. In that situation, I can only recommend starting a new drawing from a different perspective. In this way, several drawings are made in one day, not just one long-drawn-out study. If the model only offers long-term poses, it is recommended to represent the expressiveness of the human figure from all possible angles and turns. This is incredibly important for animation.

There are also the famous studies of Walt Stanchfield, the drawing instructor at Disney (Walt Stanchfield, "Drawn to Life" Vol.1 & 2, 2009).

Walt was a master of his craft. Not necessarily one of the best animators in the studio, but he was an incredibly good teacher. He could really get you to think about what he was saying, and he corrected drawings with great clarity and empathy.

Was he still working when you were in the studio?

Yes, actually for a very long time. I also attended his courses back then. In the early 80s. He just died a few years ago, perhaps ten or fifteen years ago (2000). Walt was teaching unconventional figure drawing courses. Later on, I occasionally taught figure drawing in the studio as well, and I used some of his methods. It was about some ideas, with which he had experimented back then: For example: the model takes a position, everyone looks at the pose for two, three minutes, but no one begins to draw yet!

Then the model leaves, and you draw what you have seen from memory.

Figure drawing can be taught in very exciting ways. There are many ways to challenge the brain somehow. This does not always have to be very academic, old-fashioned or even boring.

We often do this as well, that we actually study only movement sequences in figure drawing or very short poses and so on.

It's extremely important.

After all, for the animator it is not a priority to deal with textures and light studies all the time. Of course, it must be part of an artist's overall repertoire. But when it comes to animation itself, it is actually about the line in motion.

That's certainly true for 2D animation. The medium has evolved in such a way that 2D animation has been challenging the illustrator's acting skills for the last 60 years. In live-action film there are roles, definite characters. The challenge is to express yourself through acting. There is also effect animation or abstract films, which is a different thing.

Which is great, because it elegantly leads me to the next question - keyword: acting. I would be very interested to know, if there are examples from live-action film, where you would say that these are exemplary scenes or films, in which we really see acting at the highest level? This is, of course, a wide-ranging field, but maybe you can name a few personal favorites? Particularly as it relates to animation. Roles or films that also permit conclusions about the acting in animation?

That would usually be roles or films, which are "character-rich", in which the characters are very expressive. But I briefly want to make reference to the drawing ability: At one time, I had the misconception thinking that, if I could ever learn to draw well, I would be a good animator. Of course this is not true at all! When I first started working at Disney, they thought my drawings were wonderful and

Additional animal studies by Andreas Deja.
© Copyright Andreas Deja

said: "We have never seen such a portfolio, it looks as if you were working here for ten, twelve years," I was immediately accepted to the studio. But good animation was something I had to learn during the years to come.

My single-frame drawings looked good at that time. But after they were videotaped, I saw that everything was moving really badly! It had nothing to do with acting. And then, at some point I had an epiphany: Okay, now that you know how to draw, you can focus less on it. Now it's really about acting. Then I started studying drama students, and analyzing films with regard to good roles and expressive power. To give you an example of something that inspired me, even for certain things I did later: In Germany, they used to show the movies with Margaret Rutherford as "Miss Marple" (adapted from Agatha Christie), and I thought this woman was fascinating, the composition of her face, various expressions and grimaces ... There is no other person who looks like that.

(Laughing) No, probably not.

She was so fascinating and expressive, her body language and her humor as well, I was completely fascinated! I always hoped to create a similar character in the future, with a funny, quirky personality. And I tried to do that later with the character of Mama Odie, in "The Princess & the Frog" (Clements, Musker 2009).

Which brings me to the following: Very often, acting is also about interaction - almost always?

Yes.

And in "Miss Marple", there is, of course, Mr. Stringer, Miss Marple's partner. I believe that this element of contrast is also very important here, and how action and reaction are balanced.

And they were both very different. They were a team in their "crime fighting", but she was the adventurous one, and Mr. Stringer always said: "Miss Marple, I don't know, are you sure? Please don't go there". This is exactly what makes such a scene or such a sequence or a movie so rich: when characters are different. Frank Thomas used to say the following: When you have two characters in a scene and both characters think alike, then you have a problem.

Yes, exactly, because then you're lacking contrast. Then you have nothing that stands out, that is interesting or exciting.

Exactly. That is a very simple statement, but if you seriously think about it: It's really true.

You are, of course, one of the great masters in that respect. What I find incredibly difficult, something I actually still have not adequately mastered as an animator, is to achieve this subtlety in timing: In other words, if it's about things like: action, reaction, how do you balance that correctly so that it works? Do you have a tip for someone who is still relatively new to animation, as to how he can learn the ropes of this incredibly challenging topic? Is it through observation, or film analysis, through trial and error, or all of it together?

It's all of it together. Timing was the last big problem area for me. I learned good drawing through years of intense figure and animal drawing. But you actually learn timing by shooting a scene and then, if there is something wrong, hopefully noticing that certain sequences appear either too fast or too slow. Then you correct the timing. But if you are at a loss and don't know why the animation seems unnatural, then you show the scene to a colleague, a fresh pair of eyes, who can help out with his opinion. You learn good timing by doing, redoing, re-timing. The good thing is: You can just time the same drawings differently without redrawing or animating the scene anew. Sometimes you need to make graphical changes that fit better with the new timing. Perhaps push the action line a bit more, rework the rough animation. Overall, however, you can work with the first roughs from the first pass of the scene. If you need a break in the flow, then you say, okay, I will hold this drawing a little longer now, maybe not four, but twelve frames, then I have a small break. Over time, you will develop an approach to timing, you know when it works and when it doesn't.

I think that this has a lot to do with experience, of course. This fits well with what you said about drawing: Something that in my experience is one of the typical beginners' mistakes, is that there is always too much action packed in too short a time, in other words, a whole lot of poses, and somehow there is the temptation that, if poses look great,

then this is going to work somehow; then someone videotapes it and then... then it ends up looking really awful.

Too much information in a scene can complicate the clarity of the animation. You have to ask yourself: What is important about this character, what is the essence, what is it all about? Superfluous drawings are omitted, the scene is simplified. I experienced this once with Eric Larson. Too many poses, too many statements. Then I got him to take a look at the scene and he said: "Okay, we keep this drawing, we omit the other one, and here we need a break". Eric picked out the most important drawings and gave them new timing. My jaw dropped a few times, because suddenly the whole thing was clear and distinguishable.

Yes, I think this is one of the most important aspects that is often neglected, which many students do not realize: The viewer does not know what is in the artist's head, and he is the one who must be able to understand it later.

The viewer sees the scene only once, there must be clarity, the audience needs to know what it is about. If the communication from the screen is confusing, you will lose the interest of the audience.

Something else that's interesting - although it's a bit off the topic, but it also has to do with those fundamentals or beginnings: When it comes to drawing: In think what you said at the beginning was incredibly good, that you as an illustrator always make a selection from what "reality" has to offer you. You wrote yourself that even, or especially, someone like Milt Kahl - about whose drawings so many would say, that they look quite "real" - made an incredible number of design decisions.

All the time. With each stroke you make a decision. One of the most incredible characters, for which details were omitted, is Merlin by Milt Kahl (from "The Sword in the Stone", 1963, directed by Wolfgang Reitherman). You could have added a lot of detailed folds into the design for Merlin's robe, - yet he reduced it to the bare essential. And it all comes off the screen so lightly and smoothly... He has learned to reduce it, so that only the essence remains. A second character was the panther in "Jungle Book" ("The Jungle Book", 1967, directed by Wolfgang Reitherman), its design consisting of only very, very few lines, almost only one outline, though Milt Kahl knew exactly where the hip bone, the shoulders etc. were in each drawing. But then everything was omitted and reduced to the essentials. Somehow breathtaking.

I believe Milt Kahl himself has said (cited in Williams, 2002): "Well, I know where the weight is on every drawing"

Exactly.

How does everything move, and where exactly is what now, because weight in motion is constantly shifting? I would also like to hear your opinion on the following: Weight in animation is often shown or taught like this in books: Someone is shown who needs to lift a stone, and that is supposed to demon-

strate the animation of weight. But actually, the topic of weight or gravity in animation is so much more comprehensive, isn't it? It is constantly present.

Constantly. This is already the case for a normal walk, that's where it starts: After the contact drawing, where the heel first makes contact with the ground and the foot comes down, then the knee should also bend. A shift in weight must be shown by the change in position and shape: The knee will bend when bearing weight on the leg, and to what extent, depends on how heavy the character is.

I would also like to talk about the correct use of live-action reference. For many computer animators, it is almost something like the "holy grail" always to use a reference of a (frequently self-produced) live-action film.

Even filming yourself as a reference for the scene.

Exactly! Live action reference is, of course, something that can make sense. But what do you think about that? How did you use that in your work? And if you use it: How should it be implemented?

I always had my own way of using live-action film. I did not use it like the old animators. Because back then, they had these printed photographs of each filmed frame. They picked out key frames and traced drawings from live-action frames. The animator then reinterpreted them, changing proportions and timing as well. I never worked with photographs, I found it more exciting to watch things on video. Studying these individual takes in this manner in order to find out whether the actor or actress represented something, which would have never occurred to me. You say to yourself: 'Okay, the acting is really good, I would have never thought of this on my own. I can include this in the animation.'

Then I would sit down and draw sketches, small thumbnail sketches, in front of the monitor. This way I avoid tracing film frames, which can result in lifeless animation. But you can also say: 'okay, this part in the real-live scene works well, and I can do a better job with the other part.' You view the live-action film in a discerning manner. Some ideas come from the actor, others from the animator.

I believe that Jeremy Irons (in "The Lion King") was such an example, wasn't it?

No, that did not work with Jeremy Irons, because he was a lion (in the movie). (laughing)

Yes, sure, but let's put it this way: in disposition, the little mannerisms?

In the face, just a little bit. I did not necessarily sketch Jeremy Irons in the studio, but I studied him in the studio in front of the microphone, and I studied his behavior. With Scar it was very much about restraint, because he was a very poised evil and not "crazy evil". Initially, it was like this with Jafar ("Aladdin", 1992) as well: I did not know how to interpret the character. In some storyboards he was portrayed as very active, for example in the desert during the frustrated search for the lamp. Then there were other scenes, in which he was very subtle and just stood there thinking about some-

thing. There was very little happening graphically.

But Jafar was already very much - which I personally loved - somehow closer to a caricature, a strong caricature...

Oh yes! With him I did not need a live-action movie, I always had an idea how I could implement it. There were live-action scenes for realistic characters like Jasmin and Aladdin. With Jafar, I was always able to figure out his behavior by myself.

But with Jafar - was he influenced by Jaffar, enacted by Conrad Veidt in the live-action movie "The Thief of Baghdad"? (Berger, Powell, Whelan 1940)

Not at all. In fact, I am familiar with the film, which used to be on German television occasionally. The story has some similarities. Sabu (main character from "The Thief of Baghdad") is a bit like Aladdin, and Jaffar (villain from the "Thief") has similar characteristics to Jafar. Then there was (in the older film) the Sultan with his toys - so there are similarities. Although I knew the film, I did not study it while I was working on Jafar.

I thought it was absolutely insane, because I have looked at it several times now frame-by-frame, at least some scenes, and I noticed how little the actor actually does. He is almost always vertical in his posture, and hardly moves out of this rigidity. Yet, he looks incredibly intense and threatening, perhaps because of that.

For that reason.

I don't know.

It looks much more dangerous when you see someone thinking, who has evil thoughts. When it comes across with subtle eye movements it looks much more evil, as if someone were dealing out blows right and left.

Too much fidgeting would make it perhaps even a bit ridiculous.
That is exactly right. And there are some really fantastic actors who can do that. The camera shows only the eyes, nothing else, and you know what they are thinking, you know somehow what is going on inside of them. Jeremy Irons is such an actor, Judi Dench is such an actress - she can do so much with just one glance.

But how does the animator actually accomplish that the viewer can see that a character is thinking? What are the tools? Is it timing? How do I achieve that?
To put it in a nutshell: A thought process becomes clear only when a mood change occurs on the screen. If the character in the scene is only happy, in other words, is only showing one emotion, then there's no thought process in that case. Okay, you have a certain mood. But when a character, let's say, is writing a love letter and really getting into it and smiling, and suddenly you hear a loud bang in the background, then you can perceive a mood change. First, the loving mood, then all at once the realization that something dangerous is happening. By changing the emotions you can show a thought process.

This involves timing again, because a change or a thought process usually requires a reaction time. That is, if I show something, let's say, something happens, and at the same time I show the reaction to it, then it usually does not work, right?
It depends on how the whole thing is structured with regard to timing. The question that is constantly asked, especially by young animators: I would like to animate a test scene and also try to show that I can draw a character that really thinks. How can I do that? The answer I give each time is: Make sure you have an emotional change somewhere in the scene, show more than just one kind of emotion. You won't get there otherwise.

What skills should a student actually practice most, or already have, or try to obtain during the training, in order to become a good animator?
The main thing, even for hand-drawn films, is actually not the drawing, but the acting ability and a sense of character, entertainment and character development. That is actually more important than beautiful drawing. There are indeed animators who can draw wonderfully, but they are not actors. The scenes look very polished, the animation works, but somehow it does not convey any emotion. That is because the acting choices or the acting are flat. It is more important that you immerse yourself into the character and and try to understand it! If you have this ability, then you're on your way. Drawing really becomes secondary.

This means that acting abilities are of major importance. And each person has his own way of getting there. Some people need real acting lessons, including theory and analysis of how to create distinctive characters. For others, this task is easier, they work intuitively. For me, it was the constant observation of people that provided me with a foundation for animation. Just as the study of live-action films, not for the entertainment value, but for the analysis of a character throughout the entire film. Learning from classic animation films is of equal importance. How were these fantastic scenes accomplished technically? Why do they look so natural? Together with Hans (Bacher), we started the single-frame study of many Disney films back in Essen.

What he always likes to talk about, are the...
...the beer drinking nights we used to have, where we looked at all these things frame-by-frame. That was incredibly helpful! At that time we watched Disney 2D animation films in movie theaters, on the big screen, and we had no idea why these scenes looked so good. How they were drawn, where the key frames were. But later we had movies on Super8 or 16mm, which made it possible to view them frame-by-frame. Click, click, click - you could hear the penny drop, one after the other. This was fantastic training. Nowadays this type of study is so easy to do. You can really get anything that has ever been animated.

One click, yes.
You can get everything, and get it cheap too.

Yes, it's cheap to get. Ironically, when I tell this to my students, they often look at me in disbelief: What do you mean? They are supposed to sit down at night and watch a movie frame-by-frame? (laughing)
Yes, exactly! (laughing)

Then they look at me, as if they had just encountered a ghost.
That's called homework.

Yes, of course. I also happen to believe that nowadays, everything is a little too easy...
That you no longer have to search for things yourself anymore.

In the 70s and 80s, on the other hand, there was almost no literature or reference material.
Nothing, hardly any books.

Back then, it was like a gift when you got your hands on something.
If there was ever an article in the magazine "Die Bunte" about a new release of a Walt Disney film - that was worth gold, you immediately cut it out and almost framed it. And today, we have access to everything. This search for information is really easy today. If students would only realize that the old films virtually offer a real school - it's all there, you can see everything. And if you're curious enough to investigate why a scene, an old classic scene looks

good, then you can find out right now! At one time, you could not do that, or less so.

There is one more thing, something I always really liked about the Richard Williams books: conveying the importance of a breakdown, in other words, the question of which interesting intermediate position can get me from Key A to Key B?

Although, a very important breakdown is actually a key too.

Precisely.

If there is something creative happening, something new, which can not be mechanically filled, then it is actually a key. The animator should actually be drawing the main breakdowns too. For example, if the head moves from left to right, then you can not omit the center position. This breakdown is actually the front position. This is not a breakdown, this is actually a key.

The question students frequently ask, is: Where does a breakdown stop being a breakdown, and is actually a key? I think it's a bit of an academic discussion, Richard Williams also says: Key frames are just the storytelling drawings, and the others are extremes, the actual poses. But I think somehow, this is probably basically secondary.

You are absolutely right. We can have a lot of discussions about the philosophical interpretation. In the end, each animator has to find his own style and way of working. Whether it's straight ahead or pose-to-pose, everyone has to learn that for himself. You can study the sys-tem of the old animators and then take parts that work for you, which make sense to you. That is how I did it. When I started at Disney, we had access to the archive. I then checked out key scenes from "Bambi" (Hand, 1942) and "Dum-bo" (Sharpsteen, 1941). I could sort out the inbetweens, so I had only the keys in front of me. This was relatively easy, because most of the artists had circled the number to identify a key. If you just flip the keys, then the process is very smooth. If, on the other hand, you flip the inbetweens, then the sequence is bumpy, since the strong extremes are missing. Milt Kahl's mode of thinking appealed to me most. He drew only the most important keys. All drawings that did not require creative decisions were done by the inbetweener. That's how he constructed his scene. He often drew only a partial drawing, e.g. mouth changes during a dialogue scene. The rest of the face was finished by the in-betweener. And that somehow made sense to me. Why should I draw head and eyes each time, when an inbe-tweener can actually do this much more carefully?

It was quite different with Frank Thom-as. He hardly had any keys or inbe-tweens in his animation, for him, all drawings were important. Frank basi-cally created all the drawings of a scene. And then clean-up people had prob-lems with his scenes in trying to make out any kind of structure at all. It was difficult to use a conventional clean-up procedure, because each drawing had the same degree of importance.

This means that they are probably very close together...

Exactly. Frank Thomas was a fantastic actor, but in his animation he rarely focused on one important pose to be seen for any certain length of time. His characters are constantly moving, often very subtly. But the end result is always fantastic.

A constant flow.
A constant flow.

Then it gets slower or comes much closer together, becomes much more subtle in change.
But somehow something keeps moving. When Mogli yawns at the beginning of the movie ("The Jungle Book", Reitherman 1967), and says to the panther, 'ah, I'm tired now', and he stretches - nothing comes to a standstill. Milt Kahl would have found a certain inbetween to lead in the movement, and then to lead out of it again. With Frank Thomas, everything is designed in such a way that it always continues to flow smoothly, and it looks fantastic. The effect is not blurry or soft. It works and looks very natural. I knew Frank very well and I believe that he adapted this technique, because he never quite trusted his own drawing. He never saw himself as a top illustrator and never actually came to a point where he said, 'okay, this exactly is the drawing, which says it all' - it's more like a group of drawings.

This is also related to the difference between straight ahead and pose-to-pose. For me, this is always something that is difficult to explain. It is my personal experience that a beginner usually cannot

really animate straight ahead, unless he is an absolute natural talent. So for me, the question always arises: What is the definition of 'straight ahead'? Because in a way, the animator would already know about where he wants to go. Straight ahead without any idea of where it should go, actually does not work at all.
But you create the idea beforehand with your thumbnail sketches. These acting patterns, the kind of acting, are created before the animation in the form of small drawings. Because when you start with the big drawings, then you know roughly where it's all going. You are still free to make small changes during the drawing. You think, 'okay, I will do this a little different than with the thumbnails', but overall, you already have a concept that you now just draw larger. It doesn't really work without thumbnails. You're wasting time with these large drawings and throw them away if they don't work. You have to specify everything first on a small scale.

And often these drawings have already turned out well and look surprisingly good!
Because they were drawn very intuitively, not with the intention of framing them at some point, but only for the purpose of clarifying any movements and thoughts.

Finally, I would like to go back to the fact that analyzing great examples from the history of animation is a way to learn things. In closing, could you just name a few names or examples? Some names have been mentioned already, but are there other scenes from movies that come to mind, along with great animations?

The interesting characters are of course the eccentric ones. The princes and princesses in "Sleeping Beauty" (Clark, Larson, Reitherman 1959) and "Cinderella" (Geronimi, Jackson, Luske 1950), who rely heavily on live-action, are less interesting to study. The graphics are excellent, and the design of this "Sleeping Beauty" head, the graphic construction of it, and how they were able to maintain it throughout, so that every single drawing was really graphic and beautiful every time. That makes it interesting. But Cruella (de Ville) from "101 Dalmatians" (Geronimi, Luske, Reitherman 1961) is a fantastic character because of her heavy, really heavy coat, this fur coat she wears. And when she turns around, the character turns first, and the coat takes much more time, swaying backwards first, and then forward. Follow-through and weight, with respect to this fur coat, are fabulous to study. Madame Medusa (from "The Rescuers"/ Lounsberry, Reitherman, Stevens 1977) is quite wonderful in terms of bizarre expressive power and dialogue scenes. Milt Kahl animated her lips extraordinarily. When Medusa says "you", then the lips move all the way forward. There are very wide mouth openings when she screams. I was able to learn a lot from this character, as far as dialogue is concerned. The dialogue of the Indian chief from "Peter Pan" (Geronimi, Jackson, Luske 1953) is just as interesting and crazy. This Ward Kimball character has a very strange configuration of nose and mouth, and a strange, but very fascinating way to speak. And that inspired me for the character of Jafar, because I wanted to invent mouth positions and not just rely on the fact that an "M" can only look like this, and an "O" just looks like that. It is fun to design specific mouth positions for a character. But characters from other studios were influential as well. When we produced "Roger Rabbit" (Zemeckis 1988), it was more about Warner Brothers animation. At that time, I researched about Chuck Jones, of course, although he was a bit more subtle than the old Warner Brothers cartoons. There are animators like Rod Scribner or Ken Harris, who worked more with extreme poses and wilder animations too. But their work is still clear, never confusing. It is very educational to try to maintain clarity in very crazy, surreal animation scenes.

Oh, what would perhaps be nice, if you could talk about it, for the very last conclusion (laughing) - that would be really great - how the art form of hand-drawn animation continues to live on in your own project of "Mushka". I mean, there is still an incredible amount of 2D produced worldwide.

Exactly.

It has disappeared from the focus of the absolute box office of Hollywood mainstream, for now.

For now, it's gone from there. But the love is still there, definitely.

The love is still there! Perhaps you can say a little more about what your motivation was, what you want to achieve with the film, and where your main focus is, what it is that takes center stage for you?

When I left Disney two and a half years ago, I knew quite well that I had to continue working to challenge myself creatively, somehow. You can not shut it down and say 'okay, I'm retired now'. That doesn't work. I am also much too young to retire. And then I just thought about what I would enjoy doing most. I really like drawing animals - okay, but what kind of animals? Big cats have always fascinated me since "Lion King", all these studies we did in zoos and of live-action nature films. Finally I said to myself, tigers are really beautiful animals. Maybe I could develop a friendship between a tiger and a human being. A person, okay, maybe a boy? But we've already seen that in "Jungle Book" with Mogli and the panther. Maybe a girl. A young girl, so that the contrast is greater between this monstrosity, this huge dangerous animal and this innocent girl. Okay, so I knew the two main characters were already set. And then I got together with a friend who expresses himself in a variety of ways. He deals with architecture, but also writes poems, poetry and is an all-around artist. I told him that I would like to have certain story elements in the film, and asked him if he could write a script based on it. Four versions /outlines later, it was time to start storyboarding. I finished the storyboard version about two weeks ago, of course, there are still all sorts of improvements and new ideas, but overall, the story is complete. This is very exciting. Stylistically I'd like to try something new, the popular Hollywood 2D animation has indeed changed very little over the years. For decades now, the characters have clear outlines, either in black, as in the 60s and 70s, or a colored outline, and two-dimensional colors. I don't want that this time, instead, the film is going to look like one of my sketchbooks. So the whole thing is more intuitive, no clean-ups, only sketchy animation. And ever since Hans (Bacher) started posting works by the German illustrator Wilhelm M. Busch on his blog a few years ago, I have had a few aha-moments. His illustrative style is a fantastic inspiration for the design of my film. I have ordered many of his illustrated books from Germany. I would also like to base my background design a little on these very subtle, but masterly drawn book illustrations. Busch created different styles, some of them in color, others in black and white with shades of gray. I prefer his very reduced illustrations, which are really all about lines that have a spatial effect. That is how I see the aesthetics of my film.

Has it made a big difference since you have realized that you are now really responsible for everything, from directing to the story, making all the visual decisions ... your own master, so to speak?

A little. I mean, it feels good, but it's a bit risky. I believe, that you have to realize somehow where your inexperience lies, where you need help. I know very well that I need help with layouts, I need help with the story, because I've never really done story in all these years. You then ask people who can help you somehow, because you can not be good in all areas.

Yes, of course, it is also about feedback ... that you simply keep the lines of communication open with others.

Exactly. Once I finish the story in maybe two months or so, then I'll have screenings and invite people and ask them what they think, if it is clear or boring. I would not make the mistake of producing my film tucked away all alone in a cubbyhole, and then to release it.

But the beauty is that the decisions are always artistically motivated. In other words, these are not decisions that have to be made for reasons other than artistic motivation. Basically, you can really decide to make the movie the way you think is best with all the feedback you have received.

Exactly. I will make the final decisions.

Great, excellent, that was it - thank you for the conversation!

Additional sketches for "Mushka". © Copyright Andreas Deja

Guest author: Kathrin Albers

Stop Motion

Stop motion is an umbrella term for several techniques, which are all based on the fact that mostly real-built objects are manipulated frame by frame. Of all the animation techniques, stop motion is the one most similar to a live-action film shoot, especially in the version of puppet animation. Physical sets must be built, painted and illuminated. The animation is filmed with real cameras with single frame release. Stop motion, unlike any other technique, requires very complex expertise by the animator or/and must be implemented with a multi-talented team.

1) What is stop motion?

Of course, "stop motion" is a strange term. There is no movement here that is stopped and then continues. On the contrary, it is a long series of still images with rigid figures that are minimally moved frame-by-frame. Just as in traditional 2D animation, only with real built sets and characters. The illusion of the movement is created when a series of frames is played as a fast sequence. The more single frames of a movement are used per second, the smoother, softer, and more life-like the animation. The less frames are used, the coarser and more "jerky" the movement. If the frame rate is so low that the brain can perceive the individual frames as such, the illusion is no longer successful. Starting at about 4 frames, a strongly jerky animation results; at 6 or 7 frames, each frame can clearly be perceived as a still image. Generally, this is of course no reason to animate on fours, sixes or on tens. As mentioned in the intro-

ductory chapter, however, two-dimensional images are perceived at a different speed than three-dimensional images. The brain comprehends a flat drawing more easily and faster than a three-dimensional image with depth and many details.

The decision about shooting at a certain frame rate ("on ones", "twos", "threes" etc.) should be made during the conceptual phase of each film according to aesthetic and artistic aspects. This certainly applies to all animation techniques, not just stop motion.

Stop motion is not just referring to the animation with puppets à la Wallace and Gromit. It is the general term for any frame-by-frame animation of everything you can place and move in front of a camera. This can be done, for example, with flat or three-dimensional paper objects, but also with real people, furniture, cars or household items. The boundary to 2D animation can be fluid, since you can also cut out a drawn 2D animation from paper and animate it in a stop motion procedure as a constructed layer in space or lying flat. In general, there are no limitations to the adventure of experimenting and combining. This makes it the most diverse and creative form of animation.

The digital age was a kind of revolution for puppet animation. With the advent of digital cameras and the development of corresponding software, it was possible to see your current, not yet photographed image ("live image") and match it up to the previously shot frames until the continuity works. The days of blind animation with movie cameras are over, and animators finally have options for more complex movements and more precise control of individual frames.

This has strongly increased awareness of the entire post-production industry, if not to say: It only emerged in this form and concept in the first place, and has since then played an enormous part in film production, both in live-action and in animation film. Because of it, puppet animation filmmakers can plan their scenes more freely and realize the kind of animations, camera angles and set buildings that make production not only considerably easier, but also make certain ideas possible at all.

A clear division into traditional 2D animation, 3D or stop motion has therefore become more difficult since then. As already described in the introductory chapter, 3D software in particular has enormous influence on all techniques, including stop motion. In addition to camera and post-production, the use of objects modeled in 3D software, including their individual animated poses, has been particularly far-reaching. For dimensions, where the human finger and real tools cannot reach or where a form is simply too detailed and complex, a 3D printer can be used to visualize, print, and in this way, integrate almost anything beforehand into a stop motion film. However, it is worth discussing whether this is still stop motion in the traditional sense, since, in the case of thousands of printed animated frames, it has actually turned into an incarnate digital 3D animation. In the face of these new digital influences, the question is how we define stop motion in general, and what the future of the true spirit of this form of animation will look like in in the future. Is it only about how something looks afterwards, no matter how it came about, or is it also about making the manufacturing process visible for the viewer? What fascinates people about animation and stop motion in particular?

An Overview of the Various Stop Motion Techniques

Puppet Animation

This technique is the "classic" among stop-motion films with a long and rich tradition. Puppets made of different materials such as plasticine, silicone or foam are given a skeleton of wire or metal joints, called "armature" in technical jargon, with which they can be moved frame-by-frame. The scale is generally between 1:10 and ca. 1:6. But, of course, all sizes and shapes are possible.

A brief historical overview

The very first stop-motion animations were made around 1900, after George Méliès accidentally (due to a jammed camera) shot the illusion of a transformation from a car into a hearse. During the time of the malfunction, one car drove off and the other took its place. This effect, coupled with the knowledge that one can manipulate things in front of a camera between each frame, form the basis for the stop motion technique.

Early works with animated figures are, for example, those of **Ladislav Starevich** (such as "The Beautiful Lukanida", 1912), from Russia / France, who often used insects and other prepared real animals as figures, creating astounding realism through life-like animations. For many years, the former **Eastern Bloc countries** produced puppet animation films at the highest artistic level. Notably often without the label "children's film", since many artists used stop motion (as well as all kinds of animations) as an art form for different subjects, sometimes surreal, but also satirical and explicitly not for children. Well-known artists worth studying are **Jiri Trnka**, **Yuri Norstein** and **Jan Svankmajer**.

The stop motion scene grew, particularly in England, with the founding and success of **Aardman Studios** in Bristol in 1970 and, like hardly any other studio, it shaped the aesthetics as well as the humor and content of the younger generation of puppet animation film makers.

There were many stop motion films from North America, such as Rankin/Bass Productions ("Rudolph, the Red-Nosed Reindeer", Nagashima/Roemer, 1964. Produced entirely in Japan) or George Pal, who created a wonderful series of puppet animations with his "Puppetoons", which worked mainly with so-called replacements instead of jointed puppets (see section animation, page 269).

Laika Entertainment (formerly **Will Vinton Studio**) is regarded technically as the most ambitious studio at this time with its means of 3D-printing and detailed, previsualized very smooth animation (plus a lot of money), thus virtually blurring the dividing line of digital 3D to become an almost androgynous version of the two techniques. For the layperson, it is nearly impossible to tell whether for instance "The Boxtrolls" is a 3D computer animation or a stop motion film.

Pixilation

Pixilation refers to the technique in which people act as puppets. Instead of moving forward in a continuous and fluid motion, an actor moves through the set in spatial intervals in a frame-by-frame process and remains in the individual poses, which are shot in sequence. The resulting effects are mostly weird, amazing and surreal. The founding fathers of this style are, among others, Grant Munro, after whom this technique was named, or Norman McLaren ("Neighbors", "A Chairy Tale").

The surrealist Jan Svankmajer (including "Food", "Conspirators of Pleasure") uses this technique in almost all of his films and has influenced a whole generation of animation artists with his work to this day.

More recently, we have seen pixilation in playful music videos and short films. ("Human Skateboard", Pes, "Her Morning Elegance", Oren Lavie, "Strawberry Swing", for Coldplay, by Shynola, "Sledgehammer", for Peter Gabriel, by Stephen R. Johnson).

Pixilation short film "I Love Story" by Kimberly Siy Huang, developed at the School of Art, Design and Media, Nanyang Technological University Singapore.

Cutout

The word says it all: In the cutout, the figures are cut out of paper, cardboard, felt or other flat materials, placed under the camera and animated frame-by-frame.

There are two very different ways of working. If the character is put together in individual parts and animated as a jointed puppet, you achieve an effect similar to (shadow) puppetry, in which the objects and characters move mostly sideways. Popular representatives are mainly the artists of Monty Python, who cut the drawings into parts and deliberately placed little emphasis on concealing their technique, which largely contributed to the humor in the first place. The same applies

to the series "South Park", which was continued to be created in digital cutout soon after the initial release.

The worldwide "mother" of all cutout animation is undoubtedly Lotte Reiniger, who mainly used paper cutting in her films, lending her characters complex flexibility by breaking them down to finger joints and individual strands of hair. Reiniger was heavily influenced by Arabian and Asian shadow puppetry. Some titles of her works: "The Adventures of Prince Achmed", "Kalif Storch", "Papageno" and many fairy tales of the Brothers Grimm.

Another type of cutout, as already indicated above, is the blending of 2D animation and cutout animation, in which the individual

Cut-out animation with paper, from "The Animals" (2014) by Mark Wee Nai De

frames are defined and tested in advance, and only then cutout of paper and placed under the camera. After a previously defined frame-by-frame timing, they then "only" have to be shot in sequence. This is where traditional 2D animation and stop motion merge equally. You could just as well use, say, the After Effects software to digitally animate cutout and scanned characters in the manner of cutout animation.

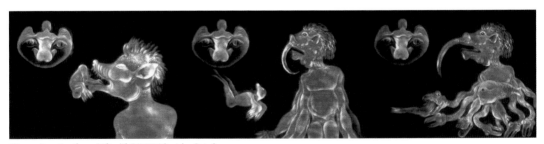

Clay animation from "Afterlife" (1978) by Ishu Patel

Sand and Plasticine Animation Techniques

Instead of rigid objects and characters, sand or plasticine are placed flat on a glass plate and animated by moving and reshaping, using the same camera set-up. The surface is usually illuminated from below, giving the material a special depth and rich color. Particularly with sand, some life-like impressions of architecture and natural representations can be achieved.

2) Concept and Pre-production

The story, even if it is visually abstract, should fit the nature of stop motion. For the initial ideas it may not matter which kind of animation you favor, but soon you should ask yourself the important question, whether stop motion is primarily stylistically, and secondly from a practical point of view, the right choice for the respective idea.

This book is primarily aimed at newcomers and those who want to realize their own projects on their own or in small teams, and as such it is advisable to set limits when starting. Of course, in a professional studio environment, even the most complex scenes can be implemented in stop motion, so I would like to contradict the general prevailing opinion that only simple ideas with few sets and characters would be suitable for this technique. This is certainly not true. Everything is possible. All stories can be told with some experience and creativity, it just depends on how you do it.

Start small.

At the beginning, and especially with little experience, it is in fact advisable to keep the story small and to limit yourself to one or two sets and puppets. Since stop motion is without question very technical even in its simplest form, I recommend a simple story that leaves enough room to get acquainted with the physical properties, the production process and, above all, the unfamiliar straight-ahead animation. A kind of finger exercise to warm up.

For starters, camera movements should be excluded and special effects should be planned - if at all - only in simple form. The same applies to talking characters. For all these topics, there are additional sections in this chapter.

As with all film projects and as already described here in the book, you first need a treatment that summarizes the idea. Then comes the storyboard stage, in which the idea is broken down into individual scenes. Unlike 2D animation, in stop motion you cannot go into too much detail of layout or camera set-up, since the live-action aspect of the various focal lengths, the size of the set and the corresponding space surrounding it will only roughly match the planned field of view and perspectives of the sketches. The storyboard should initially function only as story development. The so-called shooting board may later provide more details on the final implementation. This is where the sequence of the film shoot, all the focal lengths, required props and aids are set up, which considerably facilitate the shooting schedule. As soon as the first structures of the set have been set-up, it is recommended to shoot the planned scenes with a camera in order to test whether the scenes can be implemented as expected. Roughly cut cardboard figures instead of puppets help to recreate the scenes. These images are then imported into the so-called animatic, where the film is previsualized in terms of timing and editing. A tip for simplifying shooting is to pay attention while working in the storyboard, as to how the character will be visible in the image. Does it always have to be visible in full-length while walking?

Or can I cut it so that it will not be seen from the hip down? This would simplify the animation considerably, since, instead of a full-body

animation, it can simply be placed on a block that sits below the field of view, and is thus invisible. Moving the block up and down to simulate walking is much easier and faster as well.

Illustration: Kathrin Albers

3) From Character and Production Design to Puppet and Prop Building

Character Design for Stop Motion

Since everything has to be built in a stop-motion film, there are of course some requirements regarding design, which are ultimately subject to feasibility. On the other hand, materials and tools can be a particular source of inspiration for surfaces and shapes.

The initial approach is the same as in 2D or 3D. Sketches and silhouettes of all kinds come first. Starting out, you should not let any material feasibility restrict your creativity, but let your artistic in-tuition guide you to develop your own interesting characters that point you to the initial general direction.

While drawings are certainly indispensable, my advice is not to "fuss" over a 2D design for too long, since it will ultimately become a three-dimensional object made of real materials. As in 3D, the material selected will always affect the appearance, which is why it helps to get familiar with the available means as soon as possible and not to become too attached to the design drawing.

At this point, I deliberately exclude the technology of 3D-printing, which does not know any technical limitations, such as the size of a tool or a modeling finger, but I am focusing one hundred percent on the puppet to be made by hand. Depending on the talents of the puppet maker, his/her own artistic style will have more or less of an influence on the design.

You should change quickly into the three-dimensional world of clay or plasticine, in order to roughly test the favorite designs. It is not un-common for a snazzy 2D-de-sign to turn out boring in

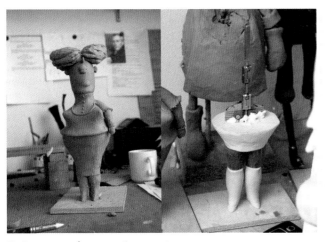

Design process of a stop motion puppet.
The first sketches are kept relatively simple, the plasticine version gives a much more accurate impression of the final design. The picture in the middle shows the armature with finished legs and a hard core made of rigid foam. The upper body was cut from soft foam and covered with fabric. The role for this puppet was limited to exclusive standing with little movement in the upper body.
Design/illustration: Kathrin Albers

three dimensions. These three-dimensional "sketches" are a much quicker way to the final design. The tools used for modeling should be adapted to the final style of the puppet. If, for example, you are aiming for a coarse plasticine look, you should not use small modeling wood sticks because such fine details will not survive, but will be pushed out of place during the animation process. Inversely, fine tools for previsualization of details should be used, if the puppet later gets sewn clothing. It is also helpful to procure fabrics and other craft materials early on in the process in order to see what is actually available, so that you do not get used to the thought of something that does not exist in real life and for which you have to look for alternatives later. You can use all kinds of tools, cutlery, pottery accessories or discarded dentist tools for modeling, which you can often buy at flea markets.

Modeling wood sticks can also be cut and filed down according to your own needs. For fabrics and other materials, the scale of the puppet world should be considered. The checks in a shirt fabric will be magnified accordingly on a puppet, the same applies to stitches of a knit sweater, the wool for hair, buttons, buckles or the wood grain for furniture. If this "size-reducing" effect is not desired, you should look for appropriate materials and patterns true to scale.

Specialists in Stop Motion

In stop motion productions, collaboration between designer and puppet maker must be very close to ensure practicability, especially at the start of production. Sometimes you can find some rather unusual specialists working in puppet animation studios, who are utilized for specific purposes. One example would be Althea Crome, who is a knitting specialist and who knitted the tiny finger gloves for the film "Coraline", among other things.

Design Planning

One special aspect is, of course, the animability of the character. In puppet animation films, everything always looks very elastic, flexible, fluttering, or wobbling. In reality, all objects are made of stiffened yet bendable materials in order to get everything in its position and keep it there. This is a special challenge for puppet and prop-builders and requires a high level of knowledge from the fields of precision mechanics, plastics processing, tailoring and carpentry.

Any novice who does not have an exceptional penchant for such techniques should use materials that do not require too much special knowledge, as this can only lead to unnecessary frustration. Multi-part shapes for silicone puppets should not be considered as a first project, rather, puppets with fabric dresses and a foam filling (foam like the one from a mattress) or made from good old plasticine.

You have defined in the storyboard what your character should do in the movie. Ask yourself when constructing the puppet, how it should best be built, so that you can implement all the scenes as planned. The purpose here is to find the most effective construction possible.

Example

- A puppet does not need to be finished on the back, if it will never be seen from behind.
- Is the puppet walking around a lot or is it just sitting down? In that case, it does not make sense to build a standing puppet, which then must be bent into a sitting pose. Build it in a sitting position right away and you will have more design options.
- Are you planning a long shot, in which the character is seen tiny in the set, and close-ups of the puppet's face? Then it is easier to build two puppets: a very small one, matching the large set of the long shot, and another one that is both suitable for whole-body and close-up shots. The small puppet does not need any details like the big one, but it should resemble her in stature, color, etc.

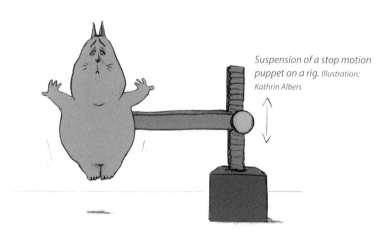

Suspension of a stop motion puppet on a rig. Illustration: Kathrin Albers

Armature Design

If you do not have an armature made of ball-and-socket joints - which is usually the case with beginners - you can build a simplified version made of wire.

All you need is aluminum wire. It is light and has great bending properties. It is available in different sizes at craft supply stores or at merchants for bonsai trees (usually less expensive on the Internet). In addition, you will need wood pieces in the size of the trunk and hips of your puppet, or alternatively two-component plasticine. With the two-component adhesive you affix the wire to the solid parts of the body. Do not use any other adhesive, because the fusion between wire and wooden parts must be as stable as possible.

For drilling holes in wooden parts, you need a small handheld or bench drill, and suitable pliers for bending, cutting and twisting the wire.

To keep the plasticine from sliding off the smooth wire later, it is advisable to wrap certain places with one layer of skin-colored textile adhesive tape (such as adhesive bandage). This tape sticks very well and allows you to push the plasticine tightly into the fabric and keep it in place.

Interior Workings

The rigging for a 3D animator is equivalent to the "armature", the skeleton for the puppet animation filmmaker.

There are various versions made of ball-and-socket joints, or more simple ones made of wire and wood. Both have their advantages and disadvantages: While ball-and-socket joints have good bending properties, wire armatures can usually perform more extreme movements. It is important that the armature is constructed as stable as possible. However, you must also realize: No armature will last forever, it will weaken somewhere in the course of the animation process, and then possibly break; the question is only when and how to to figure out the right time to repair it.

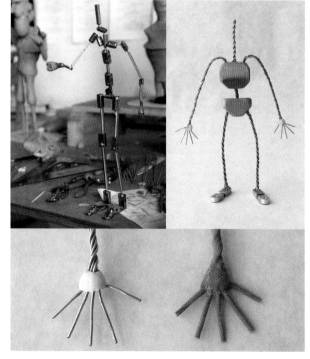

Top left: Armature with ball-and-socket joints and metal arms. The hands have a clamping device, into which thin wires for individual fingers can be clamped.
Top right: Simple wire armature with wooden blocks and twisted wires. The arms are made of five thin twisted wires, which, bent apart at the lower end, produce a hand.
Below: The palm of the hand on the left is made of two-component plasticine, which cures very quickly.
The hand on the right is wrapped with adhesive bandage, which makes the plasticine cling better.
Design: Kathrin Albers

Head and Feet

The **feet** need to be able to be anchored to the floor. If the puppet stays in one spot and does not move away, you can simply glue it down. If it walks back and forth, however, the feet must be able to be screwed to the floor. You can also use magnets that hold the feet down through the floor of the stage. For the first option you need a floor through which you can drill holes - preferably wood; for option two, you need a floor thin enough to transmit magnetism.

Option one requires feet with a small thread into which a screw can be screwed from below. For option two you need small iron pieces as "soles" that are responsive to the magnet.

For the **head**, you will need to consider whether your character is going to speak. If so, see page 272 for details on this technique. Even without speech, the character is likely to get eyes and different facial expressions.

In order to let a character look back and forth, it is easiest to integrate the eyeballs into the head, and then place the pupils and eyelids on top later. Even for a purely plasticine figure, the eyeballs should consist of a solid wooden or "Fimo" pearl - by no means of plasticine, since the small balls would deform due to frequent touching. This for one, would look quite unattractive during the movement later, and it would also make correcting the form during the animation very annoying and time-consuming.

Since the head is subject to frequent back and forth bending, it should be anchored firmly onto the neck and have a solid core. In case of a plasticine head the core must extend to just below the surface. If it does not, you again run the risk of crushing the shape during animation.

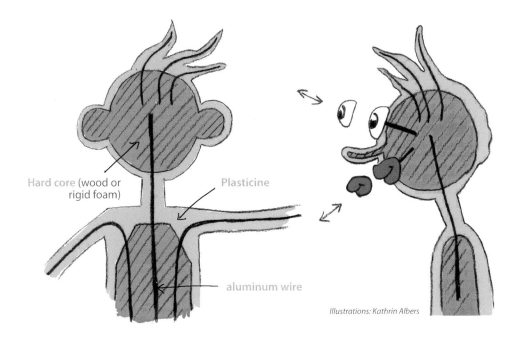

Hard core (wood or rigid foam)

Plasticine

aluminum wire

Illustrations: Kathrin Albers

Replacement Animation

Replacements are a great opportunity for circumventing the latent solidness and flexibility constraints that are inherent in a puppet. Instead of bending or modeling the character into a desired position, it is sometimes more effective and, above all, more expressive to build this new pose as a new figure and replace the previous one with the new one. It may sound like an exaggerated effort to build a whole new puppet for just one single frame of the animation. While this is true, it is still very useful when it comes to repetitive frames, for example, walk cycles, which simply look more interesting and lend more expressiveness to the animation. In addition, the popular squash and stretch can not be implemented with one single puppet. In larger productions, especially for series, replacements are also used for reasons of efficiency and saving time. In this way, part of the animation is moved, as it were, into the process of puppet making. This happens inevitably in dialogue animation, where a set of mouth pieces is built earlier and then placed on the puppet's face in sync with the recorded text. The same principle can be applied to the entire head or body.

The master and inventor of this technique was without doubt George Pal, who attracted worldwide attention in the 40s and 50s with his "Puppetoons". It is worthwhile to study these films. Replacements in plasticine can be done just as well and even easier. The series "Purple and Brown" is a classic example.

Materials

Where will a puppet be handled most during animation and how vigorously will it be handled? Especially with a plasticine puppet it pays to cheat, and not really build everything with plasticine. A modeling compound that can be cured in the oven is great to combine the appearance of plasticine with stability. In the end, you cannot tell which parts are solid and which are soft.

3D Printing

The modern form of replacement technology is 3D printing, which is now used in every major studio. The abundance of which can be seen in the feature films of Laika Studios, where mass scenes are produced with one and the same character printed hundreds of times (see e.g. circus scene with mice in "Coraline"), or where walk cycles are printed for one single character in order to get a more expressive animation on one hand, but also to create a design that could not have been implemented otherwise on this small scale (e.g. the black cat in "Coraline"). However, this technique takes facial animation to extreme levels. Thanks to this process, a main character in "The Boxtrolls" or "ParaNorman" can have up to a whopping 1.4 million facial expressions. This enormous sum is calculated from the many combinations that result from dividing the face into multiple areas.

4) Camera and Lighting

A puppet animation film is not much different than a live-action film, when it comes to camera and lighting set-up - it is only on a smaller scale. This is why, at the beginning of the set-up and during the production design stage of the animation, it is important to look for references from films showing perspectives, lighting moods and compositions that could fit into your own production.

A number of digital DSLR cameras are being used now, especially the Canon EOS-series and Nikon cameras. All these cameras work very well with current stop-motion software such as "Dragonframe" or "Stop Motion Pro". They are not just for animators, but are ideal for camera work as well. You can use them to stipulate aperture, exposure and many presets, thus setting up the entire scene.

When comparing it with a live-action set, it is important to understand that the camera in the puppet scale would be about the size of a dining table, which is therefore much larger than it would be in real life. This can inadvertently lead to opting for top view perspectives, which in turn makes the characters appear smaller and more "doll-like", thus creating a kind of human distance. There is nothing wrong with this, but the appearance of a character is often more convincing when you are "at eye level", or even below. The viewer becomes part of this world and does not remain an outside observer.

Different focal lengths also have the effect of making things appear smaller or larger. The wider the angle of the lens, the more you get into the picture. Beyond a certain size, the image becomes "bug-eyed", which may not be to everyone's taste. Nevertheless, focal lengths are somewhat different, somewhat less extreme, on smaller scales. I recommend experimenting a bit.

In lighting, a puppet is treated in the same way as an actor in live-action film, where there is a key light that defines the main lighting situation of the set, and a so-called backlight. This light is used only to make this figure stand out from the background, highlighting its silhouette.

For an average general light that does not cast strong shadows or create a certain mood, but one that provides a very soft and subtle lighting of the set, the use of so-called soft boxes is recommended. If you do not have access to a professional one, you can build one yourself. However, you should know beforehand the size of the area which is to be illuminated. Sometimes it is sufficient to throw a spotlight onto a white ceiling or wall and to use only the reflection for this purpose. This kind of indirect light is often used to fill in shadows, when one side of the character is not sufficiently illuminated. White cardboard is then positioned to reflect light on this dark side, brightening it in a subtle way.

For atmospheric enhancement of a particular mood you can also use light projections, such as projecting the outline of a window, through which moonlight shines, onto a wall. Or reflections of sunlight falling through trees onto the set.

Such effects are extremely helpful and relatively easy to build with metal foil stencils, through which a strong light shines. Some lamp manufacturers offer projection props which are placed directly in front of the lamp so that the sharpness of the outline can be adjusted with the help of adjustable lamps.

In addition, there are lighting gel filters in different colors which are clipped in front of the lamps and can provide a strong color mood. As with all visual media, the same color theories also apply here (color contrasts and color moods) that help to create the appropriate atmosphere through the use of colored light.

In lighting, the use of very long and consistently illuminating lamps is most important. The inconsistency of a light might not be visible with the naked eye, but a faulty lamp would create a strong flicker over an entire day of 8 or more hours, due to the few seconds created in the animation during that time. If a lamp does not provide constant light, it can be due to its quality or (lack of) consistent electricity in the respective shooting space. If you want to check out the quality of your lighting beforehand, you can do a test by simulating a shooting situation and taking pictures of the set lit with the lamp for two or three hours. After that, you can assess more safely whether the lamp is suitable or not.

The more advanced among you may be thinking about camera movements. This is basically a great idea, but it complicates the film shoot significantly, since it requires much more accurate planning. Technically speaking, you need a so-called motion control unit or something more simple, a camera tripod, which is moved step-by-step by cranking. This is a very tedious process and requires a lot of discipline during animation.

When working with a motion control crane, a software is used to program the camera movement, which then follows the movement frame-by-frame during the actual film shoot. The real highlight of this technique is in its use with live-action film shoots. Because programmed camera movements can be repeated indefinitely, many effects can be implemented that you normally could not do in a single take. Particularly in synchronizing multiple passes, where different scales, techniques, and frame rates (frames per second) can be combined. Also, the coordinates of these camera movements can be imported into 3D software and then mixed with digital worlds or creatures. The use of this technology is incredibly diverse, and stop motion is just one of many.

Recommended examples: the music video "Come Into My World", by Kylie Minogue (Director: Michel Gondry), advertising for Ford "Zeitgeist" (directed by Noah Harris) or many of the opening sequences of stop-motion feature films like " The Nightmare Before Christmas "," Coraline ", or many major shots in feature stop motion movies of the last years.

Set Building

It is very useful to bring the camera to the set as early as possible, so that size and scale of the stage can be planned properly. If there are different takes on the same set, it may be necessary to split it so that the camera and the animator can reach the respective place. You can even reach areas further in the back where the camera or animator's hands could normally not reach. After all, the animator needs sufficient arm maneuverability to work. This is particularly true with short focal lengths, since the camera then has to be placed closer to the character. All additional paraphernalia such as computers, small tools, notes and other support materials should be on a small table located as close as possible to the set. Long distances between the character and recording computer, showing the live image, are extremely annoying and distracting.

The stage on which the set is to be built, must be very sturdy. It is important to have a good wood construction that does not wobble and for which the board does not sag. You can also use a sturdy desk, but it should be possible to paint it, drill in holes, affix things with hot glue,

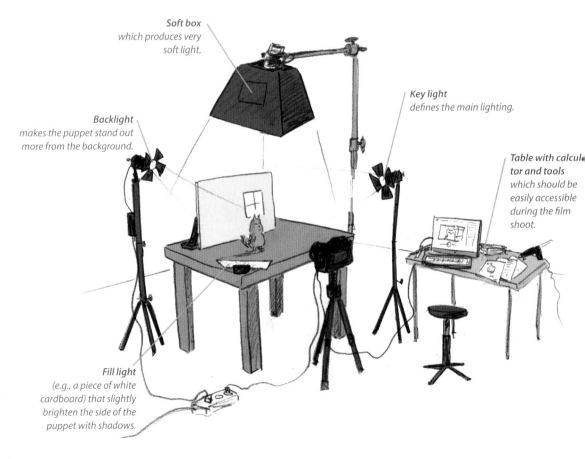

Soft box
which produces very soft light.

Key light
defines the main lighting.

Backlight
makes the puppet stand out more from the background.

Table with calculator and tools
which should be easily accessible during the film shoot.

Fill light
(e.g., a piece of white cardboard) that slightly brighten the side of the puppet with shadows.

etc. You should pay attention to the correct height of the table, because you spend most of your time standing during animation, and working at a stage that is so low that you have to bend down, is very exhausting.

I cannot stress enough: Everything on a puppet set must be fastened or completely glued down. You may not realize beforehand, how often you have to reach into the set. You are also completely focused on the puppet and may not even notice that you accidentally bumped into a small prop. Therefore, this applies to everything: fasten securely. Even objects that will be moved later by the puppet should be securely fastened until they are used. This also applies to lamps and the camera. Heavy sandbags can be placed on the base of tripods to prevent an inadvertently shifted lamp from creating major flickering of light.

5) Animation

Basically the principle of animation with puppets or objects does not differ from that of a traditional 2D animation. Here, too, there are 25 single frames per second, there are key frames, breakdowns and inbetweens. However, the production process and the requirements for stop motion are significantly different.

Just as there are no key frame animators or inbetweeners in puppet animation, there there are also no multiple animation passes, where arms or heads are animated separately at a later time or only focusing on an up-and-down moving body for a walk cycle, then adding the swinging arms, corresponding head movement and spacing etc. later. No, here everything has to happen at once, and it must happen frame-by-frame. This makes stop motion a very complex and "advanced" form of animation, as some animation experience is needed. Previous excursions into the world of 2D animation are highly recommended in order to have a grasp of the general principle of animation.

This is also why there are usually not several animators animating in one animation. On the contrary: It is worthwhile making sure that the puppets are "cast" with the same animators to maintain consistent and homogenous characteristics of the puppet throughout the entire film and not to develop a "schizophrenic" character, which acts differently from scene to scene. Many animators, like all artists, have their own styles, special preferences and strengths, which should be taken into account when assigning specific animations.

In a studio environment, the final stage of animation is preceded by extensive testing, in which the animation director together with the animators focus on the style of the movements. The director is the one who defines (together with the script writer in advance) the nature and personality of the various characters. Together with him, the animators, like actors before a film or theater production, get time to become acquainted with their characters, testing them and internalizing the style. It is also about practical aspects,

If a character is to jump, for example, thus leaving the secure floor, you can not avoid having to attach it to a support, which will be visible in the image. Sometimes you may be able hide the support. In the second picture you can see a thick wire leading from the back of the character to the rear wall. Viewed from the front, this support would not be visible. Actually, you can frequently find a solution to hide these rigs, thus keeping any retouching work to a minimum in the end.
Illustration: Kathrin Albers

such as the mobility of the skeleton and the nature of the materials. This step is particularly important in order to avoid unpleasant surprises during the animation stage and to keep from exceeding the production deadline (and above all, the budget).

Before the final animation can be executed, precise preparations must be made. The scene has to be meticulously planned in all respects. For the animator this means - in addition to preparing the puppet with the necessary support system - the planning of the animation by always making a rough dry run, called blocking. Here you animate the puppet in steps of 10 or 15 key frames through the scene, thereby determining the timing and other general aspects. In large projects, this is done at the beginning of the whole production and incorporated together with the voice recordings as part in the animatic to get as accurate an idea as possible of the film.

Blocking is often preceded by a video shot of the animator himself, in which he acts out the movement in order to analyze timing and sequence of the movement. With today's popular stop motion software (such as Dragon Frame), it is possible to import reference films and to place the blocked scene or video shot under the final animation, using it as a reference. I highly recommend that every animator observe dancers and mimes as a means for analyzing and studying movements. The control and precision that these artists exercise over their bodies is a great source of inspiration for every animator. The same applies to silent movies, of course. Actors of this genre had only their body and face to tell a story and to represent the character as clearly as possible with regard to personality and expression.

Strictly speaking, an animator is not an actor, of course, since he does not give a direct performance in front of the audience, but only the illusion of one. That is a big difference, both in terms of approach and an understanding of the two professions. Nevertheless, both art forms can strongly inspire each other.

No matter how perfect the preparation, with every beginning of a scene, the animator starts at zero - even with re-shoot - no scene will be just like the previous one. You have to be aware of this and approach it with a certain openness. In my opinion, however, it is precisely this little bit of uncertainty that also makes this form so unique and exciting.

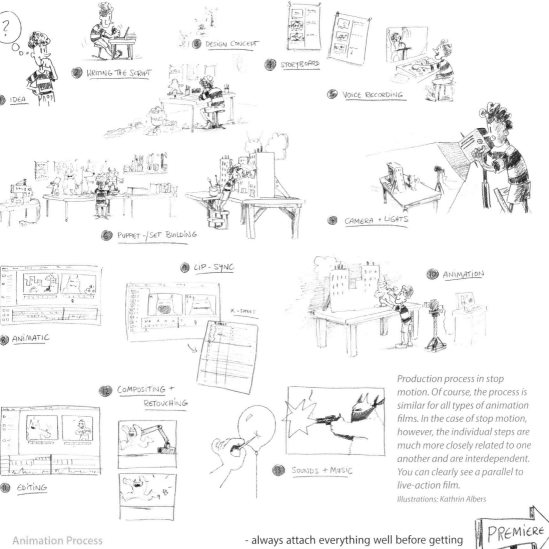

Production process in stop motion. Of course, the process is similar for all types of animation films. In the case of stop motion, however, the individual steps are much more closely related to one another and are interdependent. You can clearly see a parallel to live-action film.

Illustrations: Kathrin Albers

Animation Process

A novice in puppet animation should not start with overly complicated movements. You can move simple objects through the image as a small warm-up exercise in order to get a feel for general timing.

If you want to start with a puppet, then let the character stand or sit in one place in the beginning, and concentrate on the characteristic expression, the acting. Make sure to anchor the puppet as firmly as possible to the floor in order to avoid unwanted and unnoticed "sliding around". As already mentioned, this applies to all things on the set: Props, walls, furniture etc.

- always attach everything well before getting started.

It is easy for the animator to lose track of a movement, if he is focused too much on details. A good trick in taking a step back and reviewing the general timing of a movement is to look at the scene with slightly squinted eyes. The blurred view of the puppet filters out virtually all the small details and allows for a more simplified analysis of the movement performed.

6) Speech and Lip Syncing in Stop Motion

Giving the puppet a voice and speaking ability in the film is an essential character enhancement and clearly opens up other possibilities in the story as well as the animation. However, it not only makes puppet building more complicated, but also forces a certain timing on the animation through the previously recorded text. It is recommended that you meet with the selected actor in advance to discuss with him the character and its personality. Actors often have good ideas that can lend different nuances to the character, many of which you would not think of yourself when masterminding the story or developing the character. In addition, the animation can already develop naturally during the recording since the intonation and acting of the speaker determine specific gestures or movements. But it is important that the speaker understands that everything he says is animated later and that the physical acting is added later. This is why every animator is certainly grateful for clear intonation and somewhat exaggerated acting. Often the exaggeration in the voice recording seems much less extreme afterwards in the film.

Different ways to build replacement mouth pieces. In this character, the head was split. The dividing line runs below the nose and is covered by the mustache. This type of design requires a master mold to serve as the basis for all mouth pieces. I used the most open-mouthed one to build all the others. The difficult aspect of this design is to get all parts to fit as precisely as possible. When casting the head parts, a pin guide has to be placed from the outside into the silicone mold which will reflect the position on the body later, making sure the head always remains in the same place. The material of the mouths is dental plaster.
Design: Kathrin Albers

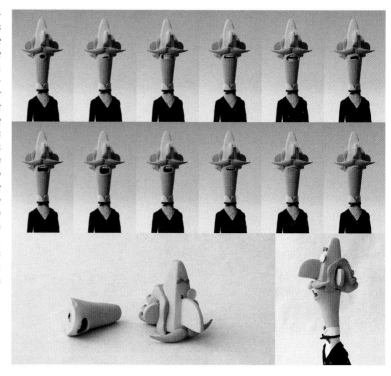

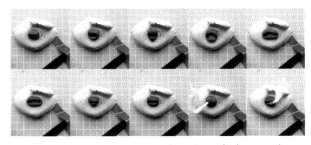

For a synchronous animation of body and mouth, the voice is recorded prior to filming and later imported into the animation software, so that the various mouth frames can be adapted to the voice recording, matching its timeline. Experienced animators are able to do this during animation. However, you must be very familiar with the expressiveness of the various mouth frames and their related facial expressions.

The number of mouth frames is a matter of style and can be achieved through the design. In general, my experience is that much less is needed than initially assumed. For a synchronous perception, it is important that key frames, such as "i", "o", "a", "m" match perfectly. Depending on the speed and expressiveness of the recording, you have to build elegant in-betweens that bridge the keys. It helps to observe yourself in the mirror while speaking and to analyze exactly how the mouth moves when speaking at different speeds.

A tip for the design: If you have the chance to make voice recordings prior to developing the final design, you can adopt the distinct dialogue, such as a dialect, into the appearance of the mouth pieces, and in doing so, develop a more convincing personality.

The final head is this one.
Design: Kathrin Albers

An easier method are mouths that are simply placed on top of the face.
In this character you can see clearly that the lips were placed on the face. For this, I had previously bent wires so that they approximately define the shape of the lips. The two ends were bent at right angles like small pins, which were then inserted into matching holes in the head. In order to build them as tightly as possible, I made a cast of the lower part of the face, and modeled the lips on top by using oven baked clay.
Design: Kathrin Albers

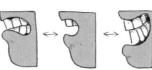

If building the molds is too complicated, and superimposed mouths are not to be used either, then interchangeable mouths can be produced just as well from plasticine. The transitional spaces between the head and the mouth part can be filled by simply using the same color plasticine.
Illustrations: Kathrin Albers

7) Post-production

Thanks to digital image post-production, you can use tools during animation that can be removed later by retouching. The most common ones are rigs. This is a support system to which the wires or articulated arms are attached that hold the puppet. They may also be small spacers which are placed under the feet during walk cycles, or retainers for objects flying through the scene. These rigs usually cannot be hidden and must be removed later by retouching.

For this purpose, a single frame of the set has to be shot without the rig and without the puppet in it right at the beginning (and for good measure, also after the animation). This so-called clean plate is placed behind the animated frame in post-production using a software such as After Effects or Nuke and fills in the gaps created by retouching.

The same principle can be used in compositing, where for example, portions of the set had to be shot separately and are then put together with the filmed animation pass. A missing wall, ceiling or piece of furniture is put into the set and photographed immediately following the film shoot.

This is a particularly good way to add special effects to an animation. For example, you can shoot the smoke of a cigarette on an "extra pass", preferably under the same lighting conditions and directly in the final set, and later composite it into the animation.

In general, the options in post-production (short: post) are far reaching, but nevertheless my advice, and also the advice of all post-production people, is to shoot as much as possible "in camera", i.e. in one take in order to ensure uniformity and to avoid extra work. The person who will do this work later must be involved in the planning of the scenes on the set, in order to estimate the camera set-up and the film shoot with regard to post-production.

This is also true of the typical post work task, for which everyone is grateful: all the mishaps that take place during the shoot, such as dirt spots, torn places on the puppet or a small piece of plasticine or tools left accidentally in the image. In this regard, you have to train yourself to be very disciplined, because any forgetfulness generates more work in post-production. Therefore, depending on the proportion and weight of the "severity of the accident", you should possibly favor a retake to post work.

Even if the post can handle a lot, the outdated phrase "fix it in the post" is clearly the wrong approach. After all, the post is not just for correcting some planning errors or minor sloppiness of a shoot, but for expanding the overall creative possibilities.

Reducing its broad capabilities to the mere function of rescuer for poorly planned and executed film shoots is the wrong approach. On the contrary, its deliberate and purposeful application enriches film projects in a creative way, making many things even possible in the first place.

Assignment:

Get a stop motion software of your choice. You can buy it on the Internet or use the free scaled-down trial version. In addition, you need a camera that is supported by it. You can find out what these are on their website.

1) First warm-up exercise:

Take small objects (dice, marbles, etc.) and move them through the frame at different speeds. Play with spacing and timing by imagining certain actions. For example:

- A marble comes speeding into the frame and bounces against an imaginary wall.
- A dice skids into the frame and slowly comes to a halt.

Always have an idea of how heavy your object is, and animate accordingly.

2) Select a brief clip from a silent movie or make a video recording of yourself. Use a very simple movement. This can be simply clapping your hands or scratching your head, leave off any running or walking for now. Now analyze the timing and transfer it to your puppet.

3) Develop and build a character design for a stop motion puppet. For this, it is helpful to write up a design idea in simple, striking phrases. For example:
"My characters are roughly modeled, expressive plasticine figures that do not obscure the material. With many fingerprints on it, giving the animation a lively, casual, deliberately unfinished look."
or
"The design follows a 50's advertising mascot to simulate its look with smooth, plastic-like surfaces."
or
"I want a found footage character consisting of cables, cutlery and buttons. I will not use elastic or manipulable materials."
or
"I will only use cotton and cardboard."
or...

Guest author: Melanie Beisswenger

Insight into 3D Computer Animation

New visual design possibilities have opened up: from stylized cartoons to photo-realistic creatures and worlds, all the way to interactive games and immersive VR - everything is possible now by means of 3D computer animation.

In less than 40 years, 3D computer animation has evolved from a gimmick of early computer pioneers to a stand-alone creative medium that has spread not only across our entertainment industry, but is also used in industries such as automotive, medicine, architecture, and many more.

The dominant and generally most visible application of 3D animation is in the field of entertainment: from animated feature films, commercials, film and TV productions with digital characters and visual effects (VFX) all the way to games for computers, consoles and mobile devices, augmented and virtual reality (AR/VR).

Since the first rudimentary computer-generated 3D wireframe animations in the late 1970s in the films "Futureworld" (1976) and "Star Wars" (1977), the artists and technicians of computer animation have provided us with fantastic imagery, such as Cyborg in "Terminator 2" (1993), the photo-realistic dinosaurs in "Jurassic Park" (1993) and the talking toy heroes Woody and Buzz Lightyear in the first fully computer animated movie "Toy Story" (1995) by Pixar Studios. No doubt, the rapid development of 3D computer animation is closely linked to the equally rapid technological development of hardware and software. Computing performance, data transfers, storage capacities and software have been - and still are - challenged and brought to the brink of their performance by the increasingly complex visual aspirations of computer graphics experts. Milestones in photo-realism were reached in films like "Final Fantasy" (1991), the digital character Gollum in "The Lord of the Rings - The Two Towers" (2002) and the aging of Brad Pitt in "The Curious Case of Ben-

Image of the stylized 3D animated short film "The Saga of Biorn" (2010) by Frederik Valentin Bjerre-Poulsen, Daniel Dion Christensen, Jonas Doctor, Jonas Georgakakis, Jesper Aagaard Jensen, Benjamin Juel Kousholt, Mads Lundgård, Steffen Lyhne, Pernille Ørum-Nielsen; The Animation Workshop, Denmark.

Detailed characters and worlds are created for the open-source 3D short film "Big Buck Bunny" (2008); Blender Foundation | www.blender.org

jamin Button" (2008). There are now no limits to the imagination, and computer graphics artists are increasingly turning to non-photo-realistic rendering (NPR), which invoke the visual worlds of traditional arts and 2D animation. ▦

3D animation in a 2D look - toon shading makes it possible. Poster for the film "Space Stallions" (2012) by Arna Rut Diego, Ágúst Freyr Kristinsson, Esben Jespersen, Jonatan Bruch, Polina Bokhan, Thorvaldur Gunnarsson, Touraj Khosravi; The Animation Workshop, Denmark.

Differences Between 2D and 3D Animation

3D animation is basically a continuation of 2D animation with other (technological) tools: the computer and pertinent animation software. The artistic fundamentals and design techniques are mostly the same as with traditional 2D animation, but 3D animation differs in working methods and production stages as well as the technical implementation on the computer.

As we have learned in the previous chapters, 2D animation is created primarily by drawing 12 frames (on twos) or 24 frames (on ones) per second. The following steps are clean-up and coloring.

In puppet animation or stop motion, a model is first created, painted and dressed, then positioned in a scene relative to the camera, illuminated and photographed. A process similar to puppet animation takes place with 3D animation: A three-dimensional model of a character or object and a scene is created on the computer. These models are given colors and textures, are animated, illuminated by virtual lights and finally photographed by a virtual camera. The big difference to traditional 2D animation is that the object does not need to be redrawn for each frame, but once created, can be viewed and presented from all sides. This is, of course, only a very simplified explanation of the development process of a 3D animation. We will look at the production steps in more detail below.

Soft shapes and pastel colors in the 3D graduation film "Drawing Memories" (2010) by Jerly Chang, Thom Chang, Yeo Bixia, Dionisuis Kartalaksana; School of Art, Design and Media, Nanyang Technological University, Singapore.

Strong lines and structures in the 3D animation film "The Backwater Gospel" (2011) by Bo Mathorne, Arthur Gil Larsen, Mads Simonsen, Thomas Grønlund, Rie Nymand, Esben Sloth, Martin Holm-Grevy, Tue Toft Sørensen; The Animation Workshop, Denmark.

Character pose from the short film "Load" (2011) by David Rene Christensen, Lasse Smith, Jeppe Broo Døcker, Mark Kjærgaard, Kristoffer W. Mikkelsen, Blake Overgaard and Malte Burup; The Animation Workshop, Denmark.

3D, CG, CGI - so, which one?

All these terms are used for computer animation, but what exactly do they mean?

- 3D refers to three-dimensional representation on the computer. Similar to the stop motion technique or puppet animation, it is easy to depict the volume of a body and the perspective of a scene using animation software.
  However, this is all on the computer and of course, only virtual.

- CG is an abbreviation for "computer generated".

- CGI stands for "computer generated imagery". The term CGI is often used as a generic term for digital effects in film and entertainment.

- Stereoscopic film presentations in movie theaters are often referred to as "3D". This has nothing to do with animation; it is the description of the type of projection on the big screen, i.e. 2D (without glasses) or 3D (with glasses and depth experience).

Production Work Stages in 3D Animation

This section is intended to provide an introduction to the work techniques and processes involved in creating 3D animation. Due to the complexity of the subject, however, it is only possible for this purpose to provide an overview of the various work areas. In order to be able to transfer the acquired knowledge, work techniques are explained in their basic software principles, without taking into account specific software functions.

All of the work steps and their sequence are called production pipeline; it becomes all the more important as more animators work together on one project, such as a short film, a movie or a game. The individual tasks are often in very specialized areas, which makes precise planning and the knowledge of how individual work steps are mutually interdependent and intertwined, even more important.

Storyboard panels for "Big Buck Bunny" (2008);
Blender Foundation | www.blender.org

In keeping with the focus of this book in the development process of a short film, we will also orient ourselves on the creative and technical sequence for this format with regard to 3D animation.

Idea, Story and Design - Pre-production

Ideas, stories and concepts are developed for 3D animation according to the same criteria and design steps as for 2D animation - in the early stages, the kind of technical implementation, i.e. whether 2D, 3D or stop motion animation, does not play a very important role yet. At the beginning of the design stage, however, it is sensible to think about the options of work techniques, since the design of the characters, sets and props can be optimized to the animation technique. Essential criteria when choosing a type of animation are often the familiarity with the medium of those involved, or questions about feasibility and possibilities within a technique: While a photo-realistic creature in a live-action film would not be implemented convincingly as a 2D animation or stop motion, this could be achieved with 3D animation - thus making this technique the ideal choice.

Before starting to work in the 3D software, one should have a precise idea about what wants to be achieved artistically. The Pre-production stage includes collecting reference images, creating design work such as sketches, drawings, sculptures, and color studies, as well as work on the storytelling in the form of storyboards and an animatic.

Character design sketches for the short film "Rob 'n Ron" (2013) by Magnus Igland Møller and Peter Smith; Tumblehead Animation Studio, Denmark.

Color script for the graduation film "Burger Burger" (2010) by Gavin Tan and Shicong Huang; School of Art, Design and Media, Nanyang Technological University, Singapore.

Color script by Goh Hui Ying for the short film "The Narcoleptic Boy" (2010) by Jessica Kesuma Winata, Nguyen Hieu Hanh, Pan Hui Ting, Hans Christian Sulistio, Stefani Irwan, School of Art, Design and Media, Nanyang Technological University, Singapore.

Modeling

3D modeling is one of the most fundamental tasks in 3D animation and the first step in the production pipeline, no matter what target medium, whether for film, advertising or games.

Virtual characters, landscapes, scenes and props are created on the computer, similar to modeling with clay. For this, three different types of geometry are used: polygons, subdivision surfaces and NURBS.

NURBS are very suitable for organic forms, but are difficult to manipulate. Over the years, this has made them less popular in the film industry and you actually cannot find them at all in the game industry. Today, NURBS are mainly used in virtual prototyping and product development in automotive and industrial design.

Polygons are the simplest and most commonly used type of geometry. The mesh consists of vertices (corner points), edges, and polygons. Subdivision surfaces usually have a polygon object as their basis. They have the advantage that very efficient partial details may be added, without driving up the overall polygon count and thus the render times too much. This makes them ideal for smooth and organic surfaces.

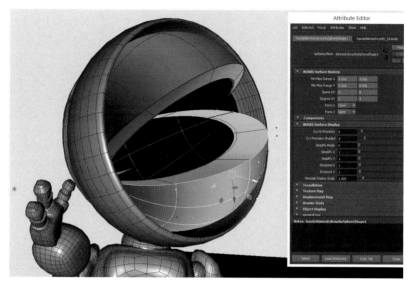

Perfect round NURBS (inside colored) compared to the square polygons (outside gray) using the example of the SIGGRAPH Asia 2009 mascot model by Yuko Oda, Brian Cannady, Leo Hourvitz (2009).

In modeling of objects, a distinction is often made between hard surface and organic forms.

Hard surface objects are defined primarily by hard edges and corners, such as machines, robots, mechanical objects and cars. Organic objects have soft curves and gentler forms, such as landscapes, plants, and above all characters, such as humans and animals.

Hard-surface prop-models for "The Narcoleptic Boy" (2010) by Jessica Kesuma Winata, Nguyen Hieu Hanh, Pan Hui Ting, Hans Christian Sulistio, Stefani Irwan, School of Art, Design and Media, Nanyang Technological University, Singapore.

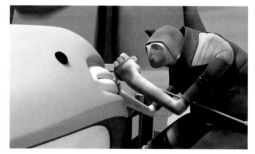

Organic forms of the two characters in the animation film "Burger Burger" (2010) by Shicong Huang and Gavin Tan; School of Art, Design and Media, Nanyang Technological University, Singapore.

Materials and Textures

In the next step, properties are applied to the model that describe the material and surface in greater detail, such as color, luminosity, reflective properties, transparency and other surface details. Various settings of these parameters allows us to perceive materials as plastic, glass or metal, for example. This process is called shading. In order to create more complexity and details into the surfaces, textures can be applied. These are images or procedural structures and patterns that are placed on the surface of the object.

Photographs of material surfaces from the real world are used for textures in order to create a particularly high degree of realism, such as

3D model of sets with different color variations by Goh Hui Ying for the animation film "The Narcoleptic Boy" (2010) by Jessica Kesuma Winata, Nguyen Hieu Hanh, Pan Hui Ting, Hans Christian Sulistio, Stefani Irwan, School of Art, Design and Media, Nanyang Technological University, Singapore.

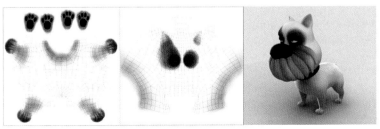

Textures for the 3D dog and finished shading: "The Narcoleptic Boy" (2010) by Jessica Kesuma Winata, Nguyen Hieu Hanh, Pan Hui Ting, Hans Christian Sulistio, Stefani Irwan, School of Art, Design and Media, Nanyang Technological University, Singapore.

wood, marble, stone, fabric structures, pores, etc., but also photographs of hair and entire faces can be projected onto geometries.

For a non-realistic and artistic look of the surfaces, real or digital brushes and pencil strokes can be used as texture as well.

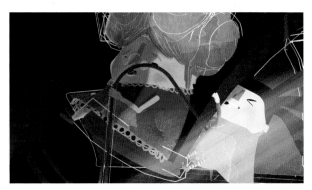

3D animation in a 2D look for the short film "Umbrella" (2014) by Brandon Chua, Tan Yin, Khoo Siew May, Sharry Kwan; School of Art, Design and Media, Nanyang Technological University, Singapore.

Diagram for generating the stylized look and white outlines in "Umbrella" (2014) by Brandon Chua, Tan Yin, Khoo Siew May, Sharry Kwan; School of Art, Design and Media, Nanyang Technological University, Singapore.

Development test for the look of "Where Do All the Lost Things Go" (2011): Color pass with outline strokes (left), ambient occlusion pass (center), final composite (right). Animation film by Hafizah Abdul Wahid, Joan Hsu Sze Yun, Kanan Abdul Kader Mohammad Ali, Bernard Su Guo Hao; School of Art, Design and Media, Nanyang Technological University, Singapore.

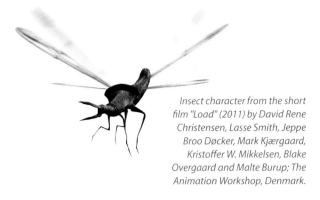

Insect character from the short film "Load" (2011) by David Rene Christensen, Lasse Smith, Jeppe Broo Døcker, Mark Kjærgaard, Kristoffer W. Mikkelsen, Blake Overgaard and Malte Burup; The Animation Workshop, Denmark.

The Agony of Choice - Which Software is Best for me?

The various software packages differ not only in performance, features and specialization, but also in price. Before deciding on a package, you should consider what you want to create, what complexity it requires, how much know-how you can contribute and how big the budget is for software. Most 3D animation software for animated features, VFX and TV are also available as trial versions or inexpensive or free student versions, which is a good way to try them out.

The Dream of a 1-Click-Does-Everything-Really-Great Software

Well, that would be nice! But I have to take this opportunity and point out that those who expect 3D animation software to rapidly implement their animation ideas "at the touch of a button", so to speak, will be bitterly disappointed. Because the computer and software - no matter how professional and complex - are just tools that have to be used in the same laborious and time-consuming manner (similar to the "traditional" animation techniques) in order to achieve the desired artistic result. Compared to 2D animation, some work steps are eliminated, while others are added.

Autodesk Maya is the most popular and widely used professional animation software for animation, VFX and TV productions. *www.autodesk.com*

Autodesk 3ds Max is also used by many studios for film and TV productions and is widely used in the games industry. *www.autodesk.com*

Autodesk Softimage is another 3D program that is used for film and TV post-production as well as game development. However, Autodesk discontinued the development of new versions in 2014. *www.softimage.com*

Cinema 4D is a 3D graphics program, mainly used in advertising and motion graphics. *www.maxon.net/en/*

ZBrush is a specialized digital modeling and painting program that allows you to intuitively create sculptures and models similar to clay or plasticine in virtual space. *www.pixologic.com*

Houdini is a procedural, node-based software, which is mainly used for high-end visual effects and simulations. *www.sidefx.com*

Blender is an open source (and free!) 3D program that contains all the functions for creating 3D animations. Extras include built-in video editing as well as a game engine.

Modo is another graphics program that mainly specializes in modeling and painting. *www.thefoundry.co.uk/products/modo*

Image from the short film "Hooked" (2010) by Yi Zhi Ang, Ying Herng Chia, Hazel Phyu Hnin Kyi and Jerome Siew Zhi Zhong; School of Art, Design and Media, Nanyang Technological University, Singapore.

Stylized look for the 3D character in "The Backwater Gospel" (2011) by Bo Mathorne, Arthur Gil Larsen, Mads Simonsen, Thomas Grønlund, Rie Nymand, Esben Sloth, Martin Holm-Grevy, Tue Toft Sørensen; The Animation Workshop, Denmark.

Screenshot of the 3D layout for "Drawing Memories" (2010) by Yeo Bixia, Jerly Chang, Thom Chang, Dionisuis Kartalaksana; School of Art, Design and Media, Nanyang Technological University, Singapore.

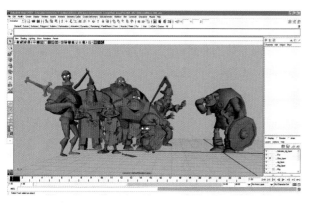

Screenshot of layout with character poses for "The Saga of Biôrn" (2010) by Frederik Valentin Bjerre-Poulsen, Daniel Dion Christensen, Jonas Doctor, Jonas Georgakakis, Jesper Aagaard Jensen, Benjamin Juel Kousholt, Mads Lundgård, Steffen Lyhne, Pernille Ørum-Nielsen; The Animation Workshop, Denmark.

Layout and Cameras

In the layout process, the previously created storyboards are transferred to the third dimension and a virtual camera is placed in the scene. 3D animation makes it possible to animate every conceivable movement of the camera, but it is advisable to use virtual tracking shots conservatively, more along our sense of viewing habits and aesthetics developed from live-action film. Excessively wild tracking shots can otherwise appear confusing, while very precisely planned cinematography can advance the narrative of the story. Studying the cinematography of live-action films is very good preparation for the virtual camera work.

Not only are image composition, camera position and animation defined in the layout, but rough movement of the characters within the scene are developed as well. Individual scenes are combined into sequences, thus forming the first more complex three-dimensional visualization of the film.

The 3D layout is an effective means to refine storytelling and check for continuity.

The layout process, which is an important step in the development of animated films, is also increasingly called previsualization - in short: previz - to plan VFX or action sequences or to prepare the shoot of complete live-action films.

Image composition for the short film "The Saga of Biôrn" (2010) by Frederik Valentin Bjerre-Poulsen, Daniel Dion Christensen, Jonas Doctor, Jonas Georgakakis, Jesper Aagaard Jensen, Benjamin Juel Kousholt, Mads Lundgård, Steffen Lyhne, Pernille Ørum-Nielsen ; The Animation Workshop, Denmark.

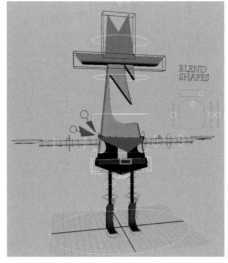

Character Rigging

Rigging creates bones, joints, and animation control objects in and around the objects and characters to be animated. The complexity of the rig depends on the character's mobility requirements within the scenes to be animated later. The scope ranges from a simple ball with only one animation control to characters and creatures with hundreds of them.

The blueprint for rigs is usually inspired by nature: Similar to the anatomy of humans and animals, virtual skeletons are integrated into the digital models, linked to the geometry surface by means of skinning and equipped with the relevant control objects for the animation. Depending on the realism or desired complexity, muscle systems can be incorporated as well as hair and clothing simulations. Another important area of rigging is equipping facial features with flexible articulation options for a wide range of facial expressions later.

Character rig with animation controls for Ron in the short film "Rob 'n Ron" (2013) by Magnus Igland Møller and Peter Smith; Tumblehead Animation Studio, Denmark.

Character rigging is one of the most technical areas of 3D computer animation and scripting skills are very useful. Creating a well-functioning and intuitive rig is an essential step in preparing for the animation and it is best done in close communication and coordination between the animators and riggers.

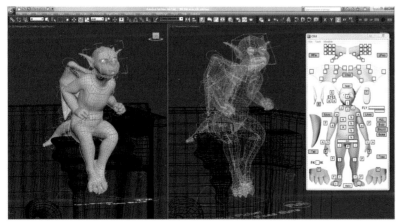

Model, rig and animation control picker for Xemerius, the 3D character in the film "Sapphire Blue". (2014);
© *Copyright mem-film, Lieblingsfilm, ARRI Film & TV, GFF, Tele München Gruppe.*

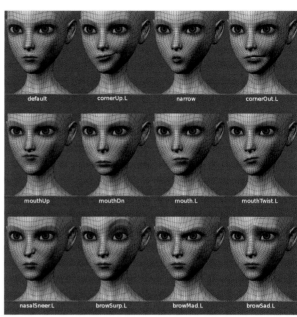

Character Animation

While the animation process breathes life into the character, it is not just about the purely physical movement, but also about the acting of the digital character. The animator has achieved his goal when the public perceives the character as thinking and feeling. The creative planning process in 3D animation is very similar to that of 2D animation, however, tools for 3D animation also differ considerably: Using the animation control objects, the 3D animator brings the character in various frames into key poses and can then play back this first rough animation - almost in real time - in order to rework and refine it in the next step.

Although the artistic principles of 3D animation are based on 2D animation, there are some clear differences between the two techniques:

- In 2D animation, the animator must be able to draw very well so that the character always looks the same and always maintains the same volume. Drawing talents, on the other hand, do not play an important role in 3D animation (similar to puppet anima-

tion); instead, the focus is placed on acting skills as well as a good understanding of movements.

- The advantage of 3D animation of having a character with constant volume can also have a disadvantageous effect when extreme shape changes and even metamorphoses are desired. These are relatively difficult to implement in 3D, since special modelling and rigging is required.

- In 2D animation, only every second frame is drawn (i.e. on 2's) to work efficiently, whereas in 3D animation, each frame is rendered (on 1's). This allows for smoother movements and more details and corresponds to our viewing habits of live-action film. Although the computer interpolates between the poses defined by the animator, a mechanically linear computer interpolation is artistically unacceptable for natural movements, so that the animator must constantly "correct" the computer and define the movements of the character down to the smallest detail.

- Animations created in 3D can be changed constantly and can quickly be rendered in preview quality. This allows for a very iterative work process, from the rough to the details of the animation, without having to wait a long time for scan or line test processes.

▓ When animating to music or dialogue, it can be played back in sync in 3D animation software. Therefore, X-sheets used in 2D animation are no longer needed.

▓ In 2D animation, details on the face are usually displayed in a very simplified manner. In 3D animation, however, a very high degree of detail can be rendered in pixel precision. This also means that a very detailed and realistic animation of the facial expressions as well as the lip sync can be created. In this case, realism refers to the credibility of facial expressions, whether in a photo-realistic or stylized and cartoony character design.

The typical work process of character animation starts with the idea and planning through sketches, self-acting of the scene and recording of video references. Afterwards, key poses for storytelling and description of movement are created in 3D software. In additional steps, more and more breakdown poses are inserted and other details are animated, including final secondary movements, such as hair and clothing (provided they are not simulated).

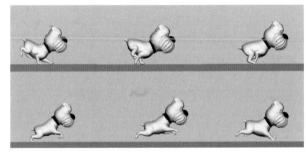

Six key frame poses for the run cycle of the dog in "The Narcoleptic Boy" (2010) by Jessica Kesuma Winata, Nguyen Hieu Hanh, Pan Hui Ting, Hans Christian Sulistio, Stefani Irwan, School of Art, Design and Media, Nanyang Technological University, Singapore.

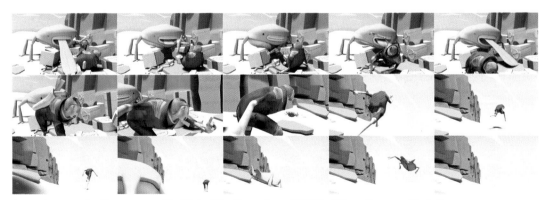

Images from an animation sequence of the 3D short film "Burger Burger" (2010) by Shicong Huang and Gavin Tan; School of Art, Design and Media, Nanyang Technological University, Singapore.

Lighting

Lighting draws attention to the action in the film and considerably influences mood and atmosphere. Similar to photography, live-action film or puppet animation, the image is further modeled with light and the viewer's gaze is purposefully directed within the scene.

Virtual lights in 3D animation software are based on those in our environment, such as natural daylight from the sun and artificial light sources, such as lamps and lights. However, since the calculation of absolutely realistic light effects is very complex and time-consuming - or is sometimes not desired for artistic reasons - light parameters such as intensity, color, casting of shadows, bouncing light, reflections, and more are individually adjusted lighting artist or TD (Technical Director). Since light interacts closely with the shading of the objects, color and surface properties are continually adapted through the lighting and compositing stage.

When creating textures for interactive games with real-time rendering, but without integrated lighting systems, lighting effects are often painted into surface textures, such as faking lamplight and shadow effects on a wall.

Classic lighting and shading set-up for "Do The Robot" SIGGRAPH Asia 2009 Mascot animation by Melanie Beisswenger (2009), model by Yuko Oda, Brian Cannady, Leo Hourvitz.

Light test for "The Narcoleptic Boy" (2010) by Hoang Long, Jessica Kesuma Winata, Nguyen Hieu Hanh, Pan Hui Ting, Hans Christian Sulistio, Stefani Irwan, School of Art, Design and Media, Nanyang Technological University, Singapore.

Lighting tests for the animation film "Sintel" (2010). ©
Copyright Blender Foundation | www.sintel.org.

Light directs the viewer's gaze in the image from the animated film "Color Theory" (2010) by Davier Yoon, School of Art, Design and Media, Nanyang Technological University, Singapore.

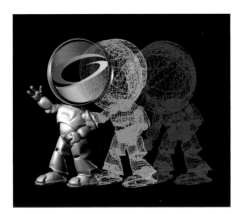

Rendered robot with wire frames for "Do The Robot" SIGGRAPH Asia 2009 Mascot animation by Melanie Beisswenger (2009).

Effects and Simulations

Effects and simulations are widely used in 3D animation and VFX projects. Due to their underlying physical laws, they can be created more complex and realistic by means of increased computer performance and software. Particle effects produce natural phenomena such as fog, rain, water and snow, even fire and explosions.

Cloth systems make it possible to depict different textile properties in virtual clothing and to calculate the movements of fabrics in a realistic manner.

Hair and skin systems are mostly used in conjunction with characters and respond to their movements. However, a fur or hair system can also be used for a meadow of grass.

All of these effects and simulations calculate physically correct the influence of natural forces such as wind and gravity on them, or even the collision of an entire group of objects with each other.

In 2D animation, partial effects are hand-drawn and animated with precise artistic control, whereas in 3D animation, they are usually simulated. While 3D software allows to obtain a first result quickly, the precise artistic design and art direction of the simulation is sometimes difficult to control and requires many repetitive steps.

CG smoke effects in "Load" (2011) by David Rene Christensen, Lasse Smith, Jeppe Broo Døcker, Mark Kjærgaard, Kristoffer W. Mikkelsen, Blake Overgaard and Malte Burup; The Animation Workshop, Denmark.

Detailed hair simulation in the 3D short film "Sintel" (2010). © Copyright Blender Foundation | www.sintel.org

Rendering

Rendering is the final step in the 3D animation pipeline, bringing together models, sets, shading, animation, lighting, and effects. Pixel images are now generated from the 3D elements and scenes, which in turn result in complete film sequences.

During the lighting process, the image is normally rendered entirely as a preview in just one pass. For the final rendering, however, several rendering passes with various image information are often created, in order to be able to change them later during the compositing process. A render pass includes individual varying attributes, such as color, shadow, and highlight, in addition, masks for transparency of individual elements are calculated, as well as channels for depth information.

Another important step before rendering is optimizing the scene with regard to rendering times. No matter how fast the performance for hardware and computing grows, the visual demands on computer graphics imagery increase at least as fast and therewith the complexity of the scenes as well. One single frame, which is one 24th of a second, may take several hours of rendering time, and with increasing complexity it can even take longer. The calculation of images is usually transferred to computer networks optimized for this purpose, so-called render farms.

Final image from "Where Do All the Lost Things Go" (2011) by Hafizah Abdul Wahid, Joan Hsu Sze Yun, Kanan Abdul Kader Mohammad Ali, Bernard Su Guo Hao; School of Art, Design and Media, Nanyang Technological University, Singapore.

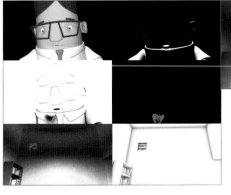

Various render layers and passes for the short film "Color Theory" (2010) by Davier Yoon, School of Art, Design and Media, Nanyang Technological University, Singapore.

Various surface structures in the 3D short film "Ride Of Passage" (2011) by Christian Bøving Andersen, Casper Michelsen, Tina Lykke Thorn, Søren Nørbæk, Allan Vadskær Lønskov, Eva Lee Wallberg, Jochen Kousholt, David Frylund Otzen; The Animation Workshop, Denmark.

A Look Beyond the Core Steps of the 3D Pipeline

The following areas and disciplines complement the 3D animation pipeline or are closely linked with it.

Motion and Performance Capture

Motion Capture is the process of capturing the motions of actors and converting this data into three-dimensional information, which is entered into 3D animation software. The movement information is then adapted to the 3D characters by motion editors and further refined by animators. This process is mainly used for realistic movements of humanoid digital characters in action and sports games as well as in VFX productions.

The term performance capture is used when facial expressions and countenance are captured in addition to body movements, thus placing the emphasis on theatrical presentation. This approach was used in films such as "Avatar" (2009) and the remakes of the "Planet of the Apes" series 2011, 2014 and 2017.

Stereoscopy – „3D" in the movie theater

Each of our two eyes perceives a slightly displaced image from which the brain calculates spatial information. In the movie theater, the stereoscopic projection simulates depth, although the screen displays only two-dimensional images. We are actually shown two superimposed images, which are assigned to each eye with the help of glasses.

This means that when filming for "stereo" all images will have to be shot twice (2 cameras mounted next to each other), as for example in "Avatar" (2009), "Hugo" (2011) and "The Young and Prodigious T.S. Spivet" (2013). However, since stereoscopic film shoots are still very demanding, a simpler method is chosen for many films: 3D conversion. The film is shot in "2D" with only one camera, i.e., only a "flat" image is created, then separated into depth layers and processed in post-production to be projected for two eyes. This process, however, does not always lead to convincing results, as in the films "Clash of the Titans" (2010) and "Alice in Wonderland" (2010), which were criticized for their 3D stereo conversion.

3D animation has a clear advantage in creating stereoscopic films: The work steps of the animation production allow for clear planning of the sequences and a coordination of the very important depth information from scene to scene. Even in the layout process, a virtual stereo camera can be created, which runs alongside and is tested in the subsequent stages. At the end of the pipeline, two separate images for each eye are rendered instead of one. The success of stereoscopic animation can be measured in the fact that for some years now, all major 3D animation film productions are created in stereo.

Characters from "Ride Of Passage" (2011) by Christian Bøving Andersen, Casper Michelsen, Tina Lykke Thorn, Søren Nørbæk, Allan Vadskær Lønskov, Eva Lee Wallberg, Jochen Kousholt, David Frylund Otzen; The Animation Workshop, Denmark.

Image from the animated film "Load" (2011) by David Rene Christensen, Lasse Smith, Jeppe Broo Døcker, Mark Kjærgaard, Kristoffer W. Mikkelsen, Blake Overgaard and Malte Burup; The Animation Workshop, Denmark.

Games and Interactive Applications

The creation of 3D models, textures and animations for real-time applications takes place with the same tools and principles as for pre-rendered films, however, their optimization to the respective game engine and a representation with a high frame rate takes top priority. Factors influencing the frame rate are, for example, the number of polygons and lights, the size of the textures, as well as the complexity of animations, effects, simulations, etc., in short: everything that loads onto the console or computer memory. For the game artist, it is also important to work closely with the designers and programmers of the game to ensure that the graphics are prepared to meet the requirements of the interactions and game logic.

Set made of cardboard and "real" hand-crafted materials (top left), 3D characters and 3D props for the foreground (upper right) and final composited image (bottom) from "Rob 'n Ron" (2013) by Magnus Igland Møller and Peter Smith; Tumblehead Animation Studio, Denmark.

Compositing

Although compositing is one of the 2D digital disciplines, it is an important step at the end of the animation and VFX pipeline, since this is where the results of the individual work steps merge into one image. The previously separately rendered elements of the 3D workflow are further processed in compositing and

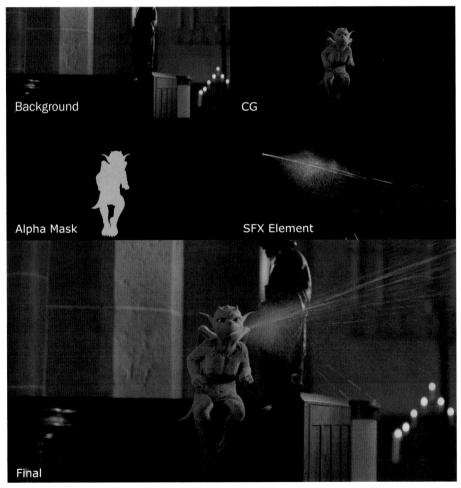

Live-action film and CG character elements for the movie "Sapphire Blue" (2014);
© Copyright mem-film, Lieblingsfilm, ARRI Film & TV, GFF, Tele München Gruppe.

merged into the final image. The image components or objects, which are separated by alpha channels (transparency masks), can be composited with one another and changed individually or together in color, brightness, contrast, etc.

Key aspects in VFX projects are the seamless integration of image sequences from live-action film shoots (often shot with a green or blue screen) with its digital elements such as set extensions and effects all the way to 3D characters.

In the next chapter we will learn more about the importance of 3D animation for visual effects productions in an interview with VFX supervisor Volker Engel.

Assignment:

Create a short animation with a ball jumping through a small obstacle course.

- Use tutorials to familiarize yourself with the basic features of the animation software of your choice.
- Develop your idea for the animation and visualize it in sketches.
- Now make a ball and a simple set with floor, wall and a box as an obstacle.
- Put materials and textures on the objects.
- Where is the camera, is it moving? Define the scene layout.
- Animate the movements of the ball. Refer to the 12 principles of animation from the earlier chapters.
- Think about a lighting situation and how the animation can best be accentuated.
- Now it's time to render everything!

"For me, animation is the ultimate fundamental training for the elementary understanding of motion."

The German Oscar winner Volker Engel is certainly one of the most renowned visual effects experts worldwide: While still attending the animation film class with Professor Ade at the Kunstakademie Stuttgart (Stuttgart State Academy of Art and Design), he formed an artistic partnership with the German director Roland Emmerich, which continues to this day. Milestones of this partnership include the Academy Award winning VFX "Independence Day" (1996), followed by "Godzilla" (1998), "2012" (2009), "Anonymous" (2011), "White House Down" (2013) and "Independence Day: Resurgence" (2016).

To start with, a basic question about the connection between animation in general and visual effects (abbreviated as VFX below) in particular: If you think about the principles of animation: What are the areas where a fundamental knowledge of the principles of animation for VFX is important? And how important is it, or where does it become important? VFX is actually an umbrella term, which includes many different disciplines.

Of course, even computer animation is already an umbrella term, because almost everything we do today - actually 100 percent now - is completely digital. With each project I get the question whether we also worked with miniature models. But unfortunately, this is usually not feasible due to high costs. In this respect, the digital domain predominates today. But everything that is done in this area can be called animation, strictly speaking. And this is where the animation principles come into play as well. This area includes, for example, computer-animated creatures, such as the animation of animals. The films we have recently made, such as "2012" (Emmerich 2012), "Anonymous" (Emmerich 2011) and "White House Down" (Emmerich 2013) again show different examples of animation. In each film, it was always about the fact that everything was photo-realistic.

These were all films by Roland Emmerich and they include more animations of objects, such as helicopters and airplanes. With "Independence Day: Resurgence" I recently finished another project with him. This is the continuation to the original "Independence Day" (Emmerich 1996). There are, of course, aliens, and they are computer-animated. And here we are already in the field of creature animation (= mythical, fictional creatures; author's note), because only a part was solved with motion capture, and a large part was still animated by hand. And even motion capture is always partially animated by hand. Therefore, a large part of the animation in the film will come from various areas. This is where I work as a supervisor with artists who need an understanding of the various areas of animation "White House Down" is a good example of a movie where you would never think that an animation supervisor was needed. My colleague Marc Weigert and I hired twelve different visual effects companies for the film, and our company "Uncharted Territory" was the hub. Everything came together at our place and we did the complete quality control and supervision. We had a modeling supervisor who checked all the CG models, rendering and shading the companies delivered. Our CG supervisor then discussed with the companies, which methods to use to improve these models. We also had an animation supervisor, Conrad Murrey, from Cape Town, with whom we have been working for a very long time.

Volker Engel in a miniature cave built by New Deal Studios in Los Angeles for the adventure film "Coronado" (2003), directed by: Claudio Fäh. The film was written by Volker Engel with his artistic partner Marc Weigert, co-produced and supervised as a VFX supervisor team.

Miniature of a bridge, built by New Deal Studios in Los Angeles for "Coronado".

Conrad already started working on the pre-visualization. We did the previz (abbreviation for previsualization; author's note) for "White House Down" in our company. A good example is the car chase, where two SUVs chase the presidential limousine around the White House. We put together an interesting mix. We used a video game engine and linked it to the "Motion Builder" software. For this, I needed somebody who was familiar with animation. We tried to automate as much as possible, and in doing so, we were able to sit there with a steering wheel of a videogame and simulate this car chase. But that was only the basis and it had to be worked out later. During this process, I constantly worked with the animation supervisor. And that was also very important for the animated shots delivered by the other companies. For example, we have a lot of helicopter sequences. You may think: Oh well, a helicopter flies from right to left, what's the big deal - but we were showing incredibly difficult maneuvers in the film: A helicopter is shot, begins to swerve, while another one just outside the White House flies upwards, is almost hit by the first one, swaying to the side. And then we received the first animation tests from very well established companies, which were by far not as good as we needed them to be. They also have their animators, of course. We then realized: Unfortunately, they don't have as good an animator like our Conrad Murrey in their company. And Conrad is the one with us who is working on these shots and finally delivers the better version, after these companies were not able to deliver good quality all the way to the end.

In other words, the previz already goes so far as to give an impression of the movement dynamics?

Yes. The important thing in such an action movie is, above all, that our previz is used for editing. Because editing runs parallel to the film shoot. Think of the aerial photographs in which you see the White House: These are all shots that we can not actually make because the airspace above the White House in Washington is a no-fly zone. So we had to produce most of the large outside shots of the White House completely digitally. They include not only Washington and the White House, but also these exciting helicopter flights and movements. In the example which I have just mentioned, there were three helicopters in the air. It was planned like a martial choreography. Conrad completely animated this one time from A to Z. We then go through it together with the director and he comments on it. For example: Yes, I know that this one has to get away now, because the other one is coming towards him. But that looks too much like a miniature model, which is much too fast, it has to be heavier and so on. This results in completely new aspects: Okay, then we have to keep one helicopter here just a little longer and it can turn away to the side later. But then, suddenly your close-up shot on the second helicopter does not work anymore, because it would be covered up by the first helicopter the entire time. And then you discuss it again with the director, because that has an effect on the editing he has planned for this sequence. We completely run through the animation once from a neutral angle with these hard-surface objects - in this case the helicopters - for about one minute of the film. Then the director goes over his cameras with us and comments: This is where I can envision the following, over there I would like to see the helicopter from this angle, back here I want to see it from there - in the end, exactly how you actually shoot a live-action movie. At one time, this was not done in previz, because it was time-consuming to render, they only did shot-by-shot previz. Today we do it differently: We design the action once completely - in previz - and then place three or four different cameras. From this we can then select the appropriate shots and, of course, change other things as well.

And this animation, how exactly is it created? You had already mentioned that it was based in part on a game engine.
We only did this for the car chase.

That means, the other is animated with key frames?
Exactly, one hundred percent.

Then, of course, for the previz stage, you definitely need someone who knows something about animation, otherwise it does not work at all.
Exactly. And previz transitions very smoothly into post-viz. Post-viz differs from previz in that the material, which was shot with the actors on the set with the blue screen, goes back to our artists. Let's take our protagonist, Channing Tatum. He runs on top of the roof because the terrorists are shooting at the helicopters with rocket launchers from the roof of the White House. He has a gun with him and tries to eliminate the terrorists, to prevent them from following through with their plan. With Channing we shot in a studio in front of a blue screen - we had a complete replica of the White House roof. But we did not have the animated helicopters in the background yet. In putting it all together, we worked with an interesting technique called Ncam - the letter N and cam for camera. With this technology, we can combine the blue screen shot live with our previz backgrounds created on the computer. The director was able to review during the film shoot on the set, what

the background image would later look like instead of the blue screen. This was tracked live the entire time, a fantastic system. We are not yet able to use a previously animated version of a helicopter together with the animated backgrounds. But I feel that this will be possible soon. To summarize it: The scene is shot in the studio against a blue screen, Channing comes running onto the rooftop, and he now thankfully has buildings and landscape in the background instead of a blue wall, which should not be too detailed, so that they can be calculated live. The filmed shot is immediately returned to our artists in post-viz. And we are working closely with the editor, who already uses our material for film editing. So the director can see immediately if the scene is working. After the film shoot, we continue to work in Los Angeles. Our animation supervisor, who himself is animating on the computer as well, is already building the helicopters into the shots. This raw form of the shot is immediately given to the editor, who then incorporates it into the cut, otherwise you would see only one actor now looking into the blue sky. Instead, the editor has to be able to apply the cut to Conrad's helicopters. And Conrad would now certainly add that he had to make 15 different versions of the shot, before everything was working 100%, because there were always corrections being made.

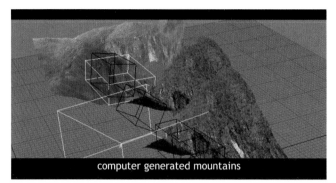

computer generated mountains

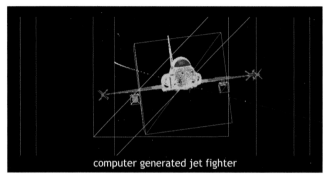

computer generated jet fighter

composite with mountains

Development of a scene from "Coronado" (2003).
Above and center are individual elements of the shot that were generated on the computer.
At the bottom is the final film image created by compositing (the virtual "putting together") of the elements.

Getting back to something I think is important with regard to motion capture: What is your position or experience with regard to the extent to which motion capture has to be post-processed nowadays? It seems logical to me that you need an experienced animator, but how is it balanced? What is the relationship between what you receive as raw data that still requires clean-up, and what still needs to be manipulated with regard to key frames?

It always depends on the task and what you are doing, how much, for example, the animated character differs from a human body. If you are dealing with a creature, for example, you will certainly have to change a lot of things: For example, if the character has six arms and looks completely different than a human being. If you just have a motion capture scene with a person moving normally, it looks different. We also made our own motion capture for "White House Down". (Although everyone always tells us that there are giant archives for motion capture data available. But for some reason, you can never find what you need). And you actually do not have to change very much.

It probably really depends on the shot, on how well the actor can be seen in the image and so on.

Yes.

If you now think of the training, how much should the knowledge of animation principles in itself be a component of the visual effects training?

3D computer animation

Image left und below: Computer animation compared to film image from "Coronado" (2003).

For me, animation is the ultimate fundamental training for the elementary understanding of motion. We encounter it in all visual effects areas. As a supervisor, I have been in charge of many films where a lot of destruction had to be animated. For example, in "2012", we had an aircraft carrier that comes rolling toward you, as the jetfighters on it are tearing away from fastening chains. The complete shot was animated by hand. Of course, the water in which the aircraft carrier floats is created by procedural animation. The White House is mowed down by the aircraft carrier, and anyone who worked on this shot has an incredible understanding of animation. And even the earthquake sequences, which we made at our company "Uncharted Territory" (a total of 400 shots for the film) use animation: For the part where the limo drives through Los Angeles, while everything to the left and right of it is collapsing, we used a software for procedural animation. However, it also caused some problems. While everything collapsed as it would happen in live-action, it happened either too fast or too slow for the scene. So we had to intervene and animate everything around it. That might not sound like a big challenge for an animator who wants nothing more than to animate

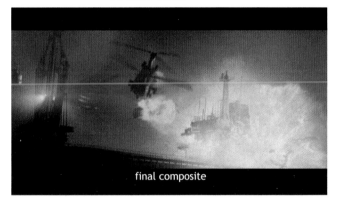

final composite

characters, for example. But continents that are breaking away, collapsing billboards and crashing freeways with cars sliding and rolling over - these are just different types of challenges! Much of this had to be animated by hand. And I worked on it with a lot of artists. Of course, not everyone has the same talents, and we certainly had our superstars for the animation. We naturally gave them the coolest shots. During this work, we also had to develop completely new skills and we virtually reinvented ourselves and our way of working.

A computer-generated Osprey helicopter flying through a real waterfall in "Coronado" (2003). The Mayan statues on both sides were digital stills of miniatures, the sea spray was achieved by using particle effects.

Regarding procedural techniques or simulation: Does the use of such techniques shift the discipline to engineering or programming? Where do you see the future trend? Will it increase, in other words, will the simulation process be somehow more artistically controllable? And will the programming become part of the training for artists working in that field? In essence, the balance between a basically digital, but still "handmade" key frame animation and that, which takes place more in processes or in simulations.

I have observed that many young people with an animation background who began working a lot with simulations, had a natural fear of the software they were working with. (laughing). My point is, that there is good news, namely, that it is getting easier for the animator to be able to use his skills - and I don't want to make it sound too easy now - in the end, by moving the correct control. He can rely on his creative instincts and does not suddenly have to encode and program a lot of things.

In other words, the trend is that the software itself is becoming a bit more intuitive and thus more user-friendly for the artist.

Exactly.

... and that the knowledge of programming per se is not a must, but a purely technical aspect that takes place more behind the user interface so that the artist can concentrate on the implementation of the artistic vision.

Yes, as with many other computer programs. They are becoming more user-friendly. You can get an artist to create something, rather than a mathematician! Because the mathematician will only provide you with something that looks absolutely terrible and has nothing to do with reality. And he will also explain to you that the computer calculated it exactly this way. It is best to have someone who basically has two heads on his shoulders, the artistic one and the mathematical one. That is how it used to be. But this is moving increasingly into the artistic world. And these are the good news.

When talking with people from the industry sector, it is apparent that they are looking for graduates who can also write their own code, their own small plug-ins for programs. I mean, ok, one does not have to exclude the other, but as an instructor you are faced with the question: Should we really push for this hybrid of artist and programmer so that someone can really, as you said, "basically have two heads on their shoulders"... in order to really merge these two things well and be equipped with both qualifications. Or could it be that the software will evolve in such a way that it becomes easier and more intuitive to use, and in turn benefit the artistic vision as well?

I think it is a slowly ascending curve. The purely technical aspect will become less important. And we continue to have people on the team (mostly in leading positions), who also write a plug-in, if needed. They write the plug-ins in such a way that it is usable for all those who can not program it. In a group of, say, seven animators, you have two who can help out and find a shortcut for something that is currently not really possible. We've seen something like this for "2012" with one of the big companies

here in Los Angeles: They were working a lot with so-called "proprietary software", i.e. an in-house development, rather than a software that was readily available off the shelf. We realized that one scene was not working very well with the in-house software: If a ship was thrown a bit to the right, for example, you completely lost the scale, and that had to be adapted somehow. To do this, the artist sat down on his keyboard and began to write. And then we thought of course: This can't be for real! He really has to program the numerical code (laughing) somehow, just to change a movement from right to left. After a while we figured out that the company was working with a dinosaur (with regard to software) at that time. But that was eight years ago. There have been so many changes since then. Sometimes these giant companies really lag behind.

Because they are just not as flexible.
Exactly, because they have developed their own products that were very expensive. An upgrade costs a lot of money again and has to be approved, because there will be 700 artists working with it in the end. You can't just say, hey, let's just quickly get this software.

A film image from Volker Engel's student short film "Re-Creation" (1993), about a mechanical "Circle of Life", animated to waltz music.
Produced at the Film Academy Baden Württemberg.

It took Volker Engel eight weeks to animate seven robots on rotating platforms for his four-minute short film.

And perhaps as a final question. I fondly remember your own film, your student film at the time, about the principles of animation. And in that respect you have always been very familiar with the classic principles of animation and have been very interested in the topic. The question would be: With all these classic principles - squash and stretch, anticipation, and everything that goes with that - do you think that new things have now been added by CG, computer animation as a whole, or things that might have to be looked at differently today, or extended terms, as far as that is concerned? Or do you believe that much of it has remained valid. Has it expanded, broadened or changed in any way?

The animation and all the classic rules of animation are certainly made easier with today's software packages. But I still have to work with people who learned all these basics. They need to know that these basics are important, and they must know the software very well to fully benefit from it. But there are hosts of untrained "animators" who may have purchased a software to try. After three weeks, these "animators" sometimes call themselves "visual effects supervisor" of their own company, because they made one small film. Something else that's very popular, is when they come to us and expect to be lead animator on a scene, and then it turns out that even working as an assistant for the animation, as third animator in the background, so to speak, they are clueless about the subject matter. That's the old story of a basic training, and as our distinguished professor Grau used to say at the State Academy of the Arts Stuttgart at the time: Before you start with abstract painting, you should have learned the basic rules of painting. (Laughing) And then you can move away from it. And in my view, this is exactly the same thing for animation. This basic knowledge as part of this training is so incredibly important for developing an understanding of movement patterns, rhythms and movement in nature. Otherwise, people animate things that just look completely wrong. Then you ask them: Why do you think that this would move this way in nature? And that's simply because they have never developed an eye for it and basically walked through life with blinders, or perhaps because they just played too many videogames.

And of course, my question certainly lumped everything together, but all these different principles have to be applied in very different ways, depending on the style which is required later. The ideal goal of visual effects is, that it actually remains "invisible" itself in most cases. The rendered images must be credibly inserted into live-action happenings. A very high degree of credibility must be achieved, and there is certainly a very broad spectrum. But much of what established the principles of animation comes from the observation of reality and is then only exaggerated or inflated.

Yes.

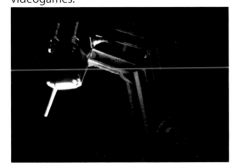

The "conductor" robot from "Re-Creation".

Volker Engel working on the "showdown scene": the 35mm Crass camera on the left and the video tab with Betacam SP deck on the right.

There is probably a big difference whether you're integrating a mythical creature into a real-world environment, where you might have more freedom as an animator - relatively speaking, although it must be credible - as compared to a purely physical-mechanical effect, which has to be incorporated into a real event.

Yes, it certainly requires more creativity when you are moving around this "creature terrain". But you'd be surprised how many artists don't manage to get a heavy vehicle driving around a fountain very quickly while swerving, due to a lack of basic training and a lack of basic knowledge. And we in turn - getting back to the example - are very fortunate to have an artist who was born to do that. We don't have to worry about whether or not he can do it. Another example on this topic is the knowledge of cinematography when working in a completely virtual space. Unless we pre-set everything precisely in previz, we often get to see camera movements that look like motion control, but in a way as if they had actually been programmed by a robot. Our catchphrase in those instances is always: This has to be more organic - which really means nothing more than: There have to be small mistakes in it! They must correspond to the movement of the helicopter, inside of which the camera is located. And this is something that no one in the audience would notice afterwards, but if it is done right, it leads to the fact that everyone thinks that it was filmed "100% real".

This goes back to the basics, that you have someone paying attention to such fundamental matters as timing and spacing. You simply have to make sure that there are also breaks in it and that irregularities are integrated, simply to avoid this "mechanical" impression so that it does not look so uniformly.

You have to place your key frames correctly, and this is done 100% manually. And I tell Conrad to imagine this with a small camera shake, which has to be integrated somehow, and that can't be done with the push of a button, which brings us back to the subject organic/real. Conrad has the appropriate knowledge and thus he has a sense of how far he has to go with it, so that it does not turn out ten times too strong and looking artificial again.

Okay, and as a real conclusion now, maybe a few words about what you think someone should focus on during their training, who wants to work in the field of VFX. It is, of course, impossible to answer this entirely across the board. VFX is the umbrella term for a very broad and diverse field, including compositing, digital matte painting, particle systems, match move and previz, which is a very big topic, of course. But if you were to try to simplify this for someone who is interested in the field of VFX as a newcomer: What would be the training areas that you would recommend as a good basis for future employment?

You should know early on, which direction you want to take. Due to their diverse nature, the requirements are becoming increasingly specialized. And the key distinction for us in the visual effects area are still computer animations on one hand, and compositing on the other. And even if you study to become a 2D artist, whether it is in the field of matte painting or as a pure compositor - and there are incredibly talented people in this area - you will still need to have a basic knowledge in the area of 3D computer animation. Simply because you're constantly working with people from that field. Your items are delivered to you by 3D artists and you have to at least understand their language, even if you yourself can not work in 3D. The same is true the other way around as well. During the intensive specialization, which you should pursue relatively early in order not to work or train for four years in the wrong area, you should still keep 30 percent of your studies for the other topic in mind.

Okay, a very small addition to this one: For many of these areas there are very clear ideas about what skills someone could or should bring to the job. An area where, in my experience, this is rather diversified or where it can vary is, for example, digital matte painting. From my conversations with industry, I know this: For this area, for example, they like to hire great photographers, they also like to take people who are very talented digital illustrators - the training background often varies greatly. This seems to be an area where a big pool of talent must come together or one very unique talent with an expandable skill set for certain additional knowledge, which can then be acquired. In other words, if someone is a tremendous photographer, he can certainly qualify for this area just as much as a great digital illustrator.

You can come from another area and still fit in 100%. In addition, we always make sure that we get artists who have good common sense, and as strange as it may sound - a sense of reality. Especially when hiring young people directly after graduating, we have made the experience that they tend to lose sight of the time factor during work. They don't understand that three days can not turn into three weeks. There are deadlines and budgets that must be met. It is not very easy to find someone who can express himself artistically, and is nevertheless able to commit to a time frame.

Great, I believe this is a good conclusion. (laughing)

"There will be a different model of doing things"

Isaac Kerlow is an independent filmmaker, artist and author. The main focus of his work is best described by the terms "changes" and "nature of man". He is developing creative projects at the Earth Observatory of Singapore which are inspired by geological science and the prevention of natural disasters. Isaac was one of the leading pioneers of digital art and animation in the initial phase of the video game industry. He worked for the Walt Disney Company for a decade and was the founding chair of the legendary Department of Computer Graphics and Interactive Media at the Pratt Institute in New York City. Isaac was also the founding Dean at the School of Art, Design and Media at Nanyang Technological University in Singapore. His filmography includes the animation and live action films "The Tsunami of New Dreams" (2015), "SHADOWS" (2014), "Genesis" (2012), "Sudden Nature" (2011) and "Mayon: The Volcano Princess" (2010). His current work, "Earth Girl 2: Preparing for the Tsunami" (2014), is available as a free download. The animated short "CHANGE" followed in October 2016.

You have written a very well-known book about computer animation, namely...
The Art of 3D Computer Animation And Effects.

Exactly, and in this book, you have expanded the traditional principles of animation to additional rules, specifically for 3D computer animation. Can you tell us more about this?
Yes, in fact, it started when I was working at Disney Interactive and we were developing the first 3D computer game for Disney. We had a lot of discussions about how to transfer the traditional principles of animation to these relatively simple 3D characters - that was still in the early days of 3D games. We had some advisors from the traditional Feature Animation Department who said, of course: This is exactly the way you have to do it! Twelve principles - end of story. This prompted me to think about how we can modify and extend these traditional principles for 3D animation to incorporate these new art forms that did not yet exist in the 1930s and 1940s. These new artforms are quite different from the purely traditional character animation. They are similar in certain ways, but are also very different in others!

One of these additional points is **limited animation**. In the context of traditional hand-drawn character animation, frame-by-frame animation is one of the most obvious and fastest ways to achieve the classic Disney-style "illusion of life". Draw as much detail as possible, achieve as much subtlety as possible. This would already account for 30% of your "illusion of life", if you know how to do it. But then, at a 180 degree turn, there is the kind of animation for anime that for long was considered sort of an inferior standard: The anime style was simple partly to achieve faster and cheaper productions, but also had a different aesthetic feeling. Then, after several decades of anime study, some were beginning to realize that a whole new style had indeed developed for acting and expression that was based on a very economical way of drawing and painting. That is when I realized that limited animation had traditionally been considered a lesser style, but on the other hand there were many examples of limited animation that presented a unique style that creates emotion in a convincing manner. You watch these movies with limited animation, where there are 3, 4 or even 10 seconds of hold with maybe one very minimal movement at most, like the hair being moved by the wind. But anime is definitely a style, and Japanese animators finally came to the conclusion that they were able to build a powerful artistic style from their production limitations. And they have continued to develop this style over the past 30 years. Anime was exported from Japan and as you know, we are now all keenly aware of anime and Japanese animators. In Europe, the United States, Latin America, everywhere! And animators worldwide began developing this supposed limitation as a style: long holds; slow motion; partial animation of body parts, while others remain still; all things that would be considered mistakes in traditional animation, but which can actually be used to express emotion.

So I thought: 'why not introduce a new principle of animation that draws attention to it'? You can use stylistic means that use limited animation in a way that would not have been approved by the traditional Disney style of the 1940s. But this is 2014, we have a completely different world, and animation audiences too are quite different. This is the interesting thing about life in general - an absolute truth of the 50's, 60's or 70's, 40 years later, no longer holds true, because people and methods have evolved.

The Little Goddess in SHADOWS, directed by Isaac Kerlow, uses her superpowers to help the villagers defeat the villains who want to destroy the forest. http://shadows-film.com.
© Isaac Kerlow

The world has changed. So I thought of the young people who grew up with video games, watched TV cartoons, most of which is done with limited animation. They have not even seen the early Pixar films, only the last, most recent ones. And for that generation, limited animation is quite normal. That's how it is. I believe that limited animation is a legitimate technique that can be used to enhance the expression of your animation.

Another aspect that I thought was worth mentioning is **cinematography**, particularly camera work. In the old days, there was a real and rigid separation between layout, camera and animation. These were very different stages, which took place at different times throughout the process. But today cinematography is considered at the very beginning of a production, and it changes during the course of production as you animate the character(s). That's why I thought it was important to bring together the artistic language of film and animation. That's why I felt that it was important to teach young people that it was not only about the performance of the character, which is, of course, the most important thing, but just as much about cinematography, about how you shoot and show the performance. Today, these two aspects are integral parts of the process, and I felt that

there should be a principle that highlighted this concept not just as an after-thought.

Facial animation is just one aspect of acting, but the traditional Disney perspective is more focused on the body's poses and silhouettes, and facial animation was not discussed very explicitly. Today we have the option of animating extreme close-ups of the face with enormous precision. In 3D animation we have software that allows us to literally control every single muscle in the face, and that is why facial animation became an extremely important way to tell a story. And I felt that it should be raised to the level of another principle of animation, because today, so much is communicated in films through facial expressions. When you compare today's films with those of 60 years ago there is a considerable difference in the number of close-ups and facial expressions that are crucial to acting. Emotions and facial micro-expressions, minimal changes in expression, are very popular in today's computer animation. It is important that young animators are at least aware of these things, that they know what options are available to them, and that they use them if they want.

Perpetual Motion is an animated short directed by Isaac Kerlow about the dynamic nature of planet Earth and human societies. This rendering test of orbiting trash is based on concept art by Victor Kerlow, modeling by Batrisya Nurul, and visual development by Mark Cheung.
© Isaac Kerlow

Blending Motion is a concept that did not exist before 2005. Motion capture has been around for 20 years, but for many years it was an imperfect, awkward and mechanical-looking technology. After two decades of motion capture, someone had the idea of the blending motion process, and today you can work with blending motion in a very sophisticated and controlled manner. So much so, that one can use the presentation of an actor to move a digital character, comparable to a puppeteer, and combine or refine it with key frame animation. This unique blend is so sophisticated that it has to be regarded as a separate technology. When I wrote about this ten years ago, it was on the verge of becoming reality. Blending motion still has limitations but today this technique is a reality, and widely used in computer games that incorporate a huge amount of character information. This animation does not look like classic Disney character animation but many of the characters in the top games have now reached a very acceptable level of acting, especially when you consider the number and range of genres and styles. And the only way to produce these games within schedule and with so many characters and such subtlety of animation is by using blended motion, and combining it with key frame animation and some motion capture. This has already become a specialized craft in itself.

This ties in nicely with the question about motion capture and how this technology is gaining importance. Do you think that in the future there will be a point, where basically the art of animation is replaced by the performance of an actor and the resulting actions that are transferred to digital characters?

I do not believe that the performance of an actor will fully replace the art of hand-drawn animation because they are two entirely different things. But it can certainly support or complement it. For me, this is like the difference between playing an acoustic guitar or an electric guitar. Both are guitars, but they sound different and you have to play them differently. I believe that the traditional key frame animation will always remain its own domain and that it will continue to evolve. But motion capture has also advanced enormously over the past 30 years and since then we have actually been able to implement things that we would never have thought possible. But I don't believe that motion capture can ever replace key frame animation, they are simply different approaches to animation. However, for certain projects motion capture offers a straightforward and feasible way to animate a large sets of characters for computer games - no question! For example, at Disney we produced baseball and football games for the ESPN brand. Producing those sport games with key frame animation was out of the question, because of the expense and effort involved. So you shoot the movements of the live-action baseball players on a soundstage and a few months later you have a game with appropriate motion. In other words, performance capture also serves the purpose of efficient production.

An isolated boy playing computer games is used to represent human alienation from nature in CHANGE, a short film by Isaac Kerlow about climate and anthropogenic change. https://art-science-media.com/change
© Isaac Kerlow

You mentioned one more additional principle?

Yes, **visual styling**. Today you can use, for example, all kinds of shaders and rendering techniques to achieve very unique and very expressive and artistic visual styles that contribute to the expressiveness of the medium. Unlike decades ago you can visualize the "look" of the finished animation before the animation is completed. This contributes to the power of your production at a basic level. We now have the ability to combine multiple visual elements with digital compositing, even on a laptop using commercial software such as Photoshop. That opened doors for many young people to try out completely new visual styles. This would have been impossible in the past, too much work, you would have needed a whole studio to get that done. I think that digital technology has brought all the production stages of animation closer together in time, you no longer have to wait 16 months between storyboarding and final rendering. You can storyboard and render in paralell. It's a different way of working. That is why I believe that we need the new principle of visual styling to reflect this changed reality.

There is not very much stylized, non-photorealistic rendering. What are the trends, how will it develop? What do you think about the current visual styles in CG-animated mainstream feature films?

In less than 30 years, rendering has been transformed from a cumbersome and barely controllable technology into an extremely sophisticated field. Today, you can render almost anything you want. It may require a complex production pipeline, but once in place, you can render almost anything convincingly, if you know how. Just think of mainstream studios like DreamWorks, Pixar, Disney, ILM, where you'll find highly sophisticated rendering solutions that combine stylized realism with painterly techniques. For example, I find "Rango" (Verbinski 2011), very interesting, because this film represents a kind of experiment. It combines realistic aspects with stylized painterly solutions. It is also unique as an animation, since it is not comparable to anything else in terms of story and animation. In "Kung Fu Panda" (Osborne/Stevenson 2008), for example, there are parts that are rendered realistically, in a classical and traditional way, and then there are small details, where that is not the case. If you look at the world of independent CG productions, you'll find even more adventurous rendering techniques. But the studios are very sophisticated and they have some incredible solutions that combine the realistic with the painterly. This aspect of CG is technically complex, and it takes quite an effort to develop this type of software. Many of the small independent productions opt for more modest rendering solutions, but that is beginning to change. There are student projects, from Germany for example, with incredibly complex and highly sophisticated rendering techniques. When I see a group of 25-year-olds coming up with these solutions, whether realistic or stylized, it tells me that the next generation of animators will be different from the previous one. These young people will be able to do more and more on their laptops. I think that's great. This opens up completely new perspectives.

What do you think a young animator should focus on nowadays? What remains important, what has changed?

I think the most important thing is and remains being familiar with the masterpieces of art, design, film and animation. This means getting acquainted with painters of the 19th or 20th century, for example, or reading literature from all over the world, from different centuries, whether from Europe, China or whatever. This is a great challenge and opportunity. Today, for example, I asked a gifted illustrator in my team whether she knew the German expressionists. She looked at me and said 'no'. I said, 'really? Have you ever heard of George Grosz?' 'No.' 'Do you know the work of Käthe Kollwitz?' 'No.' This conversation was inspired by a story in which a mother protects her child, and I thought of the classic drawings by Käthe Kollwitz. And when she said 'no', I thought, gee whiz, I really have an edge over her, just because I spent hours of my life looking at these drawings and thinking about them. Her drawing skills are excellent, but she is not aware of important works of art that can make her work better. The most important

thing young animators can do, is to gain access to the work of artists from all ages from all over the world, no matter where they come from, both in visual art and literature, since animation is about both. That is why it is very important to read poems, short stories, novels, the classics! The craft is also very important, but as a director you must know and understand the major themes of human existence. It is good to begin with it in your twenties, because sometimes it takes time to understand these topics and to master them. Otherwise, if you do not pay attention to those deep artistic literature issues, you are going to be limited to be a craftsman, and that is okay, but is not what most young people aspire to be. Most young people aspire to have the craft under their belt but also be able to tell their stories and represent their generation. So I would say, go to museums and read books. Even if you end up reading books on the iPad or look at the virtual collection of the Metropolitan Museum online - that's fine too. But you literally have to devote hours, days, weeks to it. I hope today young animators of today understand how important this really is.

Animated with a contemporary digital version of Indonesian cutout puppets, the Old Leader of the villains fights the Little Goddess in SHADOWS, a short by Isaac Kerlow. http://shadows-film.com.
© Isaac Kerlow

The bittersweet ending of CHANGE brings up the need to balance thriving human communities with a healthy natural environment. Artwork and animation by Nguyen Thi Nam Phuong and Jenevieve Ho, directed by Isaac Kerlow. https://art-science-media.com/change
© Isaac Kerlow

On to a very different topic: Convergence between live action and animation: We are very close to the point where the dividing line between these fields is barely distinguishable anymore, so it has disappeared in a way. Many Hollywood blockbusters do combine virtual sets and "real" actors" or integrate digitally created and animated characters into live action.It would be great to hear some of your thoughts about this: an outlook toward the future, how this can possibly further develop and what is happening now, what are the trends and where is that going?

That's a good question. I can think of several things. For one thing, I love watching blockbusters, because many of them are very entertaining. But also with regard to the artistic craftsmanship, the quality of the animation is sometimes really breathtaking. I love and admire good craftsmanship. And viewed from this perspective, I think that some of these accomplishments are wonderful. With the help of visual effects, you can now more than ever blur the boundaries between reality and fiction, create original worlds, and that is remarkable. Studios in Hollywood and elsewhere realize this and that is why they continue this approach. I think visual effects have developed so strongly over the last decade because studios realize that thanks to them they can earn billions of dollars within a few years. That is unlikely to change anytime soon. But this kind of work was not always interesting to me from the creative point of view. These big-budget blockbuster movies jam-packed with effects were in fact one of the reasons why I loved working at Disney, precisely because I could contribute to the process. But this was not always a challenge in the artistic sense. I always wondered how, for example, an independent film would look with this level of technology. I recently saw "Guardians of the Galaxy" (Gunn 2014).

Which is a pretty funny movie.

Yes, it's very amusing and the characters are unique, especially for this type of film. This Hollywood studio film is admirable, and many of my friends earn their livelihood with productions like this. But what if a young director wanted to shoot a film with a small team that blurred or completely eliminated the boundaries between reality and illusion? This seems impossible at the moment. I look forward to the time in a few decades when a truly independent filmmaker can fully realize the benefits of these technologies in a true independent production. Because otherwise, we will keep watching the same kind of film. These films are fun and nice to watch, but they represent only a small portion of the films we should actually be making. I would love to see what independent filmmakers would do with advanced high-end VFX technologies, once they are adapted to their means. This is not quite happening yet, even though we have excellent small "indie" productions today with great but scaled down visual effects.

I am also certain that big studios will try new stylistic approaches on a large scale. I can not predict exactly when this will happen, but something similar already happened with American cinema in the 60s and 70s. Suddenly big Hollywood studios were taking big stylistic risks to seize on the changes in technology and the viewing habits of the new audiences. I believe that what studios like DreamWorks, Pixar, Disney, Sony and Fox are doing now, is like milking a cow: Stylistically, the expectations of the audience are met and this works commercially. The look and sentiment of these films are similar, they are funny, there is some melodrama, a lot of comedy and large audiences love these films. Well. This reminds me of the Hollywood of the 30s and 40s, the Hollywood that collapsed because the old styles were not able to reflect the new realities. And films like "Easy Rider" and other films in the 1960s, and the French New Wave, all helped Hollywood to reinvent itself entirely. I cannot wait to see that. I imagine it will happen in many different types of ways, and I think it is going to happen in the most unexpected way. And that is exactly what I would like to see soon. I believe that this will happen in many different forms, and I also believe that it can happen in very unexpected ways. I would be excited to see this, because for me it would use all the technology developed since the 80s to end the first artistic chapter of 3D computer animation and then create something completely new, something that no one expected when it all started. You can already feel some of it happening in some of the games today. Today's high-end games are very interesting. It is impressive what they can achieve in a short production time. I believe this is proof that there will be a new way of doing things, for example, like using mobile phones for filming. Making a film with one tenth of the team, with one tenth of the budget and reach an audience comparable to today's blockbusters. I'm eagerly waiting for that to happen. It will be very exciting. And this will be implemented by the generation of today's 20-year-old "kids". We can help develop this "new something", and I am curious to see what the outcome will be.

Glossary

Animatic
A filmed version of the storyboard that combines storyboard drawings with limited animation and camera movements to get an impression of the final film. For this purpose, a preliminary version of the soundtrack and sound effects are added as well.
More in chapter 1.1) Script and Storyboarding.

Animation Handout
In traditional animation, it refers to a "package" consisting of storyboard, layout, dialog sheet and directional instructions, which the animator receives from the director.
More in chapter 2.2) Animated Cartoon.

Animation Pass
Repeated trials to improve animation. Each time a better version should emerge, building from the results of the previous one.

Animatronic
Puppets equipped with electronic interior life, which can be moved via motors in real time (in contrast to the single-frame technique used with animated stop-motion puppets).

Anticipation
Most movements are preceded by a preparatory movement (anticipation); good example: The golfer's backswing prior to hitting the ball. The extent of this anticipation must be scaled according to the intensity of the movement that follows.

Appeal
The quality of the animation design and/or the design of a character should have a positive effect on the audience. The design must be convincing and coherent for the relevant style.

Arcs
Movements follow the pattern of a curved arc line:
Each movement follows its own arc, which must be checked in animation: "Watch your arcs!"

Armature
Physical "skeleton" of a puppet in puppet animation. May consist of metal rods connected with joints.
More in chapter 2.3) Stop Motion.

Aspect Ratio
Refers to the screen format.
More in chapter 1.1) Script and Storyboarding.

Augmented Reality
Changing the perception of reality by using computer-generated techniques, e.g., by integrating virtual objects into live-action environments.

Blending Motion
A special technique of **character animation** widely used in games and interactive applications, whereby movements, which are based on **key frame** animation or **motion capture** can be combined, and its main features can be identified and controlled.
More in chapter 2.4) Interview with Isaac Kerlow.

Blocking
Rough work up of timing, using just a few key frames. The term is mainly used for 3D computer animation and for stop motion. More information in the respective chapters.

Breakdown
The important or crucial in-between, which defines the path from key frame A to key frame B.
More in chapter 2.1) The Principles of Animation and their Application.

Briefing
Specific artistic and/or technical definition of the task.

Cartoony
Highly exaggerated and stylized form of animation and character design: The characters are heavily caricatured, and movements usually appear very **"snappy"**.

Change of Shape
Shape change as a principle of animation.
More in chapter 2.1) The Principles of Animation and their Application.

Character Animation
Animation, which aims to produce an emotionally convincing theatrical performance of sketched, constructed or virtual characters.

Claymation
Stop Motion using plasticine as a material.
More in chapter 2.3) Stop Motion.

Clean Plate
A "clean" shot of a background setting for VFX, that is, without the character, which is later to be added in as an animated figure or live-action actor.

Clean-Up
Refers to the finalized drawing created from the previous **rough animation** in traditional 2D animation, which is most commonly reduced to a simple black outline of lead or color pencil.
More in chapter 2.2) Traditional 2D Animation.

Close-Up
A shot is placing the camera near to a character or object, making it appear big on the screen. The shot of choice to show emotion (by focusing on details in a face) or to direct attention (by showcasing a specific detail).

Color Script
Depicts the dramatically motivated color sequence across the entire movie. Resembles a colored storyboard, but has a different function.
More in chapter 1.4)What is Production Design for Animation?

Comparison Sheet
Depicts the character design in size comparison.
More in chapter 1.3) Character Design

Compositing
Combining different image elements (e.g., live action background with 3D character) into a visually convincing and uniform frame.
More in chapter 2.4) Interview with Volker Engel.

Creature Animation
Realistic animation of real or mythical creatures in the area of VFX.
Digital creatures must be credibly inserted into a live-action filmed environment.
More in chapter 2.4) Interview with Volker Engel.

Cross Cutting
Back and forth cutting between two scenes or plot threads.
More in chapter 2.2) Traditional 2D Animation.

Cutout
Flat, two-dimensionally cutout character in traditional or digital animation.

Dialogue Sheet
A tabular analysis that breaks down the dialogue to correspond with the single-frame numbers in the film.

Down Shot
Camera shot from above, e.g. from an aerial perspective. Also often referred to as "high-angle shot".

Exaggeration
Animation should exaggerate: Merely copying the forms and timing of live-action films produces unsatisfactory results.

Exposure Sheet / X-Sheet
Spreadsheet of frames (counted as single frames) and animation drawings.
More in chapter 2.2) Traditional 2D Animation.

Extremes
The extreme key, anchor or turning points of a movement. Often used interchangeably with the term key frame. Some animation experts disagree (see key frames).
More in chapter 2.1) The Principles of Animation and their Application.

Fade Out / Fade In
Means gradually decreasing or increasing the visibility of the image over time.

Field Guide
Refers to a tool of the traditional 2D animation layout, which lets you specify the camera view in relation to specific paper formats. It also defines the distance between the peg bar and the respective camera field.
More in chapter 2.2) Traditional 2D Animation.

Finish Storyboards
A highly detailed *storyboard*, which is very similar to the final "look" of a film, often in color as well.

Follow Through
A special form of **overlapping action** (listed there as well), which refers to the continuous movement of flexible and loosely connected objects. In character animation, it pertains mostly to hair, cloaks, tails, etc.

Frame by Frame
Describes the filming technique for animation and is often considered a defining criterion for animation.

Gestural Drawing
Fast, sketchy drawing, which reduces the character to the essence of its pose. Hence, an ideal training tool for animation.
More in chapter 1.2) Figure Drawing for Storyboard and Animation.

Green Screen
A green screen in front of which, for example, stop-motion characters or actors may be filmed. The green background screen can be replaced later by **keying** with a virtual or live-action filmed background in **compositing.**
More in chapter 2.4) Interview with Volker Engel.

Hard-Surface Modeling
Modeling of objects with hard, smooth, non-organic surface structures: i.e. predominantly technical objects such as machines, spaceships, buildings.
More in chapter 2.4) Insight into 3D Computer Animation.

Hold / Moving Hold
Standstill of animation as key frame/minimally animated key frame.
More in chapter 2.1) The Principles of Animation and their Application.

Inbetweens
The drawings or generated frames that connect the key frames with each other.
More in chapter 2.1) The Principles of Animation and their Application.

Key Frame
A key parameter of a movement in which a movement either ends in a pose or carries out defining directional changes. Used to structure **timing** of the animation as well as a scene, and (in traditional 2D animation) to ensure the consistency of character representation. Richard Williams strictly limits the term key frame to a step of the animation that is critical to understanding the story (storytelling drawing). In this book, however, we use the term largely interchangeable with the term **extreme**. "Extreme" and "key frame" are often used congruently in other animation reference books as well. See also the interview with Andreas Deja for a deeper discussion of this topic.
More in chapter 2.1) The Principles of Animation and their Application.

Keying
Isolating image portions, e.g. background for certain visual features, such as chromaticity or luminance. This allows for these image portions to be replaced by other image elements.

Layout
A layout or 3D layout goes one step further than the storyboard, and precisely specifies field of view, camera movements and camera angles during a **shot**. Layouts provide the basis for the subsequent animation of the shots.
The 2D layout is created in a traditionally or digitally drawn form.
The 3D layout is created as **previsualization**: generally rendered as low-resolution

versions of the character models or even with rough geometric shapes as *"stand ins"* of the characters.
More in chapters 1.1) Script and Storyboarding and 2.4) Insight into 3D Computer Animation.

Leica Reel
A Leica Reel is a type of **animatic**, in which the shots throughout the production are replaced step-by-step by the latest version of the production: in 2D, the **storyboard** drawing is replaced by **rough animation**; rough animation is replaced by **clean-up**, clean-up is replaced by the final rendered/colored version. In 3D accordingly, storyboard is replaced by **previz**, previz by **playblast**, playblast by the final rendered version.
More in chapter 1.1) Script and Storyboarding.

Lighting
Virtual lighting in 3D computer animation.
More in chapter 2.4) Insight into 3D Computer Animation.

Ligne Claire
Comic style, the best known example:
"Tintin" by Hergé.
Caricatured representation of characters with uniform black outlines is combined with detailed realistic backgrounds.

Limited Animation
A concept that is mostly used for 2D animation. It uses three or more exposures per single drawing. For example, each drawing is held for six frames. It is also used for animation, in

which characters are only partly animated (e.g., where only the mouth moves).

Line of Action
Representation of one or several main directions of movement wthin a pose.
It helps to define the essence of movement(s) within the body.
More in chapter 1.2) Figure Drawing for Storyboard and Animation.

Line Test
Filmed version of **rough animation** in traditional 2D animation to assess any improvements needed for the animation.
More in chapter 2.2) Traditional 2D Animation.

Look
The appearance of a character or a virtual world.
More in chapter 1.4) What is Production Design for Animation?

Loop
An animation that works with a limited number of frames that can be repeated endlessly: After the last frame, the first one is repeated.
More in chapter 2.1) The Principles of Animation and their Application.

Match Cut
A cut that continues a movement precisely and without a break.
More in chapter 1.1) Script and Storyboarding.

Matte Painting
Today, mostly digitally created painting that creates the illusion of a live-action setting.

Can be implemented in 2D and 3D versions. In the 3D version, the painting is often projected onto three-dimensional geometric shapes.
More in chapter 2.4) Interview with Volker Engel.

Miniatures
Reduced in size and true to scale physical models used in live-action scenes, which were mainly used in VFX shots, but are now increasingly replaced by virtual sets.
More in chapter 2.4) Interview with Volker Engel.

Modeling
The modeling of digital objects and characters in 3D computer animation.
Virtual sculpture, for organic objects such as characters increasingly carried out with more intuitive software (e.g. ZBrush).
More in chapter 2.4) Insight into 3D Computer Animation.

Model Sheet
Particularly used in traditional 2D animation for depicting a character from different perspectives and in different actions and moods.
Helps the animator to understand the vision of the character designer correctly and to implement it accordingly - the character stays "on model".
Essential, in order to ensure consistency of character representation, even with different animators.
More in chapter 1.3) Character Design.

Momentum
Dynamics of movement.

Mood Board
Compilation of visual reference materials to narrow down the look of a project in **visual development**.

Motion Blur
Rendering out of focus to create the illusion of fast movement.

Motion Capture
The modern form of rotoscoping: The movements of real actors tagged with motion markers are filmed and transferred to digital characters, using special software.
More in chapter 2.4) Interview with Volker Engel.

Motion Control
Allows for programmed execution and exact repetition of camera movement, for example, to combine different image elements. Hence, an important technique for visual effects.
Also used to enable camera movements in single-frame takes for stop-motion shoots.
More in chapters 2.3) Stop Motion and 2.4) Interview with Volker Engel.

Non-Photorealistic Rendering (NPR)
Rendering techniques, which are not concerned with photo-realism, but with the representation of artistically imaginative textures. An example would be the digital conversion of watercolor or oil painting.

Outlines

The outlines of a character in traditional and digital 2D animation.

More in chapter 2.2) Traditional 2D Animation.

Overlapping Action and Follow Through

Because of their weight and physical nature, the stomach and arms, for example, move in different rhythms, thus overlapping in time. The same applies to loose appendages of the character's body: the blowing coat, hair or the tail of the squirrel etc. The bounce of these loose pieces is called **follow through.**

Pass

see Animation Pass

Peg Bar

A bar for animated films that is used to keep the stacked sheets of drawings in register.

More in chapter 2.2) Animated Cartoon.

Pipeline also Production Pipeline

The structured production flow of all forms of digital animation. Since combinations and hybridization of animation techniques have become increasingly complex, it has become an essential part of animation and it is widely used far beyond the conventional 3D computer animation.

More in chapter 2.4) Insight into 3D Computer Animation.

Pixilation

Special stop-motion technique, in which live-action actors are animated frame-by-frame.

More in chapter 2.3) Stop Motion.

Playblast

It is a preview film version of a computer-generated animation, which is accurate to frame but lacks the final **shading** and **rendering**. Effectively the digital version of **line tests** in traditional 2D animation, which enables the assessment of animation quality and any necessary corrections.

Pose

Posture of an animation character. Usually the key or end point of a movement and often exaggerated.

Post-Visualization, also Post-Viz

Analogous to **previz**, it is the post-processing of scenes shot with VFX, thus the combination of all the image elements in a uniformly appearing film sequence.

More in chapter 2.4) Interview with Volker Engel.

Pre-Production

Everything that precedes the actual production stage, i.e. for the most part script, storyboard, character design, production design and layout. There may also be some overlap with the actual production process.

Previsualization, also Previz

Basically another name for 3D layout that is used in the area of VFX in order to plan and simulate the subsequent shoot of elaborate and (sometimes) live-action scenes with special effects. By now an indispensable part of all complex VFX-based film productions.

More in chapter 2.4) and the interview with Volker Engel.

Principles of Animation

The original 12 principles of animation, as defined by Frank Thomas and Ollie Johnson in their book "Illusion of Life" (1995) and slightly expanded and modified for this manual.

More in chapter 2.1) The Principles of Animation and their Application.

1.) Timing
2.) Spacing
3.) Slow In und Slow Out (deceleration/acceleration)
4.) Straight Ahead and Pose-to-Pose Animation
5.) Overlapping Action, Follow-Through
6.) Secondary Action
7.) Anticipation
8.) Squash and Stretch
9.) Arcs
10.) Solid Drawing
11.) Exaggeration
12.) Weight
13.) Appeal and Strong Poses
14.) Staging
15.) Change of Shape
16.) Counter-Action

Procedural Animation

Computer animations generated by simulation.

More in chapter 2.4) Interview with Volker Engel.

Prop

Object that is part of the animated film world or something characters use.

Public Domain
Term for freely available artistic works where the copyright has expired.

Puppet Animation
Stop-motion technique, which uses built puppets, mostly combined with live-action built and illuminated miniature sets.

More in chapter 2.3) Stop Motion.

Reference Map
Compilation of visual references that influence the **visual development** of a project.

Rendering
The elaborate calculation of the final surface structures and textures with the final lighting settings - required for all forms of digital animation.

Rigging
Technology in 3D computer animation: Bones, joints, and objects controlling the animation are created in and around the objects and characters to be animated. The complexity of the rig depends on the character's mobility requirements within the scenes to be animated later.

More in chapter 2.4) Insight into 3D Computer Animation.

Rotoscoping
The once frequently used process in 2D animation for realistic characters is based on frame-by-frame tracing of live-action sequences. These must be adapted to the respective animation characters. Not unlike the motion capture process, an experienced animator has to thoroughly adapt and modify the information of movement in order to obtain the desired results (masters of this craft were Disney animators Milt Kahl and Marc Davis).

Rough Animation
Not yet finalized version of the animation used for all techniques except stop motion. It is refined up to a final version prior to **clean-up** in traditional 2D animation, and prior to the final **rendering** and **compositing** in 3D computer animation.

Scripting
Special form of programming using scripts. For example, the software "Python", which is frequently used for 3D animation, can be used for scripting.

Secondary Action
A "secondary action" that supports or even counteracts the primary action of a character. It is important that this secondary action does not dominate or drown out the primary movement: It must be noticeable, but must remain secondary.

Shading
Properties applied to the digital model in 3D computer animation that describe the material and surface in greater detail, such as color, luminosity, reflective properties, transparency and other surface details. Various settings of these parameters allows us to perceive materials as plastic, glass or metal, for example.

More in chapter 2.4) Insight into 3D Computer Animation.

Shooting Board
A refined version of a storyboard that contains additional information about the position, angle, and movement of the camera. Used primarily for accurate production planning in live-action and stop motion.

More in chapter 2.3) Stop Motion

Shortcut
Key combinations on the computer keyboard.

Simulation
The animation of complex effects, such as water, storms, fire, etc., which are created with computer simulation. In contrast to **key frame** based animation, the animator has very limited control of the simulation.

More in chapter 2.4) Insight into 3D Computer Animation.

Sketch
Another name for scribble.

Skribble
Sketchy drawing, often very lively due to its intuitive nature.

Slow In und Slow Out (Cushioning)
Movements generally accelerate initially (gradual wider spacing of drawings) and slow down again (gradual narrower spacing of drawings) before they come to a standstill or go into a key pose.

Smear
Distorted drawing in traditional 2D animation, simulating motion blur.
More in chapter 2.1) The Principles of Animation and their Application.

Snappy Action
Animation, which is highly dynamic. This is achieved by strong contrast in timing and spacing.
More in chapter 2.1) The Principles of Animation and their Application.

Solid Drawing
Animated objects should always retain their original overall volume when undergoing any deformation. In computer animation, this step is performed by the computer, which calculates any relevant deformations on the basis of preconfigured volumes.
More in chapter 2.1) The Principles of Animation and their Application.

Spacing
Spatial arrangement of frames (**inbetweens**) between the **key frames** of an animation.

Special Effects
Practical effects that are produced directly on the set or in the camera: This includes traditional **matte paintings**, or **animatronics**.

Speed Lines
An abstract graphic suggestion of fast movement, primarily found in comics, but with only limited justified use in animation.

Squash and Stretch
Physically induced deformations of objects when forces act on them:
Squashing and stretching.

Staging
An action or movement is staged, so that it can be communicated best to the viewer. Here, almost all other principles of animation come into play, including the layout in relation to the specified image format.

Stereoscopy
3D technology that creates the illusion of spatial depth in projection and requires the audience to wear special glasses. The term "stereoscopic" avoids being confused with the term 3D computer animation:
The general term for computer animation that is created in virtual 3D space on the computer, but often projected two-dimensionally.
Since every 3D computer animation basically has all the necessary spatial information, it is relatively easy to create stereoscopic versions.
More in chapter 2.4) Insight into 3D Computer Animation.

Stop Motion
Frame-by-frame exposure of two-or three-dimensional (mostly physical) objects. For each exposure, the objects are gradually changed, in order to create the illusion of movement.
More in chapter 2.3) Stop Motion.

Storyboard
Converting the script into cinematic shots in the form of drawings.
At first glance very similar to a comic, but with a constant aspect ratio.
More in chapter 1.1) Script and Storyboarding.

Straights / Curves
The graphically attractive contrast of straights and curves in contouring.

Straight Ahead and Pose-to-Pose Animation
Two methods of animation that are usually combined:
In **straight ahead**, the animator works straight ahead from the first drawing in the scene, without planning the detailed movement in advance. In **pose-to-pose**, the animator plans the scene on the basis of defined key poses or **key frames**, which are connected by **inbetweens**.
More in chapters 2.1) The Principles of Animation and their Application. and 2.2) Interview with Andreas Deja.

Strong Poses
Expressive poses.

Style Guide
Visual guideline in the form of illustrations and text to ensure consistency of the production design for the animation film.
More in chapter 1.4) Production Design.

Thumbnail
Thumbnail sketch. Ideal for planning animation sequences.

Time Lapse
A single-frame technique for takes, in which time elapses between each exposure. Often used in **pixilation**.

Timing
The number of drawings/frames defines how long a movement will last "on screen".

Title Safe Area
The area within the framing, which does not overlap with a possible cut-off area when using different projections. Titles in this area are therefore not cut or blocked.

Toon Shader
Special 3D **shading** technique that creates the impression of a traditional 2D cartoon animation.
More in chapter 2.4) Insight into 3D Computer Animation.

Up Shot
Camera shot from below, e.g., the frog's eye view. Also often referred to as "low-angle shot".

Visual Development
Development process of the visual style during the production design and character design of a film.
More in chapter 1.4) What is Production Design for Animation?

Visual Effects (VFX)
Digitally generated effects - as opposed to practical effects, which are produced directly on the film set or in the camera and are correctly called **special effects**.
More in chapter 2.4) Interview with Volker Engel.

Visual Storytelling
The telling of a story with images, or in combination of text and images (comics) or dialogue/ sound /music and images (film).

Walk Cycle
A special form of **loop**, where a character can walk "in place". In combination with a (mostly) horizontal pan of the background, it creates the illusion of a character in locomotion.
More in chapter 2.1) The Principles of Animation and their Application.

Waves
Wavy movements in animation.
More in chapter 2.1) The Principles of Animation and their Application.

Weight
The animation character, which is actually weightless, needs to be "given weight" convincingly: To achieve this, timing, spacing, squash and stretch, overlapping action, anticipation, etc. all must be combined skillfully.

Wireframe
3-dimensional definition of a character in computer animation in the form of a virtual "wire frame"

Bibliography/Picture Credits

Chapter 1.1

Andrews, Mark; Chapman, Brenda (director): "Brave" (2011), animated feature film, 93 min., Walt Disney Pictures, Burbank/Pixar Animation Studios, Emeryville (production), Walt Disney Pictures (distribution), Burbank.

Baker, Cordell (director): "The Cat Came Back" (1988), animated short film, 7:40 min., National Film Board of Canada (production), Montreal.

Baker, Mark (director): "The Hill Farm" (1988), animated short film, 18 min. National Film and Television School (production), Beaconsfield.

Cochran, Robert; Surnow, Jon (creator of series): „24" (2001-2010), TV series, 8 seasons with a total of 192 episodes, Imagine Television, Universal City/20th Century Fox Television, Los Angeles/Realtime Productions, Chatsworth/Teakwood Lane Productions, Los Angeles (production), 20th Television (broadcast/distribution), Los Angeles.

Dudok de Wit, Michael (director): "The Monk and the Fish" ("Le Moine et le Poisson") (1994), animated short film, 6 min., Folimage (production), Valence.

Filoni, Dave (director (supervision/direction)): "Star Wars: The Clone Wars" (2008-2014), animated TV series, 6 seasons with a total of 121 episodes, Lucasfilm, San Francisco and Singapore (production), Trifecta Entertainment and Media, Los Angeles / New York City; Disney-ABC Domestic Television, Los Angeles; Netflix (broadcast/distribution), Los Gatos.

Fischinger, Oskar (director): "Motion Painting No. 1" (1947), animated short film, 11 min.

Gagné, Michel (director): "Sensology"
(2010), animated short film, 6 min.

Kubrick, Stanley (director): "2001: A Space Odyssey" (1968), feature film, 161 min. (release version), Metro-Goldwyn-Mayer (production and distribution), Los Angeles.

Lauenstein, Christoph and Wolfgang (director): "Balance" (1989), animated short film, 7 min., Kunsthochschule Kassel, Hochschule für Bildende Künste Hamburg (production).

Lean, David (director): "Lawrence of Arabia" (1962), feature film, 222 min, Horizon Pictures (production). Columbia Pictures (distribution), Los Angeles.

Lee, Ang (director): "Hulk" (2003), feature film, 138 min., Universal Pictures, Universal City/Marvel Enterprises, New York City/Valhalla Motion Pictures, Los Angeles/Good Machine (Production), Universal Pictures (distribution), Universal City.

Rall, Hannes (director): "Das kalte Herz" (2013), animated short film, 29 min.

Verbinski, Gore (director): "Rango" (2011), animated feature film, 107 min, Nickelodeon Movies, Los Angeles/Blind Wink, Pasadena/GK Films, Santa Monica/Industrial Light & Magic, San Francisco (production); Paramount Pictures (distribution), Los Angeles.

Chapter 1.2

Mattesi, Mike (2009), "Force: Dynamic Life Drawing for Animators (Force Drawing Series)", 2nd Edition, Focal Press, Burlington, Massachusetts.

Stanchfield, Walt (2009), "Drawn to Life: 20 Golden Years of Disney Master Classes Volume 1 + 2: The Walt Stanchfield Lectures", Focal Press, Burlington, Massachusetts.

Chapter 1.3

"British fashion plate, mostly men and boys" (1885). Public Domain. P.83, bottom left.
Image source (Download):
http://theathertonian.com/?attachment_id=545

H.A. Thomas & Wylie Litho. Co.: „Tuxedo & bowler hat" (ca. 1896), New York City. Public Domain. P.83, top right.
Image source (Download):
http://commons.wikimedia.org/wiki/File:Tuxedo_%26_bowler_hat_1896.jpg

"Overcoat (left) and topcoat (right)" (1872) from "The Gazette of Fashion". Public Domain. P.83, bottom right.
Image source (Download):
http://commons.wikimedia.org/wiki/File:Mens_Coats_1872_Fashion_Plate.jpg,

"Punch, or the London Charivari" (Magazine), Vol. 158, February 18th, 1920. Various illustrators.
Public Domain. P.83, top left and center left.
Image source (Download):
http://www.gutenberg.org/files/16401/16401-h/16401-h.htm

"Street Costumes" (excerpt) from "Antique Wanamaker's Catalog" (no date). Public Domain. P.83, right edge of image.
Image source (Download):
http://thegraphicsfairy.com/fathers-day-clip-art-victorian-family-dad/

„Victorian Gentleman".
Public Domain. P.83, far bottom right.
Image source (Download):
http://thegraphicsfairy.com/victorian-gentleman/

Chapter 1.4

Illustration of Bayeux Tapestry. Public Domain. P.114, bottom left.

Image source (Download):
*http://commons.wikimedia.org/wiki/
File:Bayeux_Tapestry,_scene_40.png*

Bacher, Hans (2013), "Light Tower"
Illustration.
P.114, image 2 from top.
*https://one1more2time3.wordpress.
com/?s=lighttower*

Bacher, Hans (2012), Color Script
for "Das kalte Herz" (2013, director:
Hannes
Rall). All images pp.129-130.

Chen, Minglou (2008), "A trip to Hills
and Lakes in Spring".
Public Domain. P.108, bottom left.
Image source (Download):
*http://upload.wikimedia.org/wikipedia/
commons/thumb/8/81/A_part_of_Gi-
ant_Traditional_
Chinese_Painting.JPG/1280px-A_part_
of_Giant_Traditional_Chinese_Painting.
JPG?uselang=de*

Emitchan (2008), "Sanqingshan".
Public Domain. P.108, center bottom.
Image source (Download):
*http://commons.wikimedia.org/wiki/
File:SanQingShan10.jpg?uselang=de*

Fang, Congyi (1365), "Sacred Mountains and Precious Groves".
Public Domain. P.108, top, image 2
from left.
Image source (Download):
*http://commons.wikimedia.org/wiki/
File:Fang_Congyi_Divine_Mountains.
jpg?uselang=de*

Keeshu (1/3/2004), "Knob of a Viking
Sword from the Haithabu Museum in
Germany".
GNU Free Documentation License.
P.112, bottom.
Image source (Download):
*http://commons.wikimedia.org/wiki/
File:Viking_sword_pommel.jpg*

Lim Wei Ren Darren; Rall, Hannes

(2014), Concept illustration for the film
"As You Like It". P.109, bottom left.

Ma Yuan (1200-1230), "Scholar with
servants on a terrace".
Public Domain. P.108, center top.
Image source (Download):
*http://commons.wikimedia.org/wiki/
File:Ma_Lin_Painting.jpg?uselang=de*

McKay Savage (3/1/2006), "China
Yangshuo 1- beautiful landscape".
Creative Commons License. P.108,
top left.
Image source (Download):
*http://commons.wikimedia.org/wiki/
File:China_-_Yangshuo_1_-_beauti-
ful_landscape_(140903344).jpg?use-
lang=de*

Meier, Michael (2008), Concept illustration for film project.
P.109, top left.

Ormston, Thomas (9/28/2007),
"Photography of Viking Longhouse
from Þjóðveldisbærinn in Iceland".
GNU license for free documentation.
P.112, top.
Image source (Download):
*http://commons.wikimedia.org/wiki/
File:Stöng_Viking_Longhouse.jpg?use-
lang=de*

Praefcke, Andreas (2/10/2013), "Fool's
Jump in Weingarten on Carnival Sun-
day, 2013, Narrenverein Wikinger 1977
e.V. (Weingarten)". Creative Commons
License. P. 113, right.
Image source (Download):
*http://commons.wikimedia.org/wiki/
File:Weingarten_Narrensprung_2013_
Wikinger_01.jpg?uselang=de*

Wergeland, Oscar (1909), "Norsemen
Landing in Iceland" Illustration in:
Guerber, H. A. (Hélène Adeline) (1909).
Myths of the Norsemen from the
Eddas and Sagas. London : Harrap. This
illustration constitutes the endpaper.

Public Domain. P.112, center.
Digitized by the Internet archive and
available on:
*http://www.archive.org/details/
mythsofthenorsem00gueruoft*
Image source (Download):
*http://commons.wikimedia.org/wiki/
File%3ANorsemen_Landing_in_
Iceland.jpg*

Rall, Jochen (2013), Design study for
the film project "As You Like It" (directed by Hannes Rall)
P.114, image 4 from top.

Yew Ee Venn (2013/14), "Wang Liui-
ang". P.108, far right.
Illustrations for URECA (Undergradu-
ate Research on Campus) project at
the Nanyang Technological University
Singapore.

Interview Hans Bacher
Allers, Roger; Minkoff, Rob (Director):
"The Lion King" (1994), animated
feature film, 88 min., Walt Disney

Feature Animation (Studio), Buena
Vista Pictures Distribution (distribu-
tion)
Burbank.

Bacher, Hans (2007), "Dreamworlds
Production Design for Animation"
(2007), Focal Press, Burlington, Massachusetts.

Bancroft, Tony; Cook, Barry (director):
"Mulan" (1998), animated feature film,
87 min., Walt Disney Feature Animation (studio), Buena Vista Pictures
Distribution (distribution), Burbank.

Clark, Les; Geronimi, Clyde; Larson,
Eric; Reitherman, Wolfgang (director):
"Sleeping Beauty" (1959), animated
feature film, 79 min., Walt Disney Feature Animation (studio), Buena Vista

Distribution (distribution), Burbank.

Dindal, Mark (Director): "The Emperor's New Groove" (2000), animated feature film, 78 min., Walt Disney Feature Animation (studio), Buena Vista Pictures Distribution (distribution), Burbank.

Geronimi, Clyde; Luske, Hamilton; Reitherman, Wolfgang (director): "101 Dalmatians" (1961), animated feature film, 75 min., Walt Disney Feature Animation (studio), Buena Vista Distribution (distribution), Burbank.

Hand, David (director): "Bambi" (1942), animated feature film, 70 min., Walt Disney Feature Animation (studio), RKO Radio Pictures (distribution), Burbank.

Trousdale, Gary; Wise, Kirk (director): "Beauty and the Beast" (1991), animated feature film, 90 min., Walt Disney Feature Animation (studio), Buena Vista Pictures Distribution (distribution), Burbank.

Trousdale, Gary; Wise, Kirk (director): "Atlantis - The Lost Empire". (2001), animated feature film, 95 minutes, Walt Disney Feature Animation (studio), (distribution), Burbank.

Chapter 2.1

Baker, Mark (director): "The Hill Farm" (1989), animated short film, 18 min. National Film and Television School (production), Beaconsfield.

Bird, Brad (director): "The Incredibles" (2004), animated feature film, 115 min, Pixar Animation Studios, Emeryville (production); Buena Vista Pictures (distribution), Burbank.

Cakó, Ferenc (director): "Ab Ovo" (1987), animated short film, 7 min.

Hubley, Faith; Hubley, John (director): "Moon Bird"
(1959), animated short film, 10 min.

Jackson, Peter (director): "The Hobbit" (trilogy):
1.) "An Unexpected Journey" (2012), feature film, 169 min.
2.) "The Desolation of Smaug" (2013), feature film, 161 min.
3.) "The Battle of the 5 Armies" (2014), feature film, 144 min.
New Line Cinema, Los Angeles/Metro-Goldwyn-Mayer, Beverly Hills/WingNut Films, Wellington (production), Warner Bros Pictures (distribution), Burbank.

Kentridge, William (director): "Ubu Tells the Truth"
(1996-97), animated short film, 8 min.

Kuhn, Jochen (director): "Neulich 1" (1998), animated short film, 4 min.

Leaf, Caroline (director): "The Metamorphosis of Mr. Samsa"
(1977), animated short film, 10 min. National Film Board of Canada (production), Montreal.

Park, Nick (director): "Wallace and Gromit" (series of animated short films):
1) "A Grand Day Out" (1990), 24 min., The National Film and Television School, Beaconsfield/Aardman Studios, Bristol (production), BBC Channel 4 (broadcast), London.
2.) "The Wrong Trousers" (1993), 30 min, Aardman Studios (production), Bristol; BBC (broadcast), London.
3.) "A Close Shave" (1995), 31 min, Aardman Studios (production), Bristol; BBC (broadcast), London.
4.) "A Matter of Loaf and Death" (2008), 29 min, Aardman Studios (production), Bristol; BBC (broadcast), London.

Patel, Ishu (director): "Afterlife" (1978), animated short film, 7:16 min., National Film Board of Canada (production), Montreal.

Petrov, Aleksandr (director): "The Old Man and the Sea" (1999), animated short film, 20 min.

Reiniger, Lotte (director): "The Adventures of Prince Achmed" (1926), animated feature film, 65 min .; Hagen, Louis (production), Berlin.

Ruhemann, Andrew ; Tan, Shaun (director): "The Lost Thing" (2010), animated short film, 10 min., Passion Pictures (production), Melbourne.

Russell, Chuck (director): "The Mask" (1994), feature film (hybrid of live action and animation), 97 min, Dark Horse Entertainment (production), Studio City; New Line Film Productions. Inc. (distribution), Los Angeles.

Švankmajer, Jan (director): "Dimensions of Dialogue" (1982), animated short film, 14 min., Kratky film (distribution), Prague.

Thomas, Frank; Johnston, Ollie, (1995), "The Principles of Illusion" in: The Illusion of Life: Disney Animation, Disney Edition, New York 1995, pp. 47-69

Williams, Richard (2002), "The Animator's Survival Kit", 2nd Edition: pp 35, 320, 323, Faber & Faber, London.

Chapter 2.2

Deja, Andreas (May 20, 2014), "Xerox" *http://andreasdeja.blogspot.de*

Geronimi, Clyde; Luske, Hamilton; Reitherman, Wolfgang (director): "101 Dalmatians" (1961), animated feature film, 103 min, Walt Disney Feature Animation (studio), Burbank; Buena Vista Distribution Company Inc. (distribution), Burbank.

Jacob (March 30, 2014), „Milt Kahl – Animator – The AristoCats", *http://adreamer49.wordpress.com/2014/03/30/milt-kahl-animator-the-aristocats/*

Trousdale, Gary; Wise, Kirk (director):

"Beauty and the Beast" (1991), animated feature film, 90 min., Walt Disney Feature Animation (studio), Vista Pictures Distribution (distribution), Burbank.

Interview Andreas Deja
Allers, Roger; Minkoff, Rob (director): "The Lion King" (1994), animated feature film, 88 min., Walt Disney Feature Animation (studio), Buena Vista Pictures Distribution (distribution), Burbank.

Bacher, Hans: "Dreamworlds Production Design for Animation" (2007), Focal Press, Burlington, Massachusetts.

Bancroft, Tony; Cook, Barry (director): "Mulan" (1998), animated feature film, 87 min., Walt Disney Feature Animation (studio), Buena Vista Pictures Distribution (distribution), Los Angeles.

Berger, Ludwig; Powell, Michael; Whelan, Tim (director): "The Thief of Bagdad" (1940), feature film, 106 min, London Films (production), London; United Artists (distribution), Burbank.

Clark, Les; Geronimi, Clyde; Larson, Eric; Reitherman, Wolfgang director): „Sleeping Beauty" (1959), animated feature film, 79 min., Walt Disney Feature Animation (studio), Buena Vista Distribution (distribution), Burbank.

Clements, Ron; Musker, John (director): "Aladdin" (1992), animated feature film, 90 min., Walt Disney Feature Animation (studio), Buena Vista Pictures Distribution (distribution), Burbank.

Clements, Ron; Musker, John (director): "Hercules" (1997), animated feature film, 93 min., Walt Disney Feature Animation (studio), Buena Vista Pictures Distribution (distribution), Burbank.

Clements, Ron; Musker, John (director): "The Princess and the Frog" (2009), animated feature film, 97 min., Walt Disney Feature Animation (studio), Walt Disney Studio Motion Pictures (distribution), Burbank.

DeBlois, Dean; Sanders, Chris (director): "Lilo and Stitch" (2002), animated feature film, 85 min., Walt Disney Feature Animation (studio), Buena Vista Pictures Distribution (distribution), Burbank.

Dindal, Mark (Director): "The Emperor's New Groove" (2000), animated feature film, 78 min., Walt Disney Feature Animation (studio), Buena Vista Pictures Distribution (distribution), Burbank.

Geronimi, Clyde; Jackson, Wilfred; Luske, Hamilton (director): "Cinderella" (1950), animated feature film, 74 minutes, Walt Disney Feature Animation (studio), Burbank; RKO Radio Pictures (distribution), Los Angeles.

Geronimi, Clyde; Jackson, Wilfred; Luske, Hamilton (director): "Peter Pan" (1953), animated feature film, 76 minutes, Walt Disney Feature Animation (studio), Burbank; RKO Radio Pictures (distribution), Los Angeles.

Geronimi, Clyde; Luske, Hamilton; Reitherman, Wolfgang (director): "101 Dalmatians" (1961), animated feature film, 103 min, Walt Disney Feature Animation (studio), Burbank; Buena Vista Distribution Company Inc. (distribution), Burbank.

Hand, David (director): "Bambi" (1942), animated feature film, 70 minutes, Walt Disney Feature Animation (studio), Burbank; RKO Radio Pictures (distribution), Los Angeles.

Lounsberry, John; Reitherman, Wolfgang; Stevens, Art (director): "The Rescuers" (1977), animated feature film, 77 min., Walt Disney Feature Animation (studio), Buena Vista Distri-

bution (distribution), Burbank.

Pollock, George (director): "Murder, She Said" (1961), feature film, Metro-Goldwyn-Mayer, Beverly Hills, George H. Brown Productions (production), Metro-Goldwyn-Mayer, Beverly Hills (distribution), Los Angeles.

Reitherman, Wolfgang (director): "The Sword in the Stone" (1963), animated feature film, 79 min., Walt Disney Feature Animation (studio), Buena Vista Distribution (distribution), Burbank.

Reitherman, Wolfgang (director): "The Jungle Book" (1967), animated feature film, 78 min., Walt Disney Feature Animation (studio), Buena Vista Distribution (distribution), Burbank.

Sharpsteen, Ben (director): "Dumbo" (1941), animated feature film, 64 minutes, Walt Disney Feature Animation (studio), Burbank; RKO Radio Pictures (distribution), Los Angeles.

Stanchfield, Walt (2009), "Drawn to Life: 20 Golden Years of Disney Master Classes Volume 1 + 2: The Walt Stanchfield Lectures" (2009), Focal Press, Burlington, Massachusetts.

Trousdale, Gary; Wise, Kirk (director): "Beauty and the Beast" (1991), animated feature film, 90 min., Walt Disney Feature Animation (studio), Buena Vista Pictures Distribution (distribution), Burbank.

Williams, Richard (2002), "The Animator's Survival Kit", 2nd Edition: P 256, Faber & Faber, London.

Zemeckis, Robert (director): "Who Framed Roger Rabbit" (1988), feature film (hybrid of live action and animation), 104 min., Amblin Entertainment, Silver Screen Partners III, Touchstone Pictures (studio), Buena Vista Pictures Distribution (distribution), Los Angeles.

Chapter 2.3

Stop Motion

Anable, Graham; Stacchi, Anthony (director): "The Boxtrolls" (2014), animated feature film, 96 min. Laika Entertainment (production), Hillsboro; Focus Features (distribution), Universal City.

Butler, Chris; Fell, Sam (director): "Para-Norman" (2012), animated feature film, 92 min. Laika Entertainment (production), Hillsboro; Focus Features (distribution), Universal City.

Gondry, Michel (director): "Come Into My World" (2002), animated music video 4.12 min.

Harris, Noah (director): "Ford Fiesta Zeitgeist" (2011), animated commercial, 1 min.

Haskin, Byron (director): "The War of the Worlds" (1953), feature film, 85 min., Paramount Pictures (production and distribution), Los Angeles.

Johnson, Stephen R. (director): "Sledgehammer" (1986), animated music video, 5:01 min.

Jutra, Claude; McLaren, Norman (director): "A Chairy Tale" (1957), animated short film, 12 min., National Film Board of Canada (production and distribution), Montreal.

Laven, Orie; Nathan, Merav and Yuval (director): "Her Morning Elegance" (2009), animated music video, 3:36 min.

McLaren, Norman (director): "Neighbours" (1952), animated short film, 8:06 min., National Film Board of Canada (production and distribution), Montreal.

Nagashima, Kizo; Roemer, Larry (director): "Rudolph the Red-Nosed Reindeer" (1964), TV Special, Rankin / Bass Productions (production), New York City.

Pal, George (director): "Puppetoons" (1932-1947), series of animated short films.

Parker, Trey; Stone, Matt (creation of series): "South Park" (1997 - ongoing) TV animation series, 18 seasons with a total of 257 episodes, Comedy Central (production and distribution), New York City.

PES(director): "Human Skateboard" (2008), animated short film, 0:31 min.

Reiniger, Lotte (director): "The Adventures of Prince Achmed" (1926), animated feature film, 65 min., Hagen, Louis (production), Berlin.

Reiniger, Lotte (director): "Kalif Storch" (1935), animated short film, 9:24 min.

Reiniger, Lotte (director): "Papageno" (1935), animated short film, 10:40 min.

Selick, Henry (director): "Coraline" (2009), animated feature film, 100 min, Laika Entertainment (production), Hillsboro; Focus Features (distribution), Universal City.

Selick, Henry (director): "The Nightmare Before Christmas" (1993), animated feature film, 76 min., Touchstone Pictures/Skellington Productions (production), Buena Vista Pictures (distribution), Burbank.

Shynola (director): "Strawberry Swing" (2009), animated music video, 4:13 min.

Starevitch, Ladislas: "The Beautiful Lukanida" (1910), animated short film.

Švankmajer, Jan (director): "Food" (1992), animated short film, 17 min.; Kallista, Jaromir (production), Zeitgeist Films (distribution), New York City.

Švankmajer, Jan (director): "Conspirators of Pleasure" (1996), animated feature film, 85 min.; Kallista, Jaromir (production), Zeitgeist Films (distribution), New York City.

Webber, Rich (director): "Purple and Brown" (2006), animated film series, 13 episodes, Aardman Animation (production), Bristol; Nickelodeon (TV broadcast), New York City.

Chapter 2.4

Insight into 3D Computer Animation

Burton, Tim (director): "Alice in Wonderland" (2010), feature film, 108 min., Walt Disney Pictures, Burbank/ Roth Films, Santa Monica/The Zanuck Company, Los Angeles/Team Todd, Burbank (production), Walt Disney Studios Motion Pictures (distribution), Burbank.

Cameron, James (director): "Avatar" (2009), feature film, 161 min., Lightstorm Entertainment, Manhattan Beac/Dune Entertainment, Los Angeles/Ingenious Film Partners, London (production); 20th Century Fox (distribution), Los Angeles.

Cameron, James (director): "Terminator 2: Judgment Day" (1991), feature film, 136 min, Carolco Pictures/Pacific Western/Lightstorm Entertainment, Manhattan Beach/Le Studio Canal + SA, Paris (production); TriStar Pictures (distribution), Los Angeles.

Fincher, David (director): "The Curious Case of Benjamin Button" (2008), feature film, 166 min, The Kennedy/ Marshall Company (production), Santa Monica; Paramount Pictures (US distribution, Hollywood; Warner Bros. Pictures (global distribution), Burbank.

Fuchssteiner, Felix; Schöde, Katharina (director): "Sapphire Blue" (2014), feature film, 116 min., Tele München Fernseh Produktionsgesellschaft (TMG) (production), Munich, Concorde Filmverleih (distribution), Grünwald.

Goedegebure, Sascha (director): "Big Buck Bunny" (2008), animated short film, 10 min., Blender Foundation (production), Amsterdam, The Geeworld Studios (distribution), Los Angeles.

Heffron, Richard T. (director): "Future World" (1976), feature film, 104 min., Aubrey Company/Paul N. Lazarus III (production), American International (distribution), Los Angeles.

Jackson, Peter (director): "The Lord of the Rings: The Two Towers" (2002), feature film, 179 min, WingNut Films, Wellington/The Saul Zaentz Company, Passaic (production); New Line Cinema (distribution), Los Angeles.

Lasseter, John (director): "Toy Story" (1995), animated feature film, 81 min, Pixar Animation Studios, San Francisco. Walt Disney Pictures, Burbank (production); Buena Vista Pictures (distribution), Los Angeles.

Leterrier, Louis (director): "Clash of the Titans" (2010), feature film, 96 min., Legendary Pictures, Burbank/ The Zanuck Company, Los Angeles/ Thunder Road Pictures, Santa Monica (production), Warner Bros. Pictures (distribution), Burbank.

Lucas, George (director): "Star Wars" (1977), feature film, 121 min, Lucasfilm (production), San Francisco; 20th Century Fox (distribution), Los Angeles.

Reeves, Matt (director): "Dawn of the Planet of the Apes" (2014), feature film, 130 min, Chernin Entertainment, Santa Monica/TSG Entertainment, Las Vegas (production); 20th Century Fox (distribution), Los Angeles.

Sakaguchi, Hironobu (director): "Final Fantasy: The Spirits Within" (2001), animated feature film, 108 min, Square Pictures (production), Tokyo; Columbia Pictures (distribution), Culver City.

Scorsese, Martin (director): "Hugo" (2011), feature film, 126 min., GK Films/Infinitum Nihil, Los Angeles (production), Paramount Pictures (distribution), Los Angeles.

Spielberg, Steven (director): "Jurassic Park" (1993), feature film, 127 min, Amblin Entertainment (production), Universal City; Universal Pictures (distribution), Universal City.

Tykwer, Tom; Wachowski, Andy; Wachowski, Lana (director): "Cloud Atlas" (2013), feature film, 171 min., Anarchos Productions/Cloud Atlas Productions/X-Filme Creative Pool (production), Warner Bros. Pictures (distribution), Burbank.

Wyatt, Rupert (director): "Rise of the Planet of the Apes" (2011), feature film, 105 min, Chernin Entertainment, Santa Monica/Dune Entertainment, Los Angeles/Big Screen Productions/ Ingenious Film Partners, London (production); 20th Century Fox (distribution), Los Angeles.

Interview Volker Engel

Emmerich, Roland (director): "Independence Day" (1996), feature film, 145 min., Centropolis Entertainment (production), 20th Century Fox (distribution), Los Angeles.

Emmerich, Roland (director): "2012" (2009), feature film, 158 min., Columbia Pictures (production), Sony Pictures Releasing (distribution), Los Angeles.

Emmerich, Roland (director): "Anonymous" (2011), feature film, 130 min., Anonymous Pictures/Centropolis Entertainment/Relativity Media Studio, Los Angeles/Babelsberg Motion Pictures, Berlin (production), Columbia Pictures (distribution), Los Angeles.

Emmerich, Roland (director): "White House Down" (2013), feature film, 131 min., Centropolis Entertainment, Mythology Entertainment (production), Columbia Pictures (distribution), Los Angeles.

Interview Isaac Kerlow

Gunn, James (director): "Guardians of the Galaxy" (2014), feature film, 122 min, Marvel Studios (production), New York City; Walt Disney Studios Motion Pictures (distribution), Los Angeles.

Kerlow, Isaac (2009), "The Art of 3D Computer Animation And Effects", 4th edition, Wiley, Hoboken, New Jersey.

Osborne, Mark; Stevenson John (director): (2008) "Kung Fu Panda" (2008), animated feature film, 92 min., DreamWorks Animation (production), Paramount Pictures (distribution), Los Angeles.

Verbinski, Gore (director): "Rango" (2011), animated feature film, 107 min, Nickelodeon Movies, Los Angeles/ Blind Wink, Pasadena/GK Films, Santa Monica/Industrial Light & Magic, San Francisco (production); Paramount Pictures (distribution), Los Angeles.

All internet sources were accessed on 06/01/2015.

Recommendations for Additional Reading

Some preliminary remarks: The following list represents only a limited selection of what we believe to be some of the most important and most useful books on their respective topics. Waging into the decision was, of course, the extent, to which this literature constitutes a meaningful addition to the book at hand. Fortunately, the number of interesting publications on animation has increased exponentially in recent years, and with so many good books on the market now, it is simply impossible to buy them all.

An animator, of course, can never have enough books, particularly when considering the very beautiful art books on special films, which are published with almost every major film production.

The Internet offers endless resources as well, often free of charge. Prompt and valuable information is available for almost every aspect of animation, including blogs and websites with artistic examples on all those topics discussed here. Almost any film imaginable is available for purchase online, and many others are available free of charge. This is especially true for many artistic short films, which are otherwise only shown at film festivals. Therefore, we can only encourage you to continue your study, particularly in the detailed (frame by frame!) analysis of these resources. And - more important than ever - keep an open mind! Animation designers should think outside the box and seek inspiration from areas other than animation, such as live-action movies, theater, ballet, modern and classical fine arts, graphic design as well as interactive applications. It's the only path to innovation and to leaving the worn paths behind!

1.1) Script and Storyboarding

Top Tip: Alexander, Kate; Besen, Ellen; Mintz, Aubry; Sullivan, Karen (2013): "Ideas for the Animated Short: Finding and Building Stories", second extended Edition, Focal Press, Burlington, Massachusetts.
One of the very few books on the market that specifically deals with the development of stories for animated short films, providing useful details with many examples.

Bacher, Hans (2015), "Sketchbook: Composition Studies for Film" Laurence King Publishing, London.

Top Tip: Beiman, Nancy (2012), "Prepare to Board! Creating Story and Characters for Animated Features and Shorts: 2nd Edition ", Focal Press, Burlington, Massachusetts.
If you want to invest only in one book on the subject, then Beiman's work is perfect: It successfully combines story development with character design and storyboard. Easy to understand, funny and superbly illustrated.

Top Tip: Brown, Blain (2011), "Cinematography: Theory and Practice: Image Making for Cinematographers and Directors", 2nd Edition, Focal Press, Burlington, Massachusetts.
An outstanding book, which uses a very comprehensive and effective combination of image and text to introduce the basics of cinematography and visual storytelling for film.

Eisner, Will Graphic (2008), "Graphic Storytelling and Visual Narrative", WW Norton & Company, New York City.
Building on that:
Eisner, Will, (2008), "Comics and Sequential Art: Principles and Practices from the Legendary Cartoonist" (Will Eisner Instructional Books), W.W. Norton & Company, New York City.

Glebas, Francis (2008): "Directing the Story: Professional Storytelling and Storyboarding Techniques for Live Action and Animation", Focal Press, Burlington, Massachusetts.

Glebas, Francis (2012) : "The Animator's Eye: Adding Life to Animation with Timing, Layout, Design, Color and Sound", Focal Press, Burlington, Massachusetts.

Hart, John (2007), "The Art of the Storyboard: A Filmmaker's Introduction, Second Edition", Focal Press, Burlington, Massachusetts.

Katz, Jason; Lasseter, John (2015): "Funny!: Twenty-Five Years in the Pixar Story Room", Chronicle Books, San Francisco.

Top Tip: Mateu-Mestre, Marcos (2010): "Framed Ink: Drawing and Composition for Visual Storytellers", Design Studio Press, Culver City.
In my opinion, simply the best book

when it comes to the concepts of composition, cinematography, lighting, lenses and film editing in the storyboard. Add to this the brilliant drawings which beautifully explain the concepts. The reader will be able to learn so much just by studying these illustrations.

Top Tip: McCloud, Scott (1994), "Understanding Comics", William Morrow Paperbacks, New York City.
Building on that:
McCloud, Scott (2006), "Making Comics: Storytelling Secrets of Comics, Manga and Graphic Novels", Harper Paperbacks, New York City.
Yes - this is about comics. And there are differences between comics and animation. Nevertheless, there are a lot of similarities in terms of visual storytelling, and animators can learn a tremendous amount here. The stroke of genius is the fact that McCloud explains the principles of visual storytelling in comic form - virtually demonstrating the relevance of his theory/theories in a practical example.

Wright, Jean Ann (2005), "Animation Writing and Development: From Script Development to Pitch", Focal Press, Burlington, Massachusetts.

Websites:
Top Tip: Kennedy, Mark: "Temple of the Seven Golden Camels", sevencamels.blogspot.com
The blog of a storyboard expert who offers an incredibly broad and valuable selection of posts on visual storytelling for (mainly) animation and comics. The best

site I have found so far on these specific topics!

1.2) Figure Drawing for Storyboard and Animation

Top Tip: Chelsea, David (1997): "Perspective! for Comic Book Artists: How to Achieve a Professional Look in your Artwork", Watson-Guptill, New York City.
Building on that:
Chelsea, David (2011): "Extreme Perspective! For Artists: Learn the Secrets of Curvilinear, Cylindrical, Fisheye, Isometric, and Other Amazing Systems that Will Make Your Drawings Pop Off the Page", Watson-Guptill, New York City.
Chelsea, not unlike McCloud, congenially uses the comic medium to explain the concepts of perspective drawing in an easy-to-understand and pragmatic manner.

Top Tip: Hultgren, Ken (1993): "The Art of Animal Drawing: Construction, Action Analysis, Caricature (Dover Art Instruction)", Dover Publications, Mineola.
Little text, but the wonderful illustrations are virtually self-explanatory. Probably the best drawings that successfully combine high realism and anatomical precision in animal representation with the stylization, exaggeration and simplification needed for animation. A master of his craft.

Top Tip: Mattesi, Mike (2009): "Force: Dynamic Life Drawing for Animators (Force Drawing

Series)", 2nd Edition, Focal Press, Burlington, Massachusetts.
Building on that:
Mattesi, Mike (2011): "Force: Animal Drawing: Animal Locomotion and Design Concepts for Animators (Force Drawing Series)", Focal Press, Burlington, Massachusetts.
Mattesi also sets a standard by showing animators with his wealth of illustrations, how to best utilize and implement drawing according to model. He then applies the same basic concepts to the drawing of animals in the second book. There is an accompanying website below.

Top Tip: Stanchfield, Walt (2009), "Drawn to Life: 20 Golden Years of Disney Master Classes Volume 1 + 2: The Walt Stanchfield Lectures", Burlington, Massachusetts.
These two volumes based on the sketchbooks and notes of the longtime drawing instructor at Disney Feature Animation, Walt Stanchfield, are an absolute must. The perfect addition and expansion to Mattesi's books - much more focused on the specific connection between the requirements of animation and the practice of figure drawing.

Websites
Mattesi, Mike, "Drawingforce. com"
http://www.drawingforce.com
The website of Mike Mattesi.

1.3) Character Design – Virtual Casting Couch for Animated Film Stars

Amid, Amidi (2006), "Cartoon Modern", Chronicle Books, San Francisco.

Bancroft, Tom (2006), "Creating Characters with Personality: For Film, TV, Animation, Video Games, and Graphic Novels", Watson-Guptill, New York City.
Building on that:
Bancroft, Tom (2012), "Character Mentor: Learn by Example to Use Expressions, Poses, and Staging to Bring Your Characters to Life", Focal Press, Burlington, Massachusetts.

Denicke, Lars; Thaler, Peter (2012), "Pictoplasma - The Character Compendium", Pictoplasma Publishing, Berlin.

Kato, Bob (2014), "The Drawing Club: Master the Art of Drawing Characters from Life", Quarry Books, Beverly, Massachusetts.

Top Tip: Mattesi, Mike (2008), "Force: Character Design from Life Drawing (Drawing Force Series)", Focal Press, Burlington, Massachusetts.
This is another book, where Mattesi pursues a very interesting and unusual concept: What does the drawing of real people bring to character design?

1.4) What is Production Design for Animation?

Top Tip: Bacher, Hans (2007), "Dreamworlds Production Design for Animation", Focal Press, Burlington, Massachusetts.
Established as the standard reference on the topic, it explains extensively the concepts for production design in animation, using beautiful illustrations throughout.

Canemaker, John (2014), "The Art and Flair of Mary Blair (Updated Edition): An Appreciation (Disney Editions Deluxe)" Disney Editions, Glendale.

Top Tip: Ghez, Didier (2015-ongoing), "They Drew as They Pleased: The Hidden Art of Disney's Golden Age Vol. 1-3", Chronicle Books, San Francisco.
A book series about the (hidden) art of the Disney Concept Artists of the 1930s into the 1990s. So relevant, because these concept studies were often much more daring, elaborate and more radical than what was later - in part due to technical reasons - seen in the completed movies. An ideal source of inspiration for designers in the digital age, who after all, have a whole new world of technological possibilities available to them. Of course, it's best to acquire all (yet to be published) volumes of this series, in order to see the full stylistic range of that period.

Polson, Tod (2013), "The Noble Approach: Maurice Noble and the Zen of Animation Design", Chronicle Books, San Francisco.

Websites:

Top Tip: Amidi, Amid, "Cartoon Brew"
http://www.cartoonbrew.com
Very important website, always with up-to-date reports about artistic developments in the mainstream and independent sector! Worth checking out daily.

Top Tip: Bacher, Hans: "One1more2three3's Weblog", *https://one1more2time3.wordpress.com*
An inexhaustible and constantly updated treasure trove for inspiration with a stylistically open perspective. Visually very analytical and always in good taste in the selection of outstanding examples of animation, film, comics, illustration and visual art.

2.1) The Principles of Animation and their Application

Top Tip: Blair, Preston (1994), "Cartoon Animation", Walter Foster Publishing, Irvine.
This book, designed in 1947 by animation veteran Blair (among others Disney, MGM), remains a stroke of genius for me: In an easy-to-grasp manner, he explains the 12 basic principles of animation with unsurpassed simplicity and clarity.

Top Tip: Goldberg, Eric (2008), "Character Animation Crash Course!" Silman-James Press, Los Angeles.
Disney Animator Goldberg (responsible, among others, for the Genie in "Aladdin") provides a comprehensive, systematic and easy-to-understand introduction to the basic principles of animation. Like Blair's book, it is an excellent introduction "from the ground up", but also of great interest for advanced animators, if only because of the excellent drawings. With accompanying DVD, where you can view the examples from the book in motion.

Hooks, Ed (2011), "Acting for Animators", 3rd edition, Routledge, London.

Top Tip: Williams, Richard (2002), "The Animator's Survival Kit," second edition, Faber and Faber, London.

The "Bible" -the undisputed standard reference, unmatched level of detail and author's wealth of knowledge. Minor limitation: Can be overwhelming for beginners and, in my opinion, focuses too much on walk cycles. Builds on this book and is therefore a great addition! Excellent DVD and iPad editions are available as well.

2.2) Animated Cartoon (traditional 2D animation)

Top Tip: Deja, Andreas (2015), "The Nine Old Men: Lessons, Techniques, and Inspiration from Disney's Great Animators", Focal Press, Burlington, Massachusetts.
Top animator Deja about the legendary "Nine Old Men", the (early) golden era at Disney. It is interesting that these masters of traditional 2D animation had fundamentally different artistic personalities. Contrary to what one might think, this work also offers great information on diverse and very different concepts.

Top Tip: Halas, John; Whitaker, Harold (2009), "Timing for Animation", Sito, Tom (Editor), Focal Press, Burlington, Massachusetts.
Another classic, which could also be listed under the heading "Principles of Animation".

Websites:
Top Tip: Deja, Andreas, "Deja View".
http://andreasdeja.blogspot.de
Excellent addition to the interview in this book. On his blog, Andreas

shows countless examples of beautifully drawn character animation. He usually combines clips with images of original drawings. Ideal for analyzing and learning!*

2.3) Stop Motion

Top Tip: Lord, Peter; Sibley, Brian (2010) "Cracking Animation- The Aardman Book of 3-D Animation", Thames & Hudson, London.
Not only for fans of the long-standing Aardman Studio in Bristol. It provides insight into the world of "Wallace and Gromit", "Gumpy" and "Shawn, the Sheep", but unlike many other making-of books (which are often nothing more than a self-promotion of studios), it is a very easy-to-read and straightforward manual. The many pictures help the reader to understand the individual production steps and to get introduced to the subject matter. Very suitable for beginners and especially those readers, who are interested in clay animation technique.

Top Tip: Priebe, Ken (2010), "The Advanced Art of Stop-Motion Animation", Cengage Learning, Boston.
This book provides a very comprehensive insight into the professional work of stop motion. And while it does not take a distinct look at the animation form itself, it provides highly practical, detailed reports on all areas of puppet animation production.

Top Tip: Purves, Barry (2007), "Stop Motion: Passion, Process and Performance", Focal Press, Burlington, Massachusetts.

A "bible" for any stop-motion filmmaker, which will never be outdated. Purvis, a renowned animation filmmaker, provides deep insight into the complex world of puppet animation, including practical tips and precise production processes. However, this book goes beyond the status of a simple "how-to-do" book and offers an intellectually engaging discussion on the subject, enriched by entertaining interviews and reports from professionals in the industry. Purvis talks about his personal experiences, which lends credence to his sincerity and enthusiasm for puppet animation in each chapter, making this an inspiring reference book! Suitable for anyone interested in animation and for every student at any level.

Top Tip: Purves, Barry (2014), "Stop Motion Animation: Frame by Frame Film-making with Puppets and Models (Basics Animation)" (2nd Edition), Fairchild Books, London.
Less extensive than the above mentioned work, and instead focusing only on production. It is based on stop-motion films by renowned filmmakers and explains various techniques and processes in an easy-to-understand and practical manner. It adequately covers every production step, but is mainly focused on character animation. Best suited for advanced beginners and animation enthusiasts in general.

Websites:
Top Tip: *www.dragonframe.com*
Website of Dragonframe, the currently most popular and

professional stop motion software. It provides many good (especially technical) tips and many links to current productions from which you can learn a lot. Professionals and beginners alike love and use this software.

2.4) Insight into 3D Computer Animation

Amin, Jahirul (2015), "Beginner's Guide to Character Creation in Maya", 3dtotal Publishing, Worcester, UK.

Top Tip: Birn, Jeremy (2013), "Digital Lighting and Rendering" Third Edition, New Riders, Berkeley.
This book not only elaborates on the software-independent practical implementation of lighting and rendering, but it also deals with the broader-reaching artistic fundamentals, in order to achieve effective image design and staging through lighting. Principles of photography, cinematography and visual arts are covered as well as the specific types of lighting used in 3D animation application.

Cantor, Jeremy (2013), "Secrets of CG Short Filmmakers", Cengage Learning, Boston.

Dunlop, Renee (2014), "Production Pipeline Fundamentals for Film and Game", Focal Press, Burlington, Massachusetts.

Gress, Jon (2014), "Visual Effects and Compositing", New Riders, Berkeley.

Top Tip: Jones, Angie. Oliff, Jamie (2006), "Thinking Animation: Bridging the Gap Between

2D and CG", Thomson Course Technology, Boston
The focus of this book is on character animation and is aimed at both 3D and 2D animators who want to transfer to and/or improve their skills with 3D animation. The authors cover special features and challenges in 3D animation and deepen the basics of animation and acting.

Top Tip: Kerlow, Isaac (2009), "The Art of 3D Computer Animation and Effects", 4th expanded and revised edition, Wiley, New York City.
Isaac Kerlow provides a comprehensive insight into the various aspects of modern computer animation and shows the historical development of techniques and their applications. This book is a good introduction into the subject matter, but is not primarily a guide for practical application.

Top Tip: Osipa, Jason (2010), "Stop Staring: Facial Modeling and Animation Done Right", Wiley Publishing, Indianapolis.
The animation of faces in 3D is a special artistic and technical challenge that Jason Osipa presents with this classic for 3D setup of faces. He presents complex facts and processes in an easy-to-understand manner, thus providing a solid introduction to a complex topic.

Roy, Kenny (2014), "Finish Your Film! Tips and Tricks for Making an Animated Short in Maya", Focal Press, Burlington, Massachusetts.

Spencer, Scott (2010), "ZBrush

Digital Sculpting Human Anatomy", Wiley, Indianapolis.

Vaughan, William (2011), "Digital Modeling", New Riders, Berkeley.

Websites:
IT'S ART
www.itsartmag.com

CGSociety
www.cgsociety.org
fxphd
www.fxphd.com

3DTotal
www.3dtotal.com

New Animation Projects by Hannes Rall

Visual development for the animated short films "All the World's a Stage" and "As You Like It"
(being developed) - based on William Shakespeare.
Director: Hannes Rall. Script: Daniel Keith Jernigan.
Visual Development: Hannes Rall, Jochen Rall and Lim Wei Ren Darren.

Character Designs by Hannes Rall (roughs) and Lim Wei Ren Darren (clean-up). These designs show the design influences of traditional art, the silhouette films by Lotte Reiniger and the minimalistic/puristic design style by designers like Saul Bass.

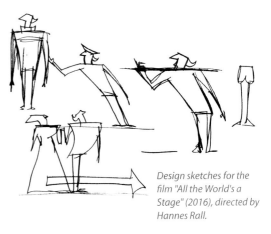

Design sketches for the film "All the World's a Stage" (2016), directed by Hannes Rall.

Production Painting for the film "All the World's a Stage" by Hannes Rall. The film has been screened at over 100 international festivals and won 4 awards.

Design study for the prologue sequence of "As You Like It" by Hannes Rall.

Prop designs by Hannes Rall (design/roughs) and Lim Wei Ren Darren (clean-up and color design).

Additional design studies for the prologue sequence by Hannes Rall.

Visual Development for the animated feature film "Die Nibelungen"

(being developed)
Director and script writer (with dialogue co-author Simon Rost): Hannes Rall.
Script Advisor: Alex Buresch.
Visual Development: Hans Bacher and Hannes Rall.

Expressionist study.
© Copyright Hans Bacher.

Production Painting:
Brunhilde confronting
King Gunther.
© Copyright Hannes Rall.

Production Painting: Siegfried in the forest
© Copyright Hans Bacher.

Character design of Siegfried.
© Copyright Hans Bacher.